WAR GAMES

A FATHER & SON MEMOIR OF WAR & SPORT

RON REED

Published by:
Wilkinson Publishing Pty Ltd
ACN 006 042 173

Ph: 03 9654 5446
www.wilkinsonpublishing.com.au

A catalogue record for this book is available from the National Library of Australia

Planned date of publication: 01-2021
Title: War Games
ISBN(s): 9781925927375: Paperback
Printed December 2020.

Design by Spike Creative Pty Ltd
Ph: (03) 9427 9500
spikecreative.com.au

Printed and bound in Australia by Griffin Press, part of Ovato

CONTENTS

INTRODUCTION

Getting paid to watch sport from the best seats in the house and to chew the fat with sportsmen every day of the week can't be called a real job – can it? That's not work – is it? That's what I told myself when I dropped out of high school at barely age 17 to take my English teacher's advice and see whether newspaper journalism and I might be a fit for each other. Initially, that involved putting a toe in the water as a proof-reader's assistant – the absolute bottom rung – while I waited for a cadetship to become available, which luckily didn't take long.

I hadn't been in my first job long at The Standard, a well-regarded daily paper in the handsome Victorian seaside town of Warrnambool, before I realised that writing about sport – and not the other staples such as council meetings, courthouse misdemeanours and sheep and cattle markets – was what I was really interested in and wanted to do, even though the crusty old chief of staff warned me that the sports section of a newspaper was the equivalent of the toyshop in a department store and I might struggle to be taken seriously if that's all I did.

For the next 50-plus years it was what I mostly did. It was, with a few exceptions, a highly enjoyable way to earn a living. The fascination for the games people play and the people who play them never faded.

In particular, the Olympic Games – once I found myself immersed in them for the first time in Los Angeles in 1984 – became a passion. This was not necessarily because of any given sport within the five-ring framework but because of that ancient institution's overall capacity for promoting excellence, goodwill and dramatic theatre, all of which, to me, far outweighed the negatives such as cheating with drugs, administrative greed and corruption and political points-scoring.

So, some four years after retiring from full-time work, I decided to attend the Games one last time, in Tokyo 2020. There was a good reason for this, beyond what had become not quite an obsession but certainly a consuming private and professional interest.

I wanted to do what I had not had the opportunity to do on my only previous visit to Japan, for the Winter Olympics in 1998, and that was to visit the memorial to the victims and survivors of the atomic bombing of the southern city of Nagasaki, the catalyst for ending the Second World War. My father, Private William Cecil Reed, of the 2nd/3rd Machinegun Battalion, Australian Imperial Forces, was a prisoner of war in Nagasaki and survived that horrific event when tens of thousands of others did not. If he hadn't, my life would not have begun. So it seemed an appropriate segue to end my professional career by giving myself a writing assignment at a tenth (nine summer, one winter) Olympics just up the road, so to speak, from where it nearly all ended for me before it had even begun.

Regrettably, the Coronavirus pandemic that plunged the world into chaos during 2020 put paid to that, forcing the International Olympic Committee and the Japanese Government to postpone the games for a year.

I still haven't been able to get to Nagasaki — but I have been encouraged by others, not least the Australian Olympic Committee's long-serving president John Coates, an old friend and professional associate, to tell Bill Reed's story anyway, and my own to some extent.

This book is the result.

It focuses on Dad's remarkable war-time experiences – the bombing was by no means his only escape from the jaws of death – and brings a form of closure for me.

I had intended it to be also a record of Australia's – and the world's – performance in Tokyo, an addition to the fairly limited written history of Australia's unbroken presence at the modern Olympics since the concept was re-invented in Athens in 1896. But that became impossible for the very good reason that there was nothing to record. Yet.

Nonetheless, it is still an observation and acknowledgement of the determination of the only country ever to be attacked with nuclear weapons to ensure that the horrors of war, especially that one, are not forgotten, even 75 years later.

War Games also revisits some of the more memorable events and people that have formed, and informed, the fabric of my working life. These stories are part of the vast sporting history of a sports-mad nation and while they reach well back into the past that doesn't mean they are no longer interesting. Some, to me, are utterly unforgettable.

Living through them has been a long and diverse journey.

From a cadetship and an early promotion to graded journalist at the *Warrnambool Standard*, I graduated to a general reporting job on the nation's pre-eminent evening paper, *The Herald*, where I stayed for 15 months before heading for London as so many young Australians did back then, and still do.

There, I worked as a sub-editor for two years, firstly at the Reuters news agency and then on Fleet Street's biggest evening daily, the *Evening News*, before *The Herald* offered to pay my airfare home if I would return to my old job. When the *Evening News* simultaneously offered voluntary redundancy, it was the perfect storm. I high-tailed it out of there with money in my pocket but not, I must admit, without a few regrets, not the least of them that I had just taken 100 wickets in a work-interrupted cricket season for Middlesex League club Shepherd's Bush and had attracted a modicum of interest from the Middlesex county club.

Back in Melbourne, I had stints as chief-sub-editor on The Herald's sports desk, a year as editor of the old 'pinky with a punch,' the Sporting Globe, and two terms as sports editor of The Herald spread across a decade, interrupted by a couple of years as a sports columnist.

When The Herald and its morning stablemate *The Sun* merged to become the Herald Sun in 1990 I returned to writing full-time, under the title of chief sportswriter. I never left the Herald and Weekly Times again and when I retired in 2016 I was the company's longest-serving employee, having been there continuously since 1971.

The job took me around the world many times.

I covered sport on every continent and in more than 30 countries. It involved multiple appearances at the Olympics and Commonwealth

Games, cricket tours to almost everywhere the noble old game is played, several editions of the Tour de France and Giro d'Italia cycling blockbusters, world title fights, major tennis and golf championships, world championships in athletics, road and track cycling, triathlon, hockey, rowing, squash and weightlifting, as well as horse racing and all the Australian football codes. One day I even found myself reporting on the arm-wrestling at the Police and Firemen Games.

In between I found time to write five books, the ghost-written life stories of star AFL footballers Robbie Flower and Wayne Johnston, the only biography written about my friend Frank Sedgman, one of the truly great Australian tennis stars, a first-hand account of the 100th Tour de France and the contributions Australian cyclists had made to that great event over the years, and a history of the Melbourne-based sportsmen's institution, the Carbine Club. More recently, I have added the first book about another more contemporary tennis champion, Ashleigh Barty.

This has resulted in a number of writing awards, including Australian Sportswriter of the Year in 1998 and the Australian Sports Commission's Lifetime Achievement award in 2013. Sports journalists are often asked — sometimes a smidgen cynically — whether they have actually played much sport themselves. In other words, do you know what you're talking about? The answer, much more often than not although with plenty of notable exceptions, is that of course we all had a crack at it growing up until the realisation sunk in that we were never going to open the bowling for Australia, kick a bag of goals at the MCG or swim the 100m at the Olympics. When those ambitions were reluctantly binned it was time to find another way to be involved.

I was as enthusiastic about cricket and footy as any other teenager and dabbled in a few other pursuits. Cricket was always No 1, but in footy I got as far as winning the club and league best and fairest awards when the Dennington Dogs won their first Warrnambool and District League premiership in 1966 and then moved up a grade to the Warrnambool Football Club in the Hampden League, which was then the strongest of the country competitions.

Then a semi-professional season with the Heidelberg club in the old Diamond Valley League in Melbourne ended with no sign of the Melbourne Football Club – for which my grandmother's brother, Percy Beames, had been a legendary triple-premiership player, captain and coach as well as a first-class cricketer and later chief footy and cricket writer for *The Age* newspaper – offering me a pathway to the big time.

So the cricket fields of England and the magnetic lure of Fleet Street, the spiritual home of journalism, looked more enticing than another season of getting roughed up in what was then a notoriously violent outer suburban competition. At 21, my footy 'career' was over. And because my job involved working at weekends, serious cricket took a back seat too.

Do I regret any of that? Hmmm, sometimes it seems a bit of a waste. But the sporting path I did choose provided a more stimulating and interesting cavalcade of experiences than kicking a goal or taking a wicket ever would have. And it lasted not just for a handful more years but for well over half a century – while saving that high school drop-out from ever having to get a real job.

For that, I am forever grateful.

VERSUS THE VIRUS

Accreditation approved, flights confirmed, accommodation booked and paid for, counting down the days on the calendar. Tokyo here we come. As the Olympic year 2020 dawned, I was ready and raring to go – seven months out.

But I didn't get past my front door. Literally.

By the time COVID-19, the deadly coronavirus, forced the International Olympic Committee and the Japanese Government to decide in mid-March to postpone the greatest sporting show on earth for 12 months, I was in lockdown in my home, unable by Government decree to go any further than the neighbourhood park for a walk with my wife and dog.

And that's where I stayed for most of what became the year from Hell.

The rest of the sporting world was similarly confined to barracks, at least initially, with no clear indication when, or if, life would return to normal – or if the old normal would ever be recognisable again.

The battle against this bastard bug has been the biggest international news story of my seven-decade-plus lifetime, certainly in Australia – a social, cultural and economic catastrophe unlike anything the vast majority of us have ever seen, no matter how old you might be.

Seen? Most of us have never imagined it.

Governments everywhere were quick to liken it to being at war, albeit it against an invisible, silent enemy. The Olympic shutdown underscored that metaphor because only the two world wars of the 20th century had been able to dismantle the famous five rings previously.

There have been a multitude of major military engagements during the 124 year history of the modern Olympics, spread over three different centuries, with casualty counts ranging from the hundreds of thousands to the tens of millions, not to mention natural disasters responsible for mass death and destruction, so the world has lived through worse.

But this vicious virus has been a game-changer in a way never experienced by anyone born this side of the second great conflict which raged between 1939 and 1945, in which time about 75 million people, military personnel and civilians did not live to tell the tale because of combat, disease and other factors.

That figure is a rough estimate because it varies considerably according to which sources you consult and specialist researchers might well offer their own give-or-take adjustments.

In its first year COVID-19 rapidly rocketed past a million deaths, not as horrendous as wartime but still tragic on a frightening scale – and with no guarantees that it would not continue its deadly work well into another year and maybe even beyond.

Like the war fought with guns and bombs it presented an existential threat to large swathes of the population of many, if not all, countries, the biggest, richest and most powerful not excepted.

For Australia, the economic ramifications have been disastrous.

Being a so-called Baby Boomer, I didn't have to live through the real war and also enjoyed the great good fortune to 'win' the lottery that decided which of my generation would be conscripted to fight – and maybe die – in the Vietnam version.

My now long-departed Dad, Bill Reed, certainly did – and he was one who did live to tell the tale.

But he never really did tell it, which is a great pity because it is an astonishing story. Which is why I was so keen to make it to Japan for the Olympics.

It would have brought a sense of closure, literally, because the closing ceremony was scheduled for August 9, which was the 75th anniversary of the Americans unleashing the second of two atomic bombs on Japan, bringing the war to an abrupt end and killing tens of thousands of people.

Three days after the first bomb flattened nearby Hiroshima, the second one descended on Nagasaki where Bill Reed was a prisoner of war along with 23 other Australian soldiers – and they all miraculously survived. If he hadn't done so, then of course I wouldn't be here to tell his tale – or any of my own.

The Games organisers had planned to use the ceremony, which is always held on a Sunday, to solemnly commemorate the two bombings as the athletes of the world waved farewell, which was something I was very keen to observe, as well as making a visit to the peace memorial in Nagasaki where Dad's name is among thousands engraved for posterity.

Hopefully this can all still happen when the Games do take place in 2021 and I am still able to bear witness to it and to salute the old man one last time – and, it must be said, with a good deal more respect than was the case while I was growing up not fully understanding, not by a long shot, what he had been through, and him, like so many returned soldiers, reluctant for a long time to speak about it.

Not many of them are left now so the eye-witness histories – the 'I was there' accounts – have nearly all been consigned to the archives, although a newspaper feature marking the 75th anniversary of the end of the war found about a dozen veterans aged 100 or more still able to provide memories.

None, living or dead, should be forgotten, which is why the Olympic commemoration would have been – and hopefully still can be, even another year down the track – an important reminder to the world.

This is not a meaningless and futile fixation on an historic tragedy that relatively few living souls can now remember. Japan is still the only country to be attacked with nuclear weapons and it doesn't want to see it ever happen to anyone else, which is why the bombings are still a live topic there.

From a broader perspective, the delayed Games will have an even bigger role to play in world solidarity – assuming they do happen – than has been the case traditionally.

IOC president Thomas Bach has described them as a light at the end of the tunnel, a rare opportunity for the entire planet to celebrate a common victory together. If the virus has indeed been stopped in its tracks by then, that will be entirely appropriate.

The title of the greatest sporting show on earth is disputed by soccer's World Cup, but while virtually every nation – more than 200 – play the most popular game ever invented, fewer than a quarter of them qualify to wave their flags at the Cup finals.

However, now that boycotts have become a distant memory, practically everybody goes to the Olympics –unless, of course, hello Russia, you have been banned for something as egregious as constant drug cheating, and even then provision is made for representation under a neutral 'clean' flag.

Just what the chaos created by the virus crisis means for the Olympics will take more than another year to become clear, as is the case for all sport, nationally and internationally. Australia is certainly no exception to that.

Australia's entire sporting economy has been forced to recalibrate from top to toe and what it ends up looking like and how long it will take to shake itself down is anyone's guess.

This is not an entirely bad thing, I would suggest – unless of course you are a footballer, cricketer or tennis player being paid multi-millions and living high on the hog.

Good luck to them, but I have long wondered whether the financial arms race in sport – not just in Australia but around the world – would one day run out of legs, whether entrepreneurial administrations could continue forever to pay increasingly absurd amounts of money to players to participate in games that have a limited purpose beyond entertaining us punters.

They have transformed most elite sport into one of showbiz's many manifestations now but it remains to be seen to what extent even that traditionally opulent industry – broadcast rights the most obvious example – might have to start pulling in the reins as national economies recede.

In Australia COVID-19 quickly became a circuit-breaker, especially for the major football codes but with cricket also finding itself in an acrimonious dispute with its broadcast partners over the true value of its product.

None of this is to say sports and entertainment is not an important part of most people's lives – of course it is and no-one would want to see it reduced to the margins or lose its capacity to motivate the best athletes to perform at the best level possible. But a bit of perspective is in order.

New Zealand cricket captain Kane Williamson, as down-to-earth an international sportsman as you're likely to find, hit it off the middle of the bat when he wrote an open letter to his country's health workers when the pandemic first arrived, in which he said: 'People talk about the pressure sportsmen and women are under to perform, but the truth is we get to do something we love every day for a living. We play games. Real pressure is working to save lives. Real pressure is going into work each day while putting your own personal safety on the line for the good of others.' Hear, hear!

In a very different context, this evoked the spirit of another champion cricketer, Keith Miller, who was a fighter pilot during the war. When asked about the pressure of playing Test cricket, he informed his questioner that 'real pressure is having a Messerschmitt (a German attack plane) up your arse.' In other words, get real!

Within weeks of Williamson's astute observation, health workers were testing positive to the virus – risking their lives while trying to protect everyone else – in their hundreds not far away in Melbourne. Most of them, certainly the nurses, were being paid a pittance compared to sports stars.

Early in the year, as happens almost every year, thousands of firefighters also put their lives on the line – some paying the ultimate price – to protect communities from massive bushfires that destroyed large swathes of Australia. Many of them were unpaid volunteers.

So it was little wonder that public sympathy became difficult to detect when some footballers began to fret about the fate of their fat contracts when their competitions were forced to shut down indefinitely, with nobody able to say for weeks on end whether there would be a season or not – let alone what the long-term future might hold.

For them, as with almost all other sectors of the community, the only certainty was that life was never going to be quite the same again.

It will be surprising if the eventual new normal, whatever that might prove to be, does not ensure a narrowing of the overblown – if not sometimes obscene – gap between the rewards on offer for sportsmen and those for the people who watch them while doing their bit to ensure the world keeps functioning in every other way.

The world will not be a worse place if – when? – the days of international soccer players earning hundreds of thousands of dollars a week are over, or cricketers can no longer pocket multiple millions for a month's 'work' at a Twenty20 tournament in India, where every ball they bowl is worth thousands to them.

That came into even sharper focus at the height of the pandemic when the world's best soccer player, Lionel Messi, 33, looked to leave his club, Barcelona, with rival outfits reportedly willing to pay him $2.5m A WEEK, all up. His Portuguese peer Cristiano Ronaldo is already a billionaire.

While the old saying 'it's only a game' is patently no longer remotely true and hasn't been for decades – professional sport is a massive industry – it's true place in the scheme of things might have now come into slightly more realistic focus, at least in Australia.

You wouldn't necessarily hold your breath for this to change in America and Europe, but we shall see.

I have watched all this unfold from Melbourne, which in this context might be the perfect vantage point given that it likes to think of itself – correctly enough, in my biased opinion – as the sports capital of the world.

There, the focus has been concentrated on the indigenous football code, the AFL, which is far and away the most successful and important domestic sport in the nation, a virtual religion in its heartland.

Mainly on the back of a massive deal with broadcasters that delivers more than $400m a year in the good times, the AFL is an impressively profitable organisation.

But when it was forced to follow many other major businesses into hibernation after just one round of the 2020 season, played without any paying customers in the grandstands, and with the rivers of gold threatening to dry up, it had to address the unsettling possibility that some of its 18 clubs might not survive in the medium term.

A lot of hard questions were suddenly being asked about why there wasn't enough money salted away to combat this threat and the short answer seemed to be that the game had been living if not exactly beyond its means in terms of bloated staff lists and gigantic payments not only to players and coaches but administrators too, then perhaps without enough regard for unforeseen calamities that might be around the next corner.

Clearly, that was going to have to change. They were going to have to pull their heads in, big-time.

The same went for their main cross-code rival, the National Rugby League, which was in an even more uncomfortable fiscal situation.

But to the credit of both bosses, AFL CEO Gillon McLachlan and his Sydney counterpart, NRL Commission chairman Peter V'landys, both competitions managed to salvage their season, or most of it.

V'landys led the way with a fearless, gung-ho approach that enabled rugby league to start playing matches again a fortnight ahead of the AFL after both had been forced to shut down indefinitely with no guarantees that a resumption would be possible at any stage.

V'landys, who also runs horse racing in NSW, quickly became regarded – especially in his home territory, where he cultivated the media expertly – as Australia's most can-do sports administrator. It was a well-earned accolade.

He and McLachlan both earned their massive pay packets as they juggled political, financial, logistical and emotional challenges most of which had never been confronted before.

As the season progressed, McLachlan had the unenviable but inevitable task of making as many as 200 of the League's massive workforce redundant, sparking an industrial relations backlash. He justified it by saying the organisation's finances were taking a $400m hit for the year.

But at least he was able to keep the ship afloat. After suspending the season after round one in March, he was able to resume 50 days later, mid-June, with the normal 23 rounds reduced to 18 and with several clubs relocated from their home states to Queensland and NSW.

But a month later, with Melbourne in the grip of a deadly second wave of the virus, all 10 Victorian clubs had to hit the road to Queensland permanently, meaning that the spiritual home of the great game would have no football at all – an unthinkable proposition at any other time. Soon, it was clear that even the Grand Final would have to move away from the hallowed MCG, with Queensland defeating the far more traditional footy states, WA and SA as well as Sydney for the privilege (and profit) of staging arguably the No 1 showpiece on the Australian sports calendar.

These were strange times indeed in many different ways.

Players and coaches found themselves making headlines for weird reasons. A club vice-captain smashed his car into multiple parked vehicles while drunk, a star's transition to a new club was interrupted when he checked himself into hospital with a stab wound that was never explained, a captain and his wife were fined after she posted a beauty treatment on social media, a coach and his assistant also had their pockets lightened for playing tennis against a former women's international star, and a couple of senior players were in strife after being filmed grabbing a team-mate in unsavoury ways while singing the team song after a big win.

And that's not to mention a former coach being arrested on the street while dressed in drag and a current star being booked by the cops over an alleged sexual assault that had happened years earlier.

Silly season doesn't begin to describe it.

But what was more worrying for McLachlan – and for V'landys for similar reasons – than any of this stuff was that personnel from almost every club were being regularly sprung for breaches of the quarantine protocols which governed the agreements for State Governments to allow the teams into their territories.

In other words, they were dancing on egg-shells – at any given time one more breach could see an entire competition shut down with the snap of a politician's fingers, putting many millions of dollars in broadcast money in jeopardy.

In Melbourne, watching footy – often referred to as the lifeblood of the city – disappear in various contexts was an intriguing exercise, no matter what level of interest you might have in the game per se.

I have often thought I could live without a footy season. Not because I don't enjoy the game. I very much do, and always have. In part, it helped keep me in a job for a long time, so to some extent I owe it.

It's just that in the town that gave birth to it and then elevated it to a status far beyond its purpose as sport and entertainment, it has always been so relentlessly in your face that it sometimes seems suffocating, impossible to escape, even when it stops.

Which it never really does, merely pausing for breath each summer. There is no such thing as an off-season. Or wasn't, until all of a sudden there was nothing but off-season – during the season.

To many hundreds of thousands of devotees, that constant out-pouring has never been a bad thing. They're the ones who can't get enough of it and who welcome being force-fed trivia on every possible platform every hour of every day of every week of every year. Cocaine junkies are less needy.

I was never really a part of that cohort, at least not to that extent.

Yep, back in the day when I was gainfully employed in newspapers as a sports editor, chief sportswriter (effectively chief football writer) and commentator/columnist, I would cheerfully attend two or even three matches almost every weekend as well as some training sessions and a steady diet of functions and social gatherings.

I even lived with a prominent League star for a fair while – more about that later – becoming a sort of de facto presence around his club, even committing the unforgivable sin of abandoning a long family allegiance to another club.

It was all grist for my mill, professionally and personally.

Eventually the appeal of that diminished. I became a faded footy fan. Not suddenly. There was no epiphany just a gradual awareness that there was a lot more to sport and life than the great game.

I didn't have to abandon it altogether, far from it. It just needed a slight perspective adjustment.

Deep into retirement that had well and truly kicked in. I was still an active fan but the number of games I found myself attending in any given season now rarely reached double figures, almost all of which involved the same club, Carlton – yes, the one by which I was kidnapped all those years, no decades, ago.

There were plenty of weekends when I didn't go at all or even watch any of it on TV, although Friday nights – when you were usually guaranteed a game of some importance – were a bit of a habit.

Don't misunderstand me. I have always remained a committed sports tragic, by upbringing, by inclination, by profession and by the influence of almost everyone around me with the notable exception of my almost completely tone-deaf (in a sports sense) better half, and when I do get involved in a game, even now, I immerse myself fully and barrack hard.

So did I really want to find out what life would be like without footy?

As everybody found out the hard way, that was no longer the hypothetical thought bubble it had been.

And the answer quickly crystallised. No, I didn't want to find that out.

Suddenly I already knew too much. I would definitely have been among the 90,000 that would have filled the MCG for the traditional season opener between Carlton and Richmond had it not been forced to take place with no spectators at all, and not having an option to do so was more disappointing than I had anticipated.

As the old saying goes, you never know what you've got until it's gone.

At first, watching it on TV was not particularly enjoyable either because it seemed like footy-lite in a range of ways, the absence of people or atmosphere, or even any noise, the main drawback.

The proceedings had the look and feel of a training drill, especially as the early part of the opening game was so one-sided that it would have been difficult to get excited even if you were there with a multitude of others.

It was a powerful reminder to all sports of how vitally important the fans are and how they must never be taken for granted.

That reality came into sharper focus when round two did not materialise and the League and its clubs began to field a few inquiries from membership card-holders about what their options were given they were now not getting what they had paid for, namely footy matches.

Media megastar Eddie McGuire, wearing his other hat as president of the leviathan Collingwood club, which has never had any trouble attracting support and nowadays wealth to match, expressed an apparently genuine fear that if too many fans queued up with their hands out 'we wouldn't have a club, we'd have a memory'.

His grim rhetoric resonated loudly because if the mighty Magpies could be seriously in mortal danger, then what of the least successful ones? It wasn't a question anyone wanted to ask or answer at that deeply uncertain juncture.

Happily, though, it proved to be a false alarm. As the rebooted season passed the halfway mark, it was reliably reported that only a very small percentage of fans had actually demanded refunds, the vast majority happy to continue to demonstrate loyalty and support in tough times for everybody.

By then, the situation was a lot less problematic in terms of what was on offer. There were two good reasons for that.

One was that crowds – small ones, but real, live people rather than the cardboard cut-outs that had made a few gimmicky appearances – were gradually re-admitted to grounds, creating some atmosphere, while the TV broadcasters had successfully experimented with artificial crowd noise, which also did the trick to a useful extent.

Secondly – and far more importantly – was that nobody was left in any doubt that footy had a massive role to play in terms of public morale and some sense of normality.

Any footy – even with substantially reduced playing minutes, an inferior spectacle created by problematic rule interpretations and a general dearth of goals – was a million miles better than no footy at all, and a 14 per cent improvement in TV ratings confirmed it.

As usual, there was no such thing as too much of it. When McLachlan's team realised they might need to outrun the pandemic, they took yet another unprecedented measure by cramming as many games into as short a period as possible.

They played 33 matches in 20 days, paused briefly and then another 31 in 18 out of 19 days, using every day of the week.

Even the busiest players ever didn't complain—in fact, the League said they were enjoying it, even though they were required to front up every four or days, as opposed to every six or seven, thereby increasing their chances of getting injured.

Some fans thought this was overkill but of course it wasn't compulsory to watch it all, or even any of it.

But for plenty of people if you were locked down in Melbourne, legally unable to walk out your front door after 8pm and with nowhere to go even if you could sneak out, this was the consolation prize, and a valued one at that.

Even I was back to being a self-proclaimed expert on every team as I found myself watching more games than I had for at least a decade, tuning in having become a post-prandial ritual every night

On the other hand, I was resigned to not watching a single game in the flesh all season, which – other than a couple of years spent living abroad – hadn't been the case since I was about 10 years old.

Life without footy – no, I definitely didn't want to see that.

And no, I didn't want a life – or even a year – without the Olympic Games, either.

But at least I didn't have a nuclear bomb coming my way.

SURVIVAL AT SEA

Country boy Bill Reed was a peaceful soul who never got into a fight in the 40 years that I knew him so it came as a surprise to learn how he chose to celebrate his 21st birthday. He walked to the Drill Hall in his home town, Bendigo, bent on joining the army – and going to war, like his father before him had done.

This was June 6, 1940, and the world's second great conflict was in full swing. It was all hands on deck, in Australia as much as anywhere else. Duty called, so my father-to-be answered promptly.

On the way, he met an old schoolmate named Don Doody who also wanted to enlist but who had a commitment that would take two weeks to clear, so Bill waited for him and they were both inducted at Melbourne's Caulfield racecourse in July.

There was no way of knowing, of course, what lay ahead – or whether either of them would have any future at all, beyond the ensuing weeks, months and, hopefully, years.

For Private William Cecil Reed, VX45894, of the 2nd/3rd Machinegun Battalion, Australian Imperial Forces, it was almost the point of no return – literally. And on more than one occasion.

He spent almost four years as a prisoner of the Japanese, during which he survived being torpedoed at sea while being transported from one prison camp to another, put himself at risk of being shot by guards over an altercation about, believe it or not, chewing gum, and, finally, miraculously, he walked away from under the atomic bomb that devastated the southern Japanese city of Nagasaki, putting an abrupt and ugly end to the war.

He did so with his physical and mental health intact, as did 23 other Australian POWs who survived the nuclear holocaust that killed tens of thousands of other people, a toll never able to be accurately confirmed. Nobody was ever able to properly explain to the survivors why they had been so lucky, if 'lucky' is the word for such an experience.

There are many thousands of stories of great escapes during all wars but his is one of the more remarkable.

Like most returned soldiers of his and earlier generations, he never spoke about it much, waiting until I was almost an adult before providing me with any detail about what he had endured. And even then, it was sparse.

He never did tell me that he was intending to write about it all for posterity. As a journalist myself, I deeply regret not encouraging him to do so, or doing it for him. However, shortly after he died at 67 in 1987, during heart surgery, my late brother Colin discovered 19 handwritten pages of unfinished memoirs, in which he referred to 'a life of hell on earth, with bashings, humiliation and starvation'.

He embarked on this after he and a handful of fellow prisoners – including his mate, Murray Jobling, who in a remarkable coincidence ended up living in the same Victorian country town of Warrnambool – returned to Nagasaki 40 years after the war, where they were emotionally reunited with the foreman of the iron and steel foundry where they had been put to work for more than a year.

After that, he began to open up more about his experiences, preaching peace and forgiveness.

His incomplete journal describes his initial deployment taking him to Colombo, Egypt, Palestine and Syria and back to Palestine, where life was 'mostly training and boredom with sand, flies and sore eyes' – and not much action.

Then it was on to Sumatra, in what is now Indonesia, where the Japanese were establishing a foothold because of the presence of valuable sources of fuel – and also because they weren't far from Australia's northern coastline, another target.

However, in what he called 'a complete schemozzle' all their gear, including weapons, was sent elsewhere on a different ship.

Before disembarking, they were paraded on deck with no guns to fight with until some old Canadian rifles and bayonets were located in the hold 'as well as, bless us, of all things, pick handles'.

'When it came to my turn,' he writes, 'I received a pick handle and 10 rounds of Tommy-gun ammunition. I said to the sergeant: "What am I going to do with these – spit them at the Japs?" His reply was: "Don't worry son, after you've been here a while, you'll be able to pick up a rifle." That was cold comfort.'

When the landing barges deposited them at the docks, the Australians were met by English Air Force chaps whose greeting was: 'Piss off, you'll be no good here, the Nips are right behind us and they have complete control of the bloody place.'

Then it was back on the boats and off to Java, where they were put under Dutch command – 'which was as good as nothing' – and issued with one gun to each four or five men.

The outcome was inevitable – surrender.

In his unfinished memoir, Private W. C. Reed takes up the story, with additional commentary from his mate Murray Jobbing:

'We fought an impossible task until the 9th March when the Dutch decided to capitulate to the Jap army. We were informed that we could make for the jungle or as an alternative there were ships in the harbour at Tilajap on the south end of the island. We started the long trek south and on reaching Tilijap there were ships there alright, but only their masts were sticking out of the water. The feeling that went around the troops was impossible to describe – no boats, no food, no hope. So it was decided to destroy arms, ammo trucks and all gear that might be of use to the enemy.

'We camped in a Dutch tea plantation until word came through from Jap HQ that we were to march ourselves to a town called Telleas where we were interned in the bicycle sheds of the school.

'This started our life of hell on earth, with bashings, humiliation and starvation, which lasted through until our release three and a half years later. Shifting from one camp to another all over Java, doing all sorts of work from cleaning up Dutch schools and barracks to make into hospitals and army barracks, to working on the wharves and growing castor oil.

'After two years of this, in May 1944, we were drafted to River Valley in Malaya, just off Singapore on the mainland.'

On June 3, 1944, three days before Pte Reed's 25th birthday, he and Jobling and about 776 other prisoners were loaded onto an unidentified ship off Singapore, according to documentation held by the Australian War Museum. Those papers say 258 of them were Australians, 281 Dutch, 196 English and 43 American, numbers which vary only slightly from those appearing in the accounts written later by Reed and Jobling.

The ship, of between 4000 and 5000 tons, was loaded with bauxite, a sedimentary rock, and was so overcrowded that 300 men slept on deck where at least they could lie straight in bed, so to speak. The ship sailed as part of a convoy of 11, three of which were carrying POWs, escorted by four small corvettes. All concerned were apprehensive of American submarines – with good reason, when the leading corvette was torpedoed three nights into the voyage.

BILL REED again:

OUT OF THE JUNGLE INTO THE SEA
River Valley Camp, Singapore, June 1944

Mud, flies, mosquitoes and bad-tempered Japs. Out of the night gloom, with Movement Orders, we were to embark on a Japanese cargo boat, headed for what we supposed (but were not sure) would be the mighty shores of Nippon.

Through lines of baton-wielding Japs, we were herded up the gangplank and down into the hold. After a few hours, up came the anchor and away we went – what was in store for us only God and the Japs had any idea. Of the 777 allied prisoners, about 260 were Australians, mostly men who had come across from Timor to Java. My own mates had left Java some months before on a craft which finished up in Burma with them sent to work on the Burma railway line.

Our convoy consisted of several ships plus a Navy escort. Our thoughts were varied as to destination, whether we would make it and what was in store for us if we did.

Even though we were hoping for freedom, we did not want it per a torpedo in the side of the ship. It was loaded to the plimsoll line with bauxite which was heavy enough to guarantee us a hasty trip to the bottom of the sea. There were all sorts of suggestions on how to vacate the ship if this occurred, never dreaming it was, later, to become a reality.

Each day we were allowed a limited time on deck to exercise and relieve our bowels over the side, which meant standing in a wooden crate fixed to the side with two boards to stand on, which wasn't too bad until we got into the China Sea and struck a typhoon. This meant when anyone used the toilets, the captain's bridge got covered in you-know-what, so we were then ordered not to use this means and had to find other ways of disposing of our excess. This, at times, was most awkward.

On the evening of the fourth day out from Singapore we were in the hold with nothing more to do than live with our thoughts when the peace was shattered by a terrific explosion somewhere on the outskirts of the convoy.

Within seconds, the chaps who were on deck came tumbling into the holds encouraged by stick-wielding Japs bellowing and kicking where they could see a body.

The ship reverberated to the sound of depth charges.

One of the chaps who was on deck said one of the corvettes exploded in a sheet of flames. A Yank near me expressed all our thoughts when he said: 'I sure hope those guys can take a hint and go home for tea now.'

From then on, until we reached Manila on 11 June no more ships were lost although there were sub scares daily and the Japs dropped depth charges as if they were tuppence a dozen. We put this down to Jap nerves rather than the presence of subs. Later we found out to our horror that this was not the case. After our initial fright we became used to the explosives.

Our ship arrived at Manila harbour and then continued its merry way on the 14th. Two days out of Manila, the convoy ran into weather of hurricane force, the seas rose mountain high, one moment the sea was several feet below us, the next minute it would be engulfing the whole

SURVIVAL AT SEA

ship and washing everything about. Some food was washed over the side, meaning we had less rations.

Strangely enough, we managed to stay afloat. Many who were in the hold were seasick and the atmosphere and stench from the people thus afflicted was almost impossible to bear.

During this storm the ship began to fall behind the convoy; she was obviously in trouble and in need of repair. We finally made it to Formosa on June 18 and we were transferred to another ship, the Tamahoko Maru.

Fate was making preparations for the dirty trick it was to play on us in the very near future.

*****

The Tamahoko Maru, which was loaded with a cargo of sugar and rice, also carried some 500 Japanese servicemen, all of whom bore the appearance of survivors themselves, according to the official documentation. Reed and Jobling recall that there were also an unknown number of women and children on board. The boat was equipped with lifebelts, although they were not actually issued to the prisoners, and a number of balsa rafts were tied to the deck.

The convoy, now consisting of 12 ships escorted by two corvettes, a minelayer and a whaling ship left Formosa, which later became Taiwan, on June 20, with all aboard pleased to be out of the tropics and in cooler weather. At 11.50pm on June 24, about 40 miles southwest of Nagasaki, the ship was hit by two torpedoes – unleashed by the American submarine Tang – just forward of the bridge on the starboard side, instantly killing many men of all nationalities. The ship took only about two minutes to sink. About 560 of the prisoners were lost.

BILL REED:
I was always optimistic enough to think that we would escape the consequences of being torpedoed.

I felt sure that Allied Intelligence in Singapore would have notified Allied Command of Allied POWs leaving Singapore and the transport they were

27 |

on, but as was proved to be in time to come, this was not the case.

We were crammed into the hold until space ran out and then the rest of us were allowed to find what space we could on the hatch cover. I did not envy the boys who were in the hold.

We were confined to our quarters in the forward part of the ship. We were on board only a short time when it was discovered that below us in the lower hold were bags of sugar, something we had not tasted for a couple of years. Boy oh boy, what joy! Lookouts were posted for the guards so we could burrow down below the top bags and fill whatever container came to hand with this precious commodity. This turned out to be unnecessary because the sugar – and the boat – finished at the bottom of the sea.

June 24th

Since leaving Formosa four days ago we had not had one sub scare. Late afternoon, land loomed in the distance. The guards were all excited and we were told that it was Japan and we would land the day after next.

While we were not overjoyed by the prospect of being incarcerated in that country, we were extremely grateful that we were still alive and not feeding the sharks. That afternoon, we were allowed to bathe under the seawater hose to wash off the accumulated sweat and grime from weeks of non-bathing.

We agreed with each other how lucky we were to have escaped the subs. How naïve can one get? As midnight approached, my mate and I were bedded down on hatch covers over the holds. Having only been asleep for what seemed minutes we were awakened by a massive boom. Sitting up, we saw the ship in front of us in the convoy sinking to the bottom of the sea. Almost immediately our ship exploded with an almighty crash and I was thrown eight or nine feet into the air and on coming down again found myself floating in the hold.

Looking up at the stars above, I could not reach the edge of the hatch, although I could feel the water rising so I let it float me up to the top where I was able to pull myself out onto the deck.

Looking up, the bridge seemed to be bearing down on me, so I said to myself, 'Bill, head for the drink quick smart or you're going to go down with *this bloody ship.' So over the side I went in the neatest dive any Olympic diver could have executed and on swimming away from the ship I had time to take stock of what was before me, which held little prospect, I assure you.*

MURRAY JOBLING:

The massive explosion woke me up. Slowly I tried to banish the sleep from my brain, subconsciously aware of a foreign sound. Around me, others were moving. 'What the blazes was that?' I thought. It wasn't left in doubt long. Even as I clambered to my feet, the hold filled with the shattering roar of a violent explosion, the decking below my feet seemed to rise and hit me in the face. The smell of explosives was in my nostrils. The dim lights went out. We were in pitch darkness.

'Jesus, we've been torpedoed,' I said to no-one in particular. Someone on my right called out: 'Righto chaps, remember your instructions.'

No sooner had I risen to my feet than water began to swirl around my legs. Trapped, my feeling was of utter hopelessness and despair. 'What hope have I got now?' I thought.

Within seconds the water was up to my chest and next moment I was floating and my head was bumping the decking above. I was completely submerged. 'What a bastard of a way to die,' I thought.

Not wishing to prolong the agony, I endeavoured to take in water and end it quickly – but somehow my efforts weren't successful. I began to swim in the direction of what I hoped was the companionway. Suddenly I realised my head was no longer bumping. Driven by desperation I began swimming upwards. After what seemed hours, my head broke the surface and I thankfully gulped in fresh air.

The scene was lit by a phosphorescent glow and although I could see no-one the air was filled with the cries of human voices. But what I could see above me was not conducive to my peace of mind. Slowly bearing down on me was the dark shape of the bridge and the funnel, nearer and nearer as the ship began to go down. I was powerless to swim clear. All my energy was being expended in the effort to stay afloat.

Suddenly I was caught a resounding blow on the chest by a portion of the bridge superstructure and, helpless, pinned by the downward surge of the ship, I was carried down to the depths again.

'This is the end,' I thought. Lights flashed past my eyes as I was carried down. Suddenly the weight on my chest was gone. I was free again. Driven more by blind instinct than lucid thought I began swimming upwards. When it seemed my lungs must surely burst my head broke the surface. I thanked my maker for the second chance.

I had emerged into complete darkness. Not a star was visible. I could feel light rain on my face. I was completely alone and far from being out of the woods yet. I began shouting in the hope of finding wreckage and another soul to keep me company. I did not relish the thought of being alone.

After what seemed hours I received an answering call. Guided by that I came upon five of my mates on a raft. That Yank voice, 'You OK, bud?' was music to my ears. I assured him I was. Then hanging on to the raft I proceeded to heave my guts into the ocean.

BILL REED:

After swimming about for what seemed ages I found a hatch cover which I climbed on and it provided buoyancy until I came across a raft which housed five chaps. I transferred to the raft which now became over-loaded and rode about a foot below the surface.

My companions consisted of a RAF doctor, W/C McCarthy, two Yanks, Jack Powell, a Texan, and a chap from New York who we knew only as Shorty. The fourth member was Murray Jobling from 13th anti-tank regiment. The fifth was a Jap seaman. After I had been in the water a few minutes, the ship to the rear of our boat also was sent to the bottom by a well-directed torpedo.

We were all hoping the sub would surface and pick us out of the sea but it was not to be. The weather, although it was summertime, did not do much to make our position very pleasant. Murray and I went into the sea in our underpants and nothing else. The water was cold, also the wind, and the action on our kidney region made us consistently urinate and pass wind which didn't make it any easier for all and sundry.

The Jap seaman was next to me on the raft and a grass mat floated by and he grabbed it and put it around his shoulder and started to breathe into it, mainly to keep us warm but I didn't appreciate the smell of his soy bean breath. Everybody was suffering with the cold – more so the Jap; he sounded like a negro minstrel playing on a set of bones.

After being in the water for about two hours we heard shouting in the distance and what was more gratifying, they were English voices – at least we were not the only survivors. Our biggest worry now was what were our chances of being picked up? Although land could be seen from the deck of the ship, we were not sure just where it had disappeared to. We knew we had little chance of reaching it unaided.

Presently we sighted a flare in the distance, perhaps 800 yards away, and as the clouds began to blow away we were able to make out thin shapes in the sea around us. Our interest centred on a hump-shaped object in the general direction of the flare. Our optimism rose at once. 'It's a sub picking up survivors,' was the unanimous verdict. We tried to will it in our direction. Later, we were disgusted to find our 'sub' was nothing but a smashed and upturned lifeboat. So much for optimism.

In the distance we heard a voice say: 'Anybody got a frying pan? I've got the daddy of a fish here.' It was an Aussie voice. I don't think he got his frying pan. Aussie humour seems to come to the surface in any situation. After the longest night I have spent in my life, the eastern sky began to get lighter, with the rising sun bursting forth in a blaze of warmth. At least I hoped to thaw out and feel warm once more.

Wing-Commander McCarthy had a watch but the only information we could gain from it was that it had stopped at 10 minutes to 12, so pin-pointing the time the ship went down. Later we found out other watches had stopped at the same time.

With the coming of daylight we were able to see who our immediate neighbours were and carry out shouted conversations. Wreckage was strung out as far as we could see and here and there little blobs that denoted the existence of human beings were in evidence. Around us were mainly allied personnel.

Through the night, Murray was bothered by a piece of wreckage bumping against his legs. After continually trying to push it away to no avail and on the arrival of daylight he found his 'piece of wreckage' to be a two-year-old Japanese child. It was wearing a lifebelt which had been no help. He towed the body away from the raft so we would not be reminded of man's inhumanity to man.

By this time, we had floated closer toward land and a faint blur could be seen in the distance. Towards afternoon, we saw two vessels patrolling about, one a Jap naval vessel and the other a converted whale chaser that had been part of the convoy. They were concentrating on picking up Japanese survivors.

Later the whale chaser came closer to our raft so I decided to swim to it. On reaching the boat, I reached up to grab the side and pull myself up and a Jap sailor came over and stamped on my fingers and pushed me back into the water. I had nothing better to do but swim around and figure out what my next move was to be. By this time, Murray and our Jap friend (?) from the raft had arrived. The Jap was taken aboard and Murray hung onto a rope which hung over the side.

Whether the Jap from the raft had anything to do with what happened next we will never know but a few minutes later we were motioned to climb on board. We were then herded up into the bows of the ship and told to stay put. As more chaps were picked up we were anxious to see if any of our friends were amongst them.

When it became apparent all survivors had been picked up the corvette came over to within 400 yards of our boat. On the deck were eight Aussies who we knew, they were told to swim over to our boat. Two brothers from Tasmania (Ashton was their name) were seen to be trying to explain that they could not swim but were unceremoniously thrown into the sea and we could only stand on deck and watch them flounder until they went down in the wake of the corvette. By the time the Japs realised they were non-swimmers and threw over bits of bamboo poles, it was too late. How ironic to have survived the torpedoing only to be murdered by a bunch of Jap bastards.

The other six reached our vessel and a count was taken and the total arrived at was 212 out of the original 777. We left Java with 268 Australians, 196 English, 43 Yanks, 270 Dutch. We now numbered 72 Australians, 42 English, 13 Yanks, 85 Dutch.

All survivors picked up by the vessels headed for land and early in the afternoon we arrived at what we were later to find out was Nagasaki on the island of Kyushu, Japan.

We made a very sorry spectacle as we were salt-encrusted and sorely in need of many comforts. We were driven to the prison camp wearing next to nothing, miserable and shivering in the cold wind. We arrived at a large wooden building with a high wall surrounding it, topped off with a liberal amount of barbed wire to convince us there was no way out.

This was Fukuoka 14 camp, situated in the heart of the industrial section in the centre of the city, and destined to be our new home. Once inside the building we soon started to thaw out and things seemed a little more cheerful. At least we were alive.

This became our home until we were released in a most unusual way fourteen months later.

Unusual? That was putting it mildly!

YOU CAN'T KILL BILL

For the prisoners of war in Fukuoka Camp 14-B in Nagasaki in 1944-45, there were many ways to die. Working as slave labour in the nearby Mitsubishi steel foundry for long hours on an inadequate diet of little more than rice and not enough warm clothing could make a man's health deteriorate to the point of breakdown. And often did. Arguing with or insulting the guards might have you beaten to death. You could wait until the Allies invaded, at which point – if it ever happened – you would surely be executed as little more than a nuisance. Which proved to be a real possibility.

Or you could, without warning, find yourself trapped on the ground when the most lethal weapon humanity had ever invented, the atomic bomb, was unleashed – on both friend and foe.

Astonishingly, none of that was enough to kill Bill Reed.

The apparently indestructible machine-gunner survived all of those experiences, having already made it through more than two years of hell on earth in earlier prison camps away from Japan and having lived to tell the tale of being torpedoed at sea.

Having endured all that – especially the bomb – you would be easily excused for making damned sure you never set foot in that country again.

But my father always wanted to go back, even if my mother, Joan, deeply disapproved, delaying his decision to do so for decades.

He had his reasons and one of them, amazingly, was to offer gratitude to one of his captors, a gesture of goodwill that transcended all the enmity, deprivation and misery of his long incarceration, which lasted five years in all.

Eventually, an invitation arrived from a TV crew to join a party of the Camp 14 alumni to revisit Nagasaki in 1985, the 40th anniversary of the bombing. One of the others was his mate Murray Jobling, who also lived in Warrnambool, where they resumed their friendship when Reed moved his family – by then, me and three younger siblings, a mongrel dog called Bull and a talkative cockatoo named Joe – there in the early sixties.

Returning to Japan, his main mission was to be re-united with the foreman of the foundry, Kojima Asagoro, who he and his mates believed had shown them kindness and mercy during their ordeal, for which they wished to thank him.

That is, if he was still alive.

He was, and their emotional, tearful re-union became the subject of a documentary called *Nagasaki Journey*, the work of Mark Stiles, which features seven other prisoners – Eric Hooper, Jack Johnson, Jack Prosser, Alan Chick, Richard Downie, Reg McConnell and Peter McGrath-Kerr.

They were among 71 or 72 (depending on your source of information) Australians who survived the sinking of the Tamahoko Maru and were taken to Camp 14. Twenty-four of them were still there – the others having been shifted elsewhere, or died – when the bomb arrived on August 9, 1945. All 24 lived through it. Not one is still alive.

There has never been any way to accurately quantify how many people were killed by the first – and still the only – nuclear attack on any country, with the larger city of Hiroshima, to the north, having been flattened three days earlier than Nagasaki.

The death tolls are complicated by the protracted impact of nuclear fall-out.

While many were killed instantly by the blasts – it is estimated that roughly half the deaths in both attacks occurred on the first day – many more died as a result of radiation sickness and injuries, long after the detonations.

Another reason for the confusion is the administrative chaos that prevailed in the aftermath.

However, in his 1984 book *Last Stop Nagasaki*, Australian author Hugh V. Clarke – himself a prisoner in a different camp in that city – says

the Hiroshima figure was 78,000 killed instantly and 60,000 injured.
In Nagasaki, an official memorial quotes 73,884 deaths and 74,909
injuries from a study by the Committee for Preservation of Atomic Bomb
Artefacts, but notes that these are estimates up until the end of 1945.

Whatever the exact truth, it was horrific to an extent the world had
never seen before – and hopefully never will again.

Set against it, it is all the more miraculous that the 24 Australians were
able to walk away, more or less unscathed, and in almost every case live
out their lives with little or no after-effects, or at least few, if any, that
could be attributed to the blast unequivocally. The truth of that may not
be as straightforward as all concerned have been led to believe in the
intervening years.

It goes without saying they were unlucky to be in the wrong place at
the wrong time at all, but that wasn't the half of it – Nagasaki wasn't even
the original target. If there was to be a target at all.

The American president Harry S. Truman – who had succeeded the
recently deceased Franklin D. Roosevelt – and the Pentagon had severe
misgivings about using such formidable force, especially for the purpose
of mass destruction, and not knowing whether it would even work
properly.

According to Australian nuclear scientist Sir Mark Oliphant, who was
working with the Americans, one school of thought favoured dropping
the bomb on the sacred Mt Fuji as a demonstration and a warning of
what lay in store if the Japanese 'were not good boys'.

Oliphant says on the *Nagasaki Journey* documentary that people
in high places began to feel dubious about it and hoped that the bomb
would not work.

Afterwards, he said, he and other scientists 'were aghast at the toll and
felt we had given away all moral right to the use of nuclear weaponry by
us or anyone in the future'.

Those words still resonate powerfully.

In the end only one concession was made, according to American
Gordon Arneson, a member of the Interim Commission for Atomic
Energy in 1945 and a high-ranking officer in the war office.

He told the documentary makers that the city of Kyoto was on a list of targets until the Secretary of War crossed it off, saying: 'I know something about that city and it is priceless to Japan. Kyoto will not be bombed.'

It was replaced on the doomsday list by Kokura, an ancient castle town not far from Hiroshima and Nagasaki. If Hiroshima had been clouded over on the day it was attacked, Kokura would have got that bomb instead. But on the morning of August 6, a Boeing B-29 Superfortress named Enola Gay, in honour of the pilot's mother, carried a nuclear bomb known as 'Little Boy' from an American Air Force base in the South Pacific. Powered by 64kg of the rare isotope uranium-235, it dropped from about 9400m onto Hiroshima at 9.15am, followed by a brilliant flash of light and an enormous mushroom cloud. About a third of the city's population died from the explosion and fire, tens of thousands more injured or doomed to succumb to cancers.

Kokura then became the primary target for the second one, but this time it was shrouded in cloud and smoke itself and so Major Charles Sweeney, in command of a second B29 Super-fortress bomber named Bock's Car carrying the weapon known as 'Fat Man' – a plutonium device three metres long with the power of 20,000 tonnes of high explosive inside its grotesque, egg-shell shaped shell – headed for Nagasaki instead.

At two minutes past 11am, the plane's bombardier released his deadly payload by sight, not by radar, and it floated silently down by parachute, its unsuspecting victims mostly oblivious to the hideous danger that was about to engulf them when it exploded in mid-air, 500m above them.

The prisoners were no exception.

For starters, they had not been told of what had happened to Hiroshima three days earlier and had no idea that nuclear weaponry even existed.

'We just didn't know what it was,' Reed said. 'You have to remember that in those days no-one had heard of such a thing as an atom bomb. When one was dropped on Hiroshima we, as POWs, were the last to learn anything.

'It's not the sort of thing you easily forget.'

He and his mates have similar recollections of the fateful day.

Reed and some others had been reassigned from foundry work to digging a tunnel into a hillside, ostensibly to build an air raid shelter because of the increasingly frequent bombing raids.

'But we knew that when the Allied invasion began the Japs were going to kill all the prisoners. We were resigned to the fact that we were digging our own mass grave,' he said.

They were right. According to one of the other survivors, Allan Chick, it emerged in later official investigations that the prisoners were due for execution in 10 days' time.

'I was told after the war that the Japanese were expecting an invasion at any time and living prisoners would have been a nuisance to their war effort. But the Japanese, of course, gave us no indication they intended to kill us,' Chick said. 'We were surviving on a day to day basis. We had no idea how long we were going to last. But I can tell you, the bomb added 50 years to my life. I'm all in favour of it.'

Having worked all night, Reed was asleep at 11am. 'The tremendous noise of the blast jerked me awake and everything crashed down around me,' he said. 'I didn't know what had happened or what was going on. My left eye was full of blood and there was something hurting my back. I couldn't stand up properly. It was pitch black, like midnight, not 11 o'clock in the morning. I was staggering and stumbling around and then one of my mates grabbed me and we all took off for the hills at the edge of town. The guards had vanished. The city was flattened. Everybody who could was getting away to the hills. Looking back, you could see this great cloud with fires burning all over what was left of the city. We thought perhaps an ammo dump had gone up. We never imagined it could be the result of just one bomb.'

The Australian and other POWs were soon rounded up again and returned to the camp. Everything had changed. In this one fearful day, the war was effectively over. Japan surrendered within days.

Chick was working on the roof of a Red Cross store, covering it with soil as protection from fire bombs, when 'suddenly there was this terrific flash of light. I didn't hear a thing, yet people further away said they thought it was a terrific noise. It sort of dazzled me. I was blinded for some time, how long I'm not sure. I didn't know what had hit me. I just came to my senses and stood up but I couldn't see a thing, it was pitch dark. How it didn't injure me I don't know. Everything was on fire. All the barracks blocks had wooden frames and there was nothing left. The telegraph poles were charred.'

Like the others, he fled to the hills. When he returned the next day to the camp, which had also housed hundreds of Chinese and 100 Japanese criminals in an enclosure next door to the Australians, he found scores, perhaps hundreds, of them lying side by side, cremated by the blast.

'One had his foot sticking up and I touched his toe – it crumbled to dust,' he said.

Murray Jobling's account is the most graphic of all.

He remembered sitting on his bed rolling a cigarette when he heard the sound of a single aircraft. 'Next moment I was hurtling through the air and landed on my feet. Through the window I could see the alleyway between the huts was filled with a sheet of flame of terrific intensity,' he said.

'Dazed and only half-conscious I staggered around and couldn't see anyone but I was aware of fires all around me. The barracks were just a tangled pile of timber and debris. Staggering to the window I tried to pull the bars out, in vain. Realising my efforts were futile I looked for another way out and almost had to laugh – the section of the wall I was trying to push over was the only part standing. I saw guards and prisoners alike heading for the hills on the east side of the city, trying to find a way through the fires. We hadn't gone far when we realised we had left without thinking about anyone who may have been injured, so a dozen of us and a guard went back but everybody had been evacuated. Japanese civilians we passed were running around aimlessly, the majority suffering from dreadful burns. Their skin was blackened and hanging from their bodies in strips. Some had huge blisters under the blackened skin. Many of the children appeared to be blinded and I observed one child with his eyes burned from the sockets. I could not help but feel pity for these children.

'As daylight faded we were puzzled as to what had happened. The entire valley was enveloped in flames and covered with a thick pall of smoke. The chaps who had been outside at the time saw one lone aircraft, very high up, and then what they thought was either a balloon or a parachute coming down. Next moment the camp was collapsing around them. Some of the boys said they heard the sound of many express trains rushing through a tunnel; others, like me, had no recollection of any sound whatsoever. Exhausted, we finally dozed off. Next morning the Japanese guards ordered us back to the camp. Amidst the burnt-out ruins our mates greeted us. A roll call (of 201 prisoners) revealed the casualties. Five prisoners killed and 30 seriously injured, some suffering from the mysterious skin burns.

'Of the 24 Australians, Peter McGrath-Kerr was the only one badly injured – he had head wounds and broken ribs but was still able to walk. (McGrath-Kerr said later that he had no memory of being rescued or of the ensuing five days.) The camp had been completely gutted. A portion of the brick wall was still standing but the large 'H' section steel girders that formed the framework were bent flat to the ground. The rice pots in the burnt-out kitchen were intact and although the rice was charred on top the remainder was edible.

'The steel framework of the factory in which we had worked was still standing upright but the corrugated iron sheets of the walls were blown inwards and wrapped around the framework like a piece of cloth in a windstorm. An eerie sight. But just 200 yards north of the factory was an even eerier sight. Where another factory had existed, there was only vacant land and a few badly burnt-out lathes to indicate what had been there. We camped in the open among the ruins that day. The bodies of the dead were cremated in the fires still burning. The civilian population were seen to be evacuating the city with what few possessions they had managed to save, plus little wooden boxes carrying the ashes of their loved ones.

'Next day, August 11, with improvised stretchers, we marched out of the ruined city. Tanaka, the little civilian interpreter, was the only member of the camp guards to be hurt and we were compelled to carry him on a stretcher also. He was groaning like hell, but to my mind the little cow looked perfectly fit. He was suffering from an acute overdose of fear. We were within sight of a camp about five miles out of the city when an air-raid siren blew. Tanaka leapt out of that stretcher and ran as though all the devils of Hades were after him. We never saw Tanaka again.

'The area we were now in was relatively undamaged. It had been protected by the terrain. Another wearying mile, we arrived at an empty army barracks. Ten days after the bombing the Japanese informed us the war was over and we were no longer regarded as prisoners of war. Red Cross representatives would arrive in due course. Our cheers must have been heard in Tokyo.'

The formal end of the war had arrived quickly, Emperor Hirohito announcing a surrender on August 15 — an inglorious defeat, after stubbornly driving his people on in a virtual kamikaze mission well after hostilities in Europe had ended with the death of Hitler and the capitulation of Germany three months earlier.

Soon afterwards, Jobling says, an American war correspondent accompanied by two airmen arrived at the camp. 'They told us that the bomb that had destroyed Nagasaki was an atom bomb, the second to be used in the war. The Yanks had come from the American air base established in Konoya in the south of the island. Planes were flying in supplies and leaving empty,' he said. 'Atom bomb? Hell, I wasn't interested in atom bombs. My eyes were fixed on Konoya. Next day, 24 Australians left the ruins of Nagasaki behind. With the directions supplied by the Yanks, we were heading towards Australia. Fast!'

The prisoners' escape was a miracle. What saved them – both from instant death, and from radiation poisoning in later life?

They just got lucky, it seems. Simple as that.

In his 1995 book *Wake Me If There's Trouble*, esteemed war correspondent Denis Warner of the *Melbourne Herald*, quotes Reed thus: 'Anyone who was under cover doesn't seem to have been affected. We didn't hang around to be affected. By being under cover we were protected from the initial effects of radiation, and we escaped other effects by moving out quickly.'

American scientists, says Warner, determined that one corner of the camp was 1420 metres from the epicentre of the explosion and that anyone there would have been exposed to 53 units of radiation. At the most distant corner of the camp they would have been exposed to 49 units.

Dr Peter Ilbury, then assistant director-general of the Australian Department of Health, and formerly a professor of radiology, discovered that the amount of radiation blood cells could accept before damage occurred was 50 units.

From the position of the Australian billets, 50 units was what the 24 men would have been exposed to.

'They were lucky,' Dr Ilbery told Warner. 'They were all under shelter and the 50 units of radiation was relatively small. Nevertheless, if they had been in the open, they would have died. Many Dutch prisoners who were caught in the open did not survive.'

Chick, who was working on the roof with not much shelter, was something of an exception – he was found to have radiation in his blood later in life but not to any serious extent. He also had heart problems but was the last one to die. Reg McConnell, who was also more or less unsheltered, eventually lost the ability to walk properly, and told Warner he blamed radiation. But he lived to 85.

In general, Warner reported, as time went on the group's health was no worse than might have been expected at their age.

However, whether later generations were unaffected is debatable.

Murray Jobling's daughter, Diane Wickson, says that her father, the second last of the 24 to die, in May 2006, always wondered whether his exposure might have been responsible for what she describes as 'health issues way in excess of the average family.'

The details of that are private, of course, but Jobling's children do seem to have been exceptionally unlucky in that regard.

Only recently, in fact since hearing about their experiences, has it occurred to me that perhaps it might not be simply bad luck that my own three siblings all died prematurely from different causes – and that perhaps I have been the lucky one, making it past the biblical allotment of three score years and ten without anything catastrophic intruding. Sadly, the other three got nowhere near that.

Precisely why, I will never know – and neither will Mrs Wickson and her siblings and their children. 'I am unaware of any research into any health problems as the years have gone on,' she told me. 'There's probably only about 100 of us, plus the next generation, and we only have to look at how hard governments fought to ignore the effects of Agent Orange in Vietnam. They are not going to look for problems.' They most certainly aren't, not after all these years.

She says there was one other issue that made life immediately after the war less pleasant for her father and others. 'The men had a special bond and stuck together because of what they went through and one thing that encouraged them to do that was that when they got back people did not believe their story.'

My own father never spoke of that but I can well believe it because whenever I tell people that he walked away unscathed from under an atom bomb, it is often possible to sense their incredulity, if not outright scepticism.

When the TV documentary of their experiences was aired, Jobling said to his family: 'Well, that might shut up the doubters.' When he was interviewed by the *Warrnambool Standard* someone said to the reporter: 'Why did you waste your time on that liar?'

That smacks of the disgraceful treatment Vietnam veterans endured many years later when they returned from that Godforsaken war only to be shunned and denigrated.

Who knows how much luck anyone is entitled to in their lifetime but my Dad certainly made some inroads into his fair share while in captivity. He not only survived the sinking of the Tamahoko Maru and the atom bomb, but life in general inside the prison camp, where, he said, it 'became a matter of survival of the fittest and mentally strong' especially during the coldest winter Japan had experienced for 70 years, when lack of warm clothing was a major issue. More than 80 Fukuoka inmates died, many of pneumonia or exposure. Infestations of fleas, body lice and bed bugs were another problem, albeit less life-threatening. Food and medical supplies were both in very short supply.

At the outset, says Reed: 'We were marched down to the foundry where we were lined up to listen to the usual bullshit about work well and be happy in your work and Nippon will treat you well and make you like Nippon.'

Most of the captors must have missed that memo.

Once, a young guard caught Reed chewing gum against an instruction that he had forgotten from the previous day. When he spat it out at the guard's feet, offending him, he was knocked to the ground.

'I was pretty upset about it and ready to spring to my feet and hit him,' he said. 'Another bloke jumped in and said "don't hit him, Bill" and then explained that I would have got a beating – and it might even have cost me my life.'

Such incidents were not uncommon. Chick said they were subjected to regular bashings from guards who revelled in meting our punishment. 'You would blink an eyelid and they would bash you and if you fell to the ground they would slip the boots in. One sergeant bashed me and fractured both my eardrums.'

Not all of the enemy were so brutally inclined.

Kojima Asagoro was not in the military, he was the foundry hancho or foreman, older than the prisoners who were mostly in their early to mid-twenties, and he was a man of more compassion than most of the guards.

'We had very small rations, very little to eat, and up against the furnaces all day, it was very hard work. Kojima realised we couldn't work if we were not fed,' Reed says on the *Nagasaki Journey* documentary.

'In three-and-a-half years he was the only Japanese I had any respect for. He was very strict but fair. He made it his business to give us extra soup and stuff. It wasn't much, but to us it was a big thing. He wasn't allowed to show it because the guards didn't like that sort of thing. It has always been in my mind to come back and seek him out because I realised he was the one person who did what he could to make our lives a little bit easier.'

So here he is on video, 40 years later, climbing the steep path to the Asogoro family home, carrying a gift. 'I feel strange, very strange,' Reed says, without elaborating.

The door opens and there the old man is, looking close to tears.

The pair embrace emotionally and at length, and speak to each other in their own languages, neither understanding the words – but totally aware of the sentiments each is conveying to the other. Namely, goodwill and gratitude on both sides. Thanks for what you did, from one, thanks for your forgiveness from the other.

Inside, joined by Jobling, a meal – a feast, really – has been prepared, and beers are poured so that toasts can be exchanged.

On the balcony, Asagoro-san is asked to point out where the factory was. It's not far. Reed and Jobling, now tourists to all intents, find their way to where a new industrial building stands – and are confronted by a uniformed guard. He just offers a friendly smile, one more thing that has changed completely.

The next day, Reed and Jobling are waiting for the train to begin the journey home when Asogoro, helped along by family members, arrives at the station, bearing gifts of his own which are presented before another emotional moment – farewell, this time forever. 'I hope you stay healthy and your family also,' were Reed's parting words.

Bill Reed waited a long time for that closure – perhaps it was all that he was waiting for. After being released he returned to Bendigo, which wasn't quite the joyful homecoming it might have been. Well before he had set out to serve his country, his parents had divorced, none too amicably apparently. His father, Percival George Reed – a grandfather I never met – was something of a war hero himself, having been awarded the Distinguished Conduct Medal for venturing out under heavy fire on several occasions to repair damaged communication lines at Fromelles and on the Somme during the First War.

The handwritten commendation, which I have, speaks of 'great coolness and courage' and 'great personal risk.'

Percival was waiting when his son arrived back but apparently got the brush-off because whatever it was that led to the divorce was still a source of anger and resentment. To my knowledge, they never met again.

After being discharged from the Army — his certificate says he was on active service in Australia for 67 days and for 1648 days abroad and he was awarded three medals – Bill met and married Joan Orr, from Ballarat, and soon had me to look after, followed by Gail, Jennifer and Colin.

A resourceful, hard-working, hands-on jack-of-several-trades, he built our first home himself and later, in partnership with my mother's parents, operated small mixed businesses in Creswick, near Ballarat, Dennington, near Warrnambool, and Albury. Most of his spare time was spent on his only hobby, fishing, and the rest of his life was much less eventful than the first bit.

He never made any money to speak of and it took a long time for him to come to terms with his wartime experiences to the point of being willing to talk freely about it, although what he did not say when I arrived home one day with a new Japanese car spoke clearly enough. However, next time I went home, he was driving one himself.

On a slightly different note, nor did he say much in 1966 when, on a Saturday morning, a letter arrived just hours before I was due to play in a country footy grand final, telling me that my number had not come out of the barrel and I would not be required to do national service and end up dodging bullets in Vietnam.

But there was no mistaking his relief that I would not have to go through anything like he had. Or my relief for that matter. Walking on air, I played the game of my life that day.

But I digress. After the return visit to Nagasaki, he lived less than another two years, dying during heart surgery within a few hours of my shaking his hand and wishing him all the best for the operation that was about to begin.

He is buried in Ballarat, not much more than walking distance from the first and only official Prisoners of War Memorial, which was opened in my original home town's superb Botanical Gardens in 2004. His name is one of 35,675 engraved in black granite, to be remembered in posterity. The name Reed appears 22 times in the section referring to World War II, one of which is my uncle Murray, who did time in Changi. And there are two listings for Penna, my wife's uncles.

In all, according to the Official War History, 7,777 prisoners of the

Japanese in various countries died – up to 600 executed and 1515 lost at sea – while 13,872 made it home. By comparison, of 7116 prisoners of Germany and Italy, only 242 died in captivity.

Bill Reed died in peace, the memory of the reunion with Asagoro still fresh in his mind, and without any trace of bitterness about all that had happened to him.

When Dr Ilbery, the radiation expert, conducted his investigation, he took what he described as testimony from my father, who told him that while the prisoners considered their general treatment to have been 'far below' what it should have been, he had eventually arrived at the view that for the captors 'it hadn't been a bed of roses either.'

In a report to the Nagasaki authorities in 1979, Dr Ilbery wrote: 'After being told the war was over he, like most of the others, felt reborn and cried like a baby to relieve the pent-up feelings of three and a half years of uncertainty, frustration and sometimes moments of despair.'

The report said that after being kept in Manila for two weeks until they gained weight and their general appearance had improved enough for them to be seen by their families, returning to normal routine 'was as one can imagine much more difficult than it first appeared'.

He says Pte Reed told him: 'To go into details about this phase in our lives would only leave the reader the thought that he was listening to some weak-minded individual looking for somebody's shoulder to cry on. It was a long way back and a hard road. If the fellows could be made to admit it in all honesty many would agree they haven't arrived there yet.'

Like all of his comrades, he agreed that the bombing, for all its destruction, had been a good thing, not a bad thing, because it had prevented many thousands more deaths on all sides if the war had dragged on.

It also saved their own lives because the plan to execute them never had time to be carried out.

'There were a lot of Japanese high school students working with us in the Mitsubishi foundry,' he said in another interview. 'In their spare time they were all making knives and swords and pikes because they were expecting an invasion and were getting ready to die for their country and their emperor. They told us that and they meant it, too. If the Allies had invaded Japan they would have found themselves fighting every man, woman and child in the country. The war would have dragged on for another year or more and millions of lives would have been wasted. But that's all past now. We're living in a different world. The Nagasaki bomb was a mere peanut compared to the modern weapons. It's no longer a question of wiping out a city; today we're talking about destroying a planet. There is no point in being bitter about the past. It's the future we have to be concerned with. I've seen one mushroom cloud. I never want to see another.'

He never did – and thankfully, no-one else ever has.

FORGIVING AND FORGETTING

How long does it take to forgive and forget the agonies of war? That probably depends on your perspective. For old soldiers it might take the rest of their lives, if even that is enough. But history would suggest, surely, that the peace-making process is often accelerated through the theatre of sport, not war. That's why the 1964 Olympics in Tokyo are fondly remembered by both the hosts and the visitors, the large team of Australian athletes, coaches and officials certainly no exception.

The Games of the XVIII Olympiad were, of course, less than 20 years after the atomic bombings of Hiroshima and Nagasaki abruptly ended hostilities in the Pacific region and brought World War II to a close. The generation that fought the war in all its theatres, on all sides, were still more or less in the prime of their lives so it might have been no surprise if old grudges and tensions were still lurking just below the surface, absorbed by the Baby Boomers who followed. But, if so, it is difficult if not impossible to find anyone who wore the green and gold Australian colours throughout the two hot and humid weeks between October 10 and 24 who has any recollection of any reluctance to fully embrace their hosts as friends and fellow sportsmen – and vice-versa.

Most regard that as a recognisable triumph of the intangible Olympic spirit.

Of those still alive, the best-known of them is legendary swimmer Dawn Fraser, now in her mid-eighties, as are many of her surviving team-mates, and although the visit was preceded by personal tragedy and ended unhappily and controversially for her out of the pool – for absolutely no fault of her Japanese hosts – it was a total triumph in the pool and she looks back on it as one of the most enjoyable experiences of her long and extremely successful career.

'I have only beautiful memories of those Games,' she said. 'People just wanted to preach forgiveness to each other.'

Basketball father-figure Lindsay Gaze, also in his eighties, agrees wholeheartedly. 'The healing process had been very rapid and we enjoyed ourselves in every way,' he said.

For the Japanese nation, this was symbolically the announcement that it had recovered from the war and was well and truly on the way back to becoming the cultural and financial – and sporting – force that it has been ever since. In the only English-language book ever written about it, *1964: The Greatest Year in the History of Japan*, Japanese-American author Roy Tomizawa called it 'the greatest year in the history of Japan' – and he means since the war as well as before it.

The Games were a major success and provided a range of developmental milestones on and off the playing fields.

It was the first time the Olympics had been held in Asia, which would have been Tokyo's privilege already but for political problems. It had been awarded the 1940 Games but because Japan had invaded China this honour was passed to Helsinki before being cancelled because of the war. Helsinki then picked up the baton in 1952, after London had reignited the flame in 1948, and before Melbourne became the first city in the Southern Hemisphere to do so in 1956, followed by Rome in 1960 – all of which played their part in restoring international goodwill.

It wasn't an altogether easy transition with many nations unable or perhaps unwilling to join in. Only 59 countries – and 4064 athletes – competed in London, 69 and 4879 in Helsinki, 72 and 3258 in Melbourne, 83 and 5348 in Rome and 93 and 5081 in Tokyo, where the absentees included South Africa, exiled for the first time because of its apartheid policies – but allowed to participate in the Paralympics the same year.

Since Sydney in 2000 there has never been fewer than 200 nations in attendance – there are currently 206 National Olympic Committees, not all of them independent countries – and from Atlanta in 1996 at least

10,000 have competed every time.

Like all Olympic cities, Tokyo was determined to present itself as positively as possible – whatever it took. New buildings, highways, stadiums, hotels, airports and transport systems sprung up at vast expense.

Some of the outcomes were not necessarily desirable or even visible to the visitors, according to American author Robert Whiting, who was stationed in the city as an Air Force intelligence operative for the two years leading into the Games and has lived there with his Japanese wife, as well as in California, ever since.

In an article published in the *Japan Times* in 2014, Whiting said there had been a 'profound negative impact' and 'waste, destruction and human misery' from what were deemed to be organisational necessities.

He wrote that $1billion was spent on the construction of a high-speed railway from Tokyo to Osaka – the fastest in the world – not because Osaka had any role in the event, but simply to impress the world with the high level of Japanese technological achievement.

He said large numbers of people were harassed and intimidated into moving from residential areas required for new facilities and 200,000 stray cats and dogs were destroyed. Corruption was rife.

Nonetheless, the Games were, for the Japanese people, 'a blaze of glory,' Whiting said.

According to Tomizawa, who has taken a much more positive view of the event and its legacy, the locals were hell-bent on regaining the trust of the world and expunging the sense of shame that they had been left with in the aftermath of the ultimately futile fighting.

It was, he wrote, 'a symbol of the immense collective joy of the time, a cathartic release from the psychological purgatory of defeat in the Pacific war, of subjugation by the enemy, and the painstaking recovery from destitution and despair.

'Never was the nation more aligned, never was the nation prouder than in 1964 – rising from the rubble to embark on the greatest Asian economic miracle of the 20th century. The only thought most Japanese had in October 1964 was to convince the world that Japan was peaceful, friendly, productive, innovative and modern – that they belonged to the global community as much as any other nation.'

Every man, woman and child, he said, prepared to welcome the world, believing it was their civic duty to ensure that foreigners who came to town were not deprived of any necessity or assistance. People were told to convert hole-in-the-ground toilets in their homes to flush toilets on the off-chance a foreigner might visit them.

Many studied English in case they ever had to help a visitor.

Not surprisingly, given this mindset, they became known afterwards as 'the Happy Games'.

Among the ground-breaking achievements, the Games were the first to be telecast internationally – without the need for tapes to be flown overseas – using satellites, and the first in colour, if only for sports that were big domestically, such as judo and volleyball, which were played at the Olympics for the first time.

For swimming, a new timing system started the clock by the sound of the starter's gun and stopped it with touchpads and photo-finish equipment determined the result of sprints.

They were the last to use a traditional cinder track for athletics, with an all-weather synthetic version employed in Mexico City four years later.

Of the 93 competing nations, 16 made their Olympic debut, while one became the only country to start an Olympic campaign with one identity and finish it as another – Northern Rhodesia declared its independence as Zambia on the day of the closing ceremony.

The cauldron was set ablaze by one Yoshinon Sakai, who was born in Hiroshima on August 6, 1945, the day his city was bombed, setting the scene for his countrymen to punch above their weight in the 19 sports and 25 disciplines – as all host nations invariably do.

The 328 Japanese athletes were outnumbered only by the 346 Americans and the 337 competing as the United Team of Germany – before they separated into east and west – while the Soviet Union fielded 317.

As usual, the Americans, with 36 gold and 90 in all, and the Soviets with 30 and 96, dominated the medal count, with Japan third with 16 and 29, a vast improvement on their four and seven in Rome four years earlier.

The home-town gold medals were celebrated with an almost religious fervour and when the women's volleyball team upset their physically superior opponents, the Soviet Union, in the final, almost every TV in the country was tuned in. There has still never been a higher-rating program.

Among the American gold medallists was heavyweight boxer Joe Frazier, who matched the performance in Rome of his soon-to-be arch rival Muhammad Ali, while sprinter Bob Hayes – later to become a Superbowl winner with the Dallas Cowboys football team – won the 100m in world record time: 10 seconds flat, which wouldn't get him out of the heats these days. He did that in borrowed shoes because one of his own had been inadvertently 'lost' under a bed by a nervous Frazier, who was throwing things around in a visit to Hayes's room to try to calm himself down before his own big event.

Comparatively speaking, these were a good Games for Australia – as, perhaps, they should have been, given that the team numbered 234, according to the official Australian Olympic historian, the late Harry Gordon, although other references put the figure at 243 and 250. Whichever is correct, it was the fourth largest visiting contingent and the most ever to leave home – there had been 325 in Melbourne in 1956.

There had been a long and heated debate over the selection policies, centred on whether it was appropriate to nominate young, fringe athletes simply to give them experience. 'An Olympic team should not be inflated to gratify immature ambitions of sports and individuals,' thundered the formidable Syd Grange, the president of the Australian Olympic Federation, as it was then. 'The Olympic Games is not a testing ground … the time to gain experience is between Olympics.'

An original list of more than 300 nominations was significantly pruned but nevertheless it seems to have been that anybody who qualified got a guernsey, and so, for instance, 10 boxers won four fights between them, while 18 fencers, 11 gymnasts, eight shooters, seven weightlifters, eight wrestlers, an uncompetitive water polo team and a few other individuals in more prominent sports were making up the numbers – big numbers.

Strangely, then, the management team consisted of only three – and unsurprisingly they had their hands very full. 'The numbers were far beyond what they should have been,' the much-respected Judy Patching, assistant to chef de mission Len Curnow, admitted to Gordon later. 'As a consequence, we had a lot of trouble, some of it concerned with poor discipline.'

The trouble took various forms, including many quarrels and, more seriously, the theft of electronic goods and pearls from a van in the athletes' village, which were swiftly returned when Patching, a former Naval officer, laid down the law.

But for all that, there was still a fair bit to like.

Australia won six golds and 12 minor medals to finish eighth on the table – in other words, better than 85 other countries, including Great Britain (4 and 18).

Two of the golds have taken their place in posterity as immortal chapters in Australia's proud sporting history – Fraser's third consecutive win in the 100m freestyle, and Betty Cuthbert's inspirational comeback from injury-induced retirement to win the first edition of the women's 400m, the event that carried Cathy Freeman to the status of national hero in Sydney 36 years later.

The swimmers accounted for three of the others – Robert Windle in the 1500m, Ian O'Brien in the 200m breaststroke, Kevin Berry in the 200m butterfly – while yachtsmen Bill Northam, Peter O'Donnell and James Sargeant saluted in the 5.5 class, making the affable Northam, 59, Australia's oldest medallist ever.

Fraser, who also helped win silver in the 100m relay, retired after Tokyo, having established herself – first in Melbourne, then in Rome – as such a superstar that when the Sport Australia Hall of Fame was established in 1985, she was the second inductee, behind only the immortal cricketer Don Bradman, and the first woman. She later served a term as chair of the organisation, the most prestigious sporting 'club' in Australia.

But Tokyo, while triumphant, was certainly a mixed experience for her.

Seven months before the Games, shortly after the national championships, Fraser was driving home from a dinner engagement at a rugby league club when her mother Rose was killed in a car crash and her sister and a friend injured. She suffered severe injuries herself, causing her neck and back to be encased in a steel brace for nine weeks. She still managed to come back and swim inside the minute in her 100m freestyle semi-final in Tokyo – the first woman to do so – and then win the final in Olympic record time, making her the first person of either gender to win three Olympic gold medals in the same event.

She did so under enormous pressure. 'If any of those competitors had been able to see inside my head or my heart they would have been able to get an edge,' she wrote in her autobiography. 'No doubt about it. I was frightened. I wanted to vomit and run to the toilet. It was just the most crushing pressure. This race was so important to me and I felt an immense desire to win it for mum.'

She led from start to finish and when she arrived on the victory dais to collect the historic third medal – the first of the Games for Australia – 'I couldn't have felt prouder. The tears were just too hard to hold back so I stopped trying.'

In the circumstances, it is little wonder she has always regarded that as her finest moment.

'It is a beautiful memory because I was having a hard time coming up to Tokyo,' she said. 'Without the help of my team-mates, I don't think I would have made it, but they were very good and supported me. When you're in a team you're never alone.'

The Japanese also admired her courage and spirit as well as her immense talent. 'When we got to Tokyo it was like another world,' she said. 'It was magnificent. The Japanese people treated us so well and made us feel right at home. The atmosphere was "OK, let's forget the wars we've had, the Pacific wars". The mood was "here we are now in a country that is opening up to the whole world" and the Japanese wanted to show they could put on a good show and they certainly did. The people were very courteous – if you wanted to catch a train or go shopping for a camera, they were extremely helpful – and I think the Australian team were very hospitable towards them too. I guess we knew what some of our people had gone through fighting for our country – it was horrendous.

'I think even today there are people old enough to know what it was like and who would never, ever forgive or forget. There is still that little bit of nastiness from some people. But the Olympic team wanted people from both countries to just get on with it, it was in the past and no-one wanted to see it in the future.'

Even the Japanese police were eventually called on to make sure Fraser was treated like the international sporting icon that she was, but they couldn't prevent her visit – and her entire career – ending in chaotic, controversial circumstances that even now, more than half a century later, are still difficult to live down in some official circles.

Always a larrikin and a rebel, Fraser had a colourful history of clashing with the pedantic swimming officials of the time and it was no different in Tokyo. She had been banned from marching in the opening ceremony in Rome and now she defied another order not to do so because it was deemed too close to her first event. She then refused to wear the official swimsuit in her final and threatened not to swim if she didn't get her wish, but was eventually persuaded by Judy Patching who appealed to her sense of team.

It then became clear that while the swimming officials were at war with her, Curnow – in charge overall – was not, because he invited her to carry the flag at the closing ceremony, a significant personal endorsement made in the knowledge that swim manager Bill Slade had formally reported her for disobedience and improper behaviour.

On the day before the ceremony Fraser had moved out of the village and into a hotel, where she proceeded to party with other team members, kicking on to well after midnight with the men's hockey players.

One of them, Des Piper, team doctor Howard Toyne and Fraser decided to go in search of a flag to souvenir, which led them to the Emperor's Palace, where there were many of them flying on poles.

Fraser was minding blazers while Piper and Toyne bunked each other up and cut loose the object of their desire with a pair of nail scissors. But the cops were onto them and the men threw the flag to Fraser and told her to run for it, which she did, until she saw a bike and took off on it, not realising it belonged to her uniformed pursuers. Panicking, she scaled a wall and jumped two metres into a moat set in concrete and badly hurt her ankle.

Without identification, she struggled to convince the police that she was a world famous gold medallist, but when a friend arrived with proof they not only sent her on her way, gladly, but gave her the purloined flag as a gift and agreed to hush up the incident. Only a few hours later there she was with the flag – the official Australian one this time – in the stadium but walking with a limp no-one could explain. By the time she arrived back in Sydney, the ankle was so sore she was in a wheelchair – but she had not one but two flags in her bag.

It didn't end there, of course.

Fraser took the blame when the escapade became known and did not mention Piper and Toyne by name in her book *Gold Medal Girl* and that's the way it stayed until Piper publicly confessed in 1988.

Then early in 1965 the Amateur Swimming Union of Australia – and not the Olympic authorities – decided that its reputation had been sullied and that disciplinary measures were necessary. So it banned three of Fraser's cohorts in the opening ceremony rebellion, Linda McGill, 19, Marlene Dayman, 15, and Nan Duncan, 17, for four, three and three years respectively, which seemed well over the top, if not draconian, for three teenagers – until the coup de grace was revealed: Fraser, 27, was banned for 10 years! This was unbelievably savage and sent shockwaves around the world, especially as there was no clarity about which offences – marching, the wrong swimsuit, the flag incident – she was being punished for. According to Gordon's book, *Australia at the Olympic Games*, the report by the ASUA's Bill Slade, on which the decision was based, is now stored away in AOC archives but has been mutilated with scissors, all reference to Fraser's behaviour deleted.

The penalty was later reduced to four years, but it effectively ended her career anyway, with many experts believing she could have won for a fourth time in Mexico City in 1968.

Fraser has always been bemused by her treatment, saying: 'I know I offended some officials and at times I did some foolish things (but) I still can't match the severity of the sentence with anything I did.'

Like Fraser, Cuthbert considered Tokyo to be her finest moment, which is not surprising given that she had been instructed to come out of retirement, she said, by God – and the winner of three gold medals at 100m and 200m in Melbourne in 1956 was now moving up to the metric quarter-mile, never before contested by women at the Olympics. Afterwards, she thanked the Lord and asked him if she could now rest, mission accomplished.

Sadly, she contracted multiple sclerosis in 1969 and spent the rest of her life in a wheelchair. Having been part of a selection panel that included her among the 10 subjects of the first batch of statues to be erected outside the MCG, I visited her at her home in Mandurah, south of Perth, where she told me that she was confident God would allow her to run again before he called her to the pearly gates. She meant it too, such was her faith. However, she went to meet her maker in 2017, aged 79, without that ever happening. As personalities, the God-fearing Cuthbert and the free-spirited Fraser could scarcely have been much different – but as far as Australia is concerned, they have always been the headline acts, the defining performers, of the Tokyo Olympics.

Lindsay Gaze, who was at his second Olympics as a basketballer – he played at three and coached for another four – also enjoyed Tokyo. That was partly because he believes it was the first international tournament in which Australia was taken seriously by the American and European powerhouses in the sport, and partly because the general atmosphere was so pleasant. 'There was a lot of frivolity and friendship, everyone at pains to understand each other,' he said.

But to Gaze, the post-war healing process really began in Melbourne. 'London in 1948 was still war-affected, Helsinki in 1952 was still difficult for many countries to attend, but Melbourne … that was when people started saying "we're ready to play again, let's embrace the Olympics,"' he said. Gaze may well be right about that – they were dubbed 'the friendly games' afterwards – but that doesn't mean they were free of political tensions or unanimously embraced by the world. For various reasons three different boycotts led to Egypt, Iraq, Lebanon, the Netherlands, Cambodia, Spain, Switzerland and China refusing to attend.

This was only 11 years after the war ended and Japan sent a team of 110 athletes, the fifth biggest visiting contingent, who competed without problems, winning four gold medals and 15 others. One of the most significant moments came in the pool, when the great Australian freestyler Murray Rose narrowly beat Japan's Tsuyoshi Yamanaka in the 1500m, with the crowd applauding both men as they went neck and neck down the final lap.

Rose recalled later: 'For years there was still some resentment in Australia toward the Japanese. I knew the crowd was watching us closely. Then, simultaneously, we both smiled, fell over the lane lines and warmly embraced. Behind us we heard the crowd cheering. But the true significance of our race and what happened afterward was on the front page of every newspaper the next day. One of the captions read, "The war is finally over".'

According to both Fraser and Gaze, and others in the team, by the time Tokyo rolled around eight years later there were no negative attitudes about going there, not even any official briefings about how to deal with the locals. None were needed – which wasn't necessarily always the case in other Games cities.

Gaze laughs and adds: 'It certainly wasn't like Moscow in 1980 when we were all told not to fraternise with the Russian women because venereal disease was, allegedly, rife – and when we got there we saw an English language newspaper warning the local women not to fraternise with us, because VD was rife among us. It was classic propaganda. In Tokyo, there were no barriers to romance.'

Gaze recalls he and other basketballers going to watch Fraser's historic race without passes to get in, so they wore tracksuits, carried towels, wet their hair, said they were swimmers and brushed past the lone ticket collector and then scattered, knowing he would not be able to leave his post. 'There was no anger, no-one chased us, it was just typical of the whole experience – people wanted us to enjoy ourselves, and to enjoy themselves with us,' he said.

A lot of things change in 56 years – but as Tokyo prepared to revisit the Olympic hosting duties and the world prepared to return, that sentiment was never going to be one of them. An extra year won't make any difference.

WHY THE OLYMPICS MATTER

Most people remember the beginning of a significant love affair in their lives. For one of mine, it was a warm summer's evening in Los Angeles in August 1984, and the girl involved was a little-known Australian athlete of several diverse talents, who I had never met – and never did get to know.

Her name was Glynis Nunn and she had just won the heptathlon – a new track and field event involving seven disciplines – at the first Olympic Games to which I had been assigned as a sportswriter. It was the first time I had witnessed an Australian athlete from any sport earn one of those precious little golden discs, live and up close.

You didn't get many chances to do that in those days. There were only three other Australian golds at those Games, there had been only two in Moscow four years previously and, calamitously, none at all in Montreal four years before that.

But as the dusky twilight turned to darkness over the old Coliseum – an iconic art-deco stadium that was hosting the Olympics for the second time and which will for a third time in 2028 – the 24-year-old physical education teacher from Toowoomba, Queensland, was being presented with her prize for having narrowly upset the hot favourite, American Jackie Joyner.

Up in the Press tribune, we hadn't been expecting to see this. Joyner was a superstar – she went on to win the event at the next two Olympics – and while Nunn had triumphed at the Brisbane Commonwealth Games two years earlier, she was regarded as no match for the mighty American. But she got there 6390 points to 6385, or the equivalent of a third of a second in the 800m race, or about 3cm in the long jump.

In other words, it was desperately close.

What wasn't surprising was the tears that streamed down her face as she mounted the top step of the podium for the presentation, holding a toy kangaroo aloft. It was a moment of pure joy for her and one you couldn't help basking in yourself – if you were Australian.

Or even if you were not.

Because as the national anthem rang out, something else completely unexpected happened. In the row immediately in front of us, a group of black African journalists, about eight or 10 from memory, stood up, turned around, grinning broadly, and shook the hands of each Australian reporter. They were congratulating us, as if we had won the gold medal.

The significance of that gesture took a little time to sink in. But when the penny did drop, I realised that this was what was meant by the term the Olympic spirit. These guys didn't say where they were from – they didn't say much at all, possibly not being English speakers – and it didn't matter. This was a demonstration of the power of sport to bring nations together, on and off the field of play.

It was affirmation that for all its many problems and failings – the political posturing, the commercial corruption, the never-ending issues with drugs, the win-at-all-costs attitudes, the avarice, the cynicism and the one-upmanship – the Olympic movement has always had much to offer the world, and hopefully always will.

The Africans were telling us that in this environment friendship and goodwill were positives worth focusing on.

It was exactly the right time for me to be reminded of this.

I had come to LA to experience the greatest sporting show on Earth – and it is that, whatever protests soccer might wish to put forward in defence of its own World Cup – not knowing what to expect, but well aware this was not exactly the most propitious moment to be joining in.

These were deeply troubled times for the movement.

Boycott followed boycott. Some African nations refused to go to Montreal because of the presence of New Zealand, who were engaging in sporting contact with the still deeply racist South Africa. The United States pulled out of Moscow, taking others with them – and weakening the Australian team – because Russia had invaded Afghanistan. The Soviets and all their allies predictably responded by giving LA a big, cold miss.

In a climate of great political and financial uncertainty there were no guarantees the Olympic Games would survive at all.

Happily, the Americans were able to prevent the cracks from widening any further and got the whole show back on track, albeit not without a self-indulgent 'look-at-us' dynamic that formed part of the backdrop as they dominated the action, winning four times as many gold medals, 83, as the next best nation, Romania, with 20.

Not only were Russia and East Germany absent, but China had still not returned to the fold after a long stand-off and South Africa were banned. But 140 nations attended, 60 more than had gone to Moscow. That number kept increasing until the Games came to Sydney in 2000, when it reached 200.

I arrived in LA with a mix of curiosity and cynicism and departed … well, hooked.

That condition proved permanent. I did not miss another summer Games until Rio de Janeiro in 2016, by which time I had retired from full-time newspaper work, and took in the 1992 Winter Games in Nagano, Japan, in 1998. Unwilling to end the affair, I planned to return for a 10th summer assignment in Tokyo 2020 to write this book. That was put on hold by the Coronavirus but not abandoned.

It has been an inspirational journey, not always involving winners or even active athletes. It has resulted in a number of friendships, none more based on admiration –- or more genuine – than with Peter Norman, the Melbourne schoolteacher who is a central figure in one of the most famous and important images in all sporting history.

Norman won the silver medal – in a time, 20.06, that was still the Australian record until his death nearly 40 years later – in the 200m at the Mexico City Olympics in 1968, splitting two black Americans, Tommie Smith and John Carlos, who then performed a Black Power salute on the medals dais, bowing their heads and raising their gloved fists during the national anthem as a civil rights protest.

In a courageous gesture of brotherhood that the two Americans never forgot, and endangering his own future in the sport, Norman supported them by wearing a civil rights badge on his uniform, instead of the 'Jesus saves' type of religious messages he sometimes wore in accordance with his devotion to the Salvation Army.

The Americans were sent home and vilified and ostracised for years while Norman was given a good-humoured ticking off by the team manager of the day for breaking Olympic protocol, which suggested he had done nothing seriously wrong. Which he hadn't. But when the next Olympics rolled around, he wasn't selected even though he was still the best sprinter in Australia. He was still paying for what some people considered his sins, apparently.

Other than performing in amateur theatrics, he faded from public view – other than within the track and field community – until I came across him at a small ceremony in Melbourne one night in August 1993, where he was being presented with a participation pin, then a new gesture by the International Olympic Committee to all living Olympians.

Over the first of more than a few drinks we were to share over the ensuing years, he told me there was a reason why he hadn't been seen around much for a long time – he was just emerging, he said, from a seven-year stint in a private hell that cost him his professional career and nearly cost him a leg, his sanity, his family and his life. All without the world at large knowing until he allowed me to publish this sad story.

Mexico City was a world away and eons ago when Norman and a group of old track and field mates got together in November 1985 to participate, purely for the fun of it, in an interclub D Grade relay race at a suburban park.

Running the third leg Norman took the baton and attempted to display what was left of the explosive acceleration that had once made him the second fastest man in the world over half a lap.

He got 30 metres. Then, snap! The Achilles tendon on his right leg caved in, agonisingly.

Although he didn't know it at the time, so did his life.

He needed surgery, which took a few weeks to arrange. But when the plaster came off, it had gone horribly wrong. An infection had set in, the flesh and tissue had broken down, and he was left with a gaping hole where his Achilles had once been. He was rushed back into hospital, and this time it was serious. He remembered lying in bed in a drug-induced daze, listening to two surgeons discussing which option to take – to amputate the leg above the knee or below it.

Eventually one said: 'You can't cut his leg off. He's a physical education teacher and, what's more, he's an Olympic silver medallist.'

By luck, the surgeon turned out to be an old inter-club runner who knew who Norman was – and he suggested the less drastic alternative of grafting part of the other leg into the hole might – just might – work. And so they did.

Norman spent three long months lying in that hospital bed. When he emerged he was crippled. Confined to a wheelchair. Unable to walk, let alone run. For a former athlete known for his warm, friendly, outgoing personality, this was a nightmare.

When his wife Jan wheeled him through the door of their home in Williamstown he took one look at the pot plants, realised they had grown half a metre – and broke down. 'I didn't just sob, I bawled my eyes out,' he said. 'I knew that if I had missed seeing the plants grow that much I had missed seeing the two kids grow up, too.'

The pain was immense and coping with it without medication was impossible. He tried to get back to work but found he could teach or he could live with the agony – but not both.

'So I started to wag school, which isn't good for a teacher,' he said.

He had to give up all his hobbies – tennis, squash, skindiving – and a deep depression set in.

'I virtually went nuts,' he said. 'I had a breakdown. I'd take medication to knock out the pain then have a couple of drinks and I was a goner. I spent probably three years like a zombie. You become impatient that the medication isn't working fast enough and take more, and by the time you're convinced it is working you're so dopey you have no idea what you're doing. So you take more and more and so it goes on. I once took enough for three months in the course of a week and had a couple of pretty bad turns. I was destroying myself and I think I came pretty close to finishing the job a couple of times. It wasn't a matter of being suicidal, it was a matter of being able to control the circumstances. In the worst scenario I'd be dead by now.'

Norman finally got off the painkillers – for good. The pain did not disappear but he realised he had no choice but to learn to combat it.

He was amazed that his wife stuck it out and was tormented by what he might have been putting his pre-teen daughters Belinda and Emma through. He was also the father of three other children, Gary, Sandra and Janita, with his first wife Ruth.

'Being young girls they were certainly affected by it,' he said.

'Imagine it, seeing their dad in that condition when other dads could keep it all together. Other dads had a job, other dads could go for a ride on the bike, other dads could go to the Little Athletics and jog laps with them.

'They never came to me about it but they certainly spoke to their mother about it.

'Jan was very patient but it is a wonder she didn't throw me out. The marriage was very close to breaking up and if that had happened it would have been the end.

'Eventually she became very forceful about what I had to do. I had to pick up the ball and try to make the most of what I did have. It was my last chance. You only get one shot.'

Norman always rejected the option of wallowing in self-pity. 'It's more anger with myself for being so stupid,' he said.

'But at least I'm not buying one trouser, one sock and one shoe at a time. I'm not sure what the Australian record for a one-legged 200m is but it would be a lot slower than 20.6 seconds.'

Norman never lost contact with Carlos and Smith – nor they with him, right to the end. In 2005 a statue of the pair commemorating the two medals was unveiled at San Jose University in California. It did not feature Norman – but he was there for the unveiling, one of several reunions they had over the years.

Even though Carlos had once referred to him contemptuously as 'that little white sprinter boy,' they became and remained firm friends and corresponded regularly. They suffered more than Norman did, by far, both being vilified for years, both finding it hard to find work, both their marriages breaking up – and then Carlos's wife committed suicide.

In 2001, Carlos published his autobiography, simply and enigmatically titled WHY? and sent a copy to Norman. It carried a handwritten inscription: 'I now have a brother after 30 years. I love you my friend and I always will.'

When Norman showed it to me, I emailed Carlos to ask about the sentiment behind it. He replied immediately:

'Hi there Mr Reed, Mr Norman has always been a brother to me since 1968, that I have said many times. He was a great runner and a great person, not just to me but to the world. I am very sure that the Australian people can learn a lot from Peter. I no (sic) Peter went through hell there after the Games and he did not brake (sic) because he know what right in this life we live.'

The message went on to say that nothing happens until God wants it to and 'it took me some time to understand that'. The bronze medal didn't mean much and he was giving it to his kids to do with as they wish.

Smith tried to sell his gold medal and all his memorabilia, putting a $1m tag on it. It is not known whether he succeeded.

Norman kept his silver on the piano just as a reminder of better times. 'Having a silver medal doesn't mean a lot in life,' he said 'I was in the right place at the right time and I consider myself very lucky.'

Norman died of a heart attack on October 3, 2006, aged 64.

Smith and Carlos flew to Melbourne to join about 2000 mourners at his funeral at Williamstown Town Hall. Speaking on tape at his own send-off, Norman hoped his epitaph might feature one word: respect.

Never has a dying wish been more sincerely honoured – or deserved.

The American soul brothers were joined by a senior official from USA Track and Field, Steve Simmons, who read a written proclamation declaring the date, October 9, to be Peter Norman Day in America. I obtained a framed copy of that, which has adorned my home office study ever since.

'In the 170 year history of American athletics we have never done this before,' Simmons said, adding that the photograph of the dais salute had been listed as the seventh most famous image of all time – up there with the moon landing.

Smith, always known as an introvert, kept his eulogy short, focusing on his friend's integrity. 'He believed right can never be wrong,' he said.

Carlos's heartfelt tribute, with its strong religious theme, was a masterpiece – one of the most stirring funeral orations most mourners had heard.

He spoke of how he and Smith – 'two black individuals, disenchanted with life' – had received death threats in the ugly aftermath of the protest.

'The average young white individual would never have had the nerve, the gumption or the backbone to stand there with us,' he said. 'But not Mr Norman. He said "I stand with you and behind you". When the anger and that viciousness came I could share it with Tommie Smith and him with me. But who could Peter Norman share it with? He was a lone soldier and many in Australia did not understand how this young white man could stand there with these black individuals. He didn't stand with his fist in the air, he stood to attention – he stood for Australia.'

Carlos said he hoped everyone would 'go and tell their kids this story and the courage he showed. Remember Peter Norman the man, and make sure you use that phrase – THE MAN!'

In some ways the Peter Norman story is a contradiction of the proposition I have put forward that the Olympic movement's most uplifting reason for existing is that it promotes and perpetuates goodwill and friendship between people of all colours and creeds. In this case, the institution, especially in America, frowned heavily on what Smith and Carlos did, and to a lesser extent on Norman for endorsing it.

It wouldn't happen again now and the movement has always been rightly embarrassed that it ever did. However, if the Olympics had not provided the backdrop and the universal audience for such an eloquent gesture to be employed, seen and heard, and supported, then the long and painful struggle for human equality and dignity would have been deprived of some highly significant momentum.

That is my fearless friend Peter Norman's timeless legacy.

THE OTHER MEDAL THEY SHOULD GET

The list of winners of the Bill Roycroft Medal is not overburdened with famous names. There's a reason for that: there is no such award. But there should be.

Roycroft is one of Australia's most enduring Olympic legends, the bush horseman from the Western District of Victoria who famously checked himself out of hospital, against doctors' orders, after sustaining a range of injuries when his gelding Our Solo misjudged a jump and threw him off during the cross-country element of the three-day event in Rome in 1960.

Exactly how seriously he hurt himself depends on which version of the colourful contemporary reports you choose to believe. The injuries have been variously described as a broken shoulder, dislocated collarbone, deep bruising and severe concussion. What is not disputable is that he was in a lot of pain when he insisted on returning to the fray the next day, with his right arm virtually useless.

In a memorable display of raw courage – and considerable skill – he ignored the pain to complete the show-jumping event on the final day, ensuring that he, Laurie Morgan and Brian Crago won a gold medal that would have been forfeited if he had not defied the doctors to do his bit.

The applause never really died down. Roycroft was 45 at the time and until he passed on at 96 his performance was pretty much unanimously regarded as the personification of sporting inspiration, and the very essence of the decree by the founder of the modern Olympics, the French Baron Pierre de Courbetin, that the most important thing was not to win but to take part. Taking part in such challenging circumstances – and winning as well – was as good as it gets.

Old Bill was well before my time, although I would eventually meet him at various Olympic functions and had the pleasure of spending a pleasant day with him late in his life on his dairy farm, where he lived alone in his final years, cared for by the neighbours as country people do. He had absolutely no tickets on himself and no expectation that he should be regarded as some sort of a hero.

In the years since, there have been many, many more examples of Australian Olympians across a wide range of sports who have also either performed with singular distinction under the stress of personal injury, family tragedy or simply demonstrating an unusual level of class under pressure. At every Games there is always at least one stand-out example, often two or three.

Given the whirlwind pace with which the sporting news cycle moves on, they are of course applauded loudly on the day but then, sometimes, consigned to history, not always remembered as well as they could and should be. And with no formal, tangible recognition – other than their medals, of course, if they did win one – of how special their achievement was in its own distinct way.

That's why during the London Olympics in 2012 I bailed up the boss, the Australian Olympic Committee's long-serving president John Coates, and suggested there should be a medal for the most inspirational athlete at every Games, and that it should be named after Roycroft and perhaps be made retrospective. I followed up with a column in the team's in-house magazine, Aspire, hoping the idea might catch on with the athletes themselves. But Coates politely passed on it, without saying why. I think it's still a valid suggestion.

In the eight consecutive summer Games I attended, I would have had no trouble coming up with a worthy winner each time. Here's who they would be:

LOS ANGELES 1984: Swimmer John Sieben whose can-do attitude saw him bring down one of the greatest swimmers of his or any other generation in the 200m butterfly.

SEOUL 1988: Canoeist Grant Davies, silver medallist in the 2000m for kayaks whose philosophical reaction to having the gold snatched from him after being told he had won it made Australia proud.

BARCELONA 1992: Rower Peter Antonie, who partnered Stephen Hawkins in the double sculls in which they were physically ill-equipped to even be competitive and won gold.

ATLANTA: With apologies to swimmer Kieren Perkins who won a heroic 1500m freestyle, equestrian Gillian Rolton gets the nod for her pain-defying contribution to the three-day event team gold medal.

SYDNEY 2000: Most people would not go past Cathy Freeman's 400m track triumph but I'm going for cyclists Scott McGrory and Brett Aitken, who won the Madison in the velodrome after one lost an infant child and the other almost did.

ATHENS 2004: Swimmer Grant Hackett, for winning the gruelling 1500m gold medal while suffering a debilitating illness.

BEIJING: Rower Drew Ginn, who shared the pairs gold medal with partner Duncan Free despite back pain so fierce he could scarcely walk.

LONDON 2012: Cyclist Anna Meares, who completed a comeback from a near-fatal racing crash to win the sprint gold medal on the track.

Some of these remain household names but some have long faded back into obscurity. Davies for instance, was a complete unknown before he made a brief appearance in the headlines and you could go to a hundred pub trivia nights now and never hear his name mentioned. Much the same could be said of Sieben and Antonie and perhaps Rolton. Their stories deserve a more prominent place in posterity so here they are.

Many Australian sports fans – and I was no exception – had little or no idea who butterfly swimmer Jon Sieben was when he became one of the 240 athletes selected for Los Angeles. He certainly wasn't regarded as a prospective gold medallist, with even his parents believing that, at 17, he was at best being sent for the experience with an eye to the future. So they did not make the trip to watch him.

Sieben's only claim to fame was that as a 15-year-old international debutant he had won bronze in the 200m fly and gold in the medley relay at the Commonwealth Games two years earlier.

If the sports media focused on him at all in LA, it was only in the context of his main race, the 200, being one of the most competitive on the program, with the quality of the field not unduly weakened by the Eastern Bloc boycott.

It was headed by one of the greatest swimmers of his generation, Michael Gross, a towering 200cm German whose arms extended forever – he was known as The Albatross after his massive 225cm fingertip to fingertip wingspan – and an intimidating presence.

Gross had already won the 200m freestyle and the 100m butterfly in world record times and the 200 fly was his best event.

He was the world record holder and had dominated the event for three years – and would continue to do so for the following five – and therefore the hot favourite, although American Pablo Morales and Venezuela's Rafael Vidal were expected to provide stiff challenges.

The boy from the Queensland beaches, unemployed and on the dole, was just making up the numbers – in the eyes of everybody but himself and his flamboyant coach Laurie Lawrence.

Years later, when we came to be working in offices near each other and would have lunch together, Sieben told me that even at his relatively tender age he was not overawed by the Olympics and did not regard himself as a casting extra.

'I loved racing and I loved winning,' he told me. 'It wasn't about experience. It was an opportunity to win gold.'

That is not stating the blindingly obvious. It is defining a distinct difference in attitudes and Sieben believes it is what made him a winner on the world's biggest stage rather than just another wide-eyed teenager with plenty of talent but not enough teeth.

It had been driven home to him by a motivational speech he had heard delivered by Australian rugby star Andrew Slack. 'He said there were three things you could never get back: the spoken word, a spent arrow and a missed opportunity,' Sieben said. 'It applies to everything in life.

You miss a training session and you might train harder the next night but you've still missed one. This was an opportunity I didn't want to miss.'

At the very least Sieben knew he had put in the hard yards at training and would not be found wanting on the score of fitness. And by his side he had a can-do ally in Lawrence, the former rugby player who was on the way to becoming one of Australia's best-known sporting motivators – even if his style was seen as a bit over the top.

The first clue that Sieben might be about to tear up the script came when he finished second to Morales in his heat in Australian record time, two seconds faster than he had ever swum before. Even then, team-mates were congratulating him for making the final, as distinct from urging him to go for gold.

'That's all they were expecting out of me. They didn't think I could win. But I knew I'd done it easy in that race and that I'd done the work – and I could win,' he said.

He said as much to Lawrence, who realised his young charge was deadly serious and could scarcely contain his own excitement.

Sieben believed that to a significant extent the final was won and lost not in the pool but in the marshalling room. There the eight finalists were locked up together for nearly half an hour, an environment calculated to test anybody's susceptibility to mind games.

'Most people see only "on your marks, bang!" and the swimming but in the little room beforehand … things happen,' he said. 'Without saying a word, Gross was at his intimidating best. Just by stretching his arms in the air, he looked about nine feet tall. There was an aura about him. Without a doubt he was the greatest swimmer I had ever competed against and here he was. One of the American guys was in awe of him. He was shaking.'

That American, Patrick Kennedy, finished last.

Through this ordeal within an ordeal, Sieben's self-belief and mental steel never faltered. The coach was more on edge than the swimmer, who told him: 'Settle down, stay calm, I just want to do my own thing.'

He had a firm game plan. Knowing that Gross and Morales were a massive two seconds quicker than him over 100m and would go out fast, he decided to come from behind and depend on his fitness at the finish.

It worked. He came from seventh at the halfway mark and fourth at 150m and stormed past the three big guns to win in world record time of 1 minute 57.04, four seconds better than he had ever swum before he got to Los Angeles.

He had the gold medal – the opportunity had been grasped. Class under pressure? He had personified it.

'People used to say "I made the team and that's it,"' he said. 'Now kids could see making the team is great but performing well is even better. I always knew I could make the team but I knew there was more.'

Sieben also won a bronze in the 100m medley relay and went on to swim at two more Olympics. He was named Young Australian of the year for 1984, awarded an AOM and was later inducted into the Sport Australia Hall of Fame.

GRANT DAVIES wasn't an Olympic champion for long – but he will always be a champion Olympian. Never before and probably not since has any athlete in any sport come closer to winning a gold medal without quite doing it than the little-known kayak paddler. And yet, the last time we checked, a decade later, he remained totally bereft of self-pity, regret, frustration or even disappointment.

That is no surprise to those of us – and there weren't many – who were on hand as amazing, unprecedented scenes erupted around the laid-back but talented and determined Queenslander on and off the water one hot and steamy Saturday morning in Seoul in 1988.

He didn't quite win on the water – but he certainly did off it.

Then 24 and a stranger to most sports fans, Davies was part of an Australian canoeing team that took friend and foe alike by surprise. They were the Cinderellas of the Olympic effort that year, emerging from what was billed as a satellite branch of the Australian Institute of Sport but which, in reality, was nothing more than a strip of beach at Maroochydore on the Sunshine Coast and a backyard in which the owner let them store their kayaks at night.

Most of the focus was on their only headliner, former ironman Grant

Kenny, who had won a bronze medal in the pairs with Barry Kelly at Los Angeles four years earlier.

Kenny was competing in the fours this time, partnering Bryan Thomas, Steve Wood and Paul Gilmour, and if a medal was going to come from anywhere they were the ones expected to provide it. In fact, they finished fourth, upstaged by Peter Foster and Kelvin Graham, who won bronze in the pairs. Martin Hunter did well to make the final of the 500m sprint. And then there was Davies.

Like most of the others he was a product of the golden surf beaches to the north and south of Brisbane. Davies' father John was also an old surfie and lived for the mateship and the ambience of their local club on the Gold Coast, often leaving late at night, in the dark, and riding his bike home. One night, doing exactly that, he was hit by a car. When he woke up in hospital he was paralysed from the waist down.

That, and the fact he never had much money, seemed to mean he was destined to miss a once-in-a-lifetime opportunity to see his son compete for Australia at the greatest sporting show on earth. Somehow he and other family members begged and borrowed their way to Seoul. When they arrived, Davies senior made an ambitious promise to his son.

'If you win a medal, any medal, I will stand up in my wheelchair and applaud,' he said. That, of course, was impossible. He was a paraplegic.

Most thought it didn't matter anyway because Davies would find the opposition too hot in the 200m. It was headed by American Greg Barton, no stranger to adversity himself. Hailing from Homer, Michigan – a small town with more pigs than human beings, according to Olympic historian David Wallechinsky – he was born with two club feet, a condition aggravated rather than improved by four operations as he grew up. But he found a sport that did not require him to use his feet and made himself into a champion.

Davies completed his Olympic preparations in Europe, where he consistently finished fourth. 'But I was getting closer and closer,' he recalled. Eight weeks out, he finished within a length and a half of Barton and he and the Australian coach Brian Trouville realised that although inexperienced he was unlikely to finish any worse than fourth.

'I thought I was capable of a medal,' he said.

Maybe his old man took the tip and started practising himself.

When the moment of truth arrived, Barton and Davies produced a race to rival that other dramatic thriller of the Seoul Olympics, the women's 400m hurdles which Australian Debbie Flintoff won by a whisker. Flintoff could easily have been the nominee for the non-existent Roycroft Medal herself, as she was competing while wracked with grief following the death of her sister just before she left Australia.

As Davies and Barton crossed the line too closely locked together for the naked eye to pick the winner, it seemed Davies had emulated Flintoff's golden feat. Certainly, the electric scoreboard said so. Davies looked up and almost fell into the water with glee. He didn't know that Korean officials were about to tell Barton differently.

Davies paddled to shore, disembarked and was immediately surrounded by Australian media people with a TV crew flashing the euphoric scenes back home. He jubilantly sent a cheerio to his mates at the surf club and turned to find the heavies from the Australian Olympic Committee – late arrivals because they too were caught by surprise – rushing to add their congratulations.

And then came the first hint that something was wrong. Terribly wrong.

An official asked Davies to come with him to the judging enclosure. There, he was told that the International Canoe Federation jury had examined the photo-finish and decided that Barton had won by five one-thousandths of a second – or less than a centimetre.

It was the smallest margin in Olympic history, so much so that even the computerised timing equipment took it to the third decimal place. The difference was officially recorded as one-hundredth of a second, 3.55.27 to 3.55.28. By that infinitesimal margin the gold was gone, replaced by the universal symbol for second best, a silver medal.

So how would Davies react to this disastrous turn of events? With a tantrum? With tears? With despair or dismay?

'How do you feel?' is one of the weakest cliché questions a reporter can resort to in situations of triumph or disaster because the answer is usually all too obvious. But something about Davies' demeanour prompted me to ask it anyway.

THE OTHER MEDAL THEY SHOULD GET

He looked me in the eye and said evenly: 'If that's the worst thing that ever happens to me, I'll have a good life.'

It was a quote dripping with dignity and sportsmanship and which ensured that he retained, in many eyes, the hero status that would have accompanied the gold medal.

But still this ripping yarn wasn't over.

For those who had the right vantage points in the grandstand had witnessed an even more astonishing performance. As Davies finished talking to the media, his father arrived in the wheelchair. He was beaming – and so were the other family members surrounding him. As the two paddlers had crossed the line, John Davies kept his unlikely promise. Somehow, he stood, grasped the rail in front of him, paused while he balanced himself – and clapped. Then he fell back into the chair.

Davies returned to Australia with his profile greatly enhanced. Along with several other well-performed Olympians an airline gave him a job that allowed him all the time he needed to pursue his sport. He took a year off and when he returned the magic had gone. The results just weren't there. The best he managed was sixth at a world championship.

'I just didn't have the will to do it anymore,' he said. 'I was doing just as much training but not performing.' So he quit.

He returned to the Gold Coast, settled down with his wife, started a family, paid off a mortgage by working as a lifeguard and regularly went fishing with his proud dad. He could still be found paddling competitively for his surf club and refused to worry about anything he could not change.

'It was just one of those things,' he said. 'Looking back, I couldn't have improved my race plan any more. Maybe if I had more experience I might have done a little better, but there are no regrets.'

And no, he said, nothing worse had happened in his life so far.

His story survives as a classic example of what the Olympic spirit truly means. He gave it his best shot – and went home happy.

PETER ANTONIE was proof positive of the proposition that big things can often come in small packages. The Victorian rower was also the very personification of the Olympic ideal that participation is more important than the result. So when he finally did get the ultimate outcome – a gold medal in the double sculls with a young sidekick, Stephen Hawkins, in Barcelona in 1992 – you would have struggled to name anyone who deserved it more. Or enjoyed it more.

Antonie was 34 at the time and had been a world-class oarsman for 15 years, winning a lightweight world championship and a Commonwealth Games gold medal among many other expressions of his enormous talent, dedication and determination. But the Olympic dream appeared to have eluded him, and few believed it was achievable this time given that he was, by five years, the oldest man in the field and Hawkins, 21, was the youngest while they were conceding a combined bodyweight of between 10 and 15kg to every other crew, an enormous disadvantage for the 'pocket rockets,' as they were dubbed. They also had to overcome a lack of experience rowing together.

None of it fazed Antonie, who had spent his entire career in the no-man's-land between the lightweight class, where he had to starve himself to make the 72kg limit, and the heavyweight class, where the Olympic big boys dwelt – most of them much heavier than he could ever build himself up to be. So be it – that's where he needed to be.

Rowing against these daunting odds, the odd couple of the strongest rowing team Australia had ever sent to an Olympics or world championship, Antonie and his new best friend had little to say to each other, they just knew that somehow they were in sync. 'It was like rowing with my twin brother,' Antonie said. That proved to be the difference as they powered over the 2000m metres in a shell named John Coates after the Australian Olympic Committee president, staving off the powerful Austrian and Dutch crews by just over a second in 6 min 17.32 sec to win Australia's first rowing gold medal for 44 years. Twenty-four hours later, the coxless four who were to become forever known as the Oarsome Foursome, Mike McKay, James Tomkins, Nick Green and Andrew Cooper added another one.

This was the end of a very long road for Antonie – or was it?

He had devoted himself entirely to his sport, abandoning two university degrees and supporting himself as a labourer, lawn mower,

painter, gardener, van driver, kitchen hand and abattoir worker – you
name it – to ensure he had time to train and compete until finally the
ANZ bank, which ran a sports stars job program, took him on as a
financial adviser,

It had been a decade and a half of relentless hard work,
uncompromising dedication, financial sacrifice and a struggle against the
physical odds. Antonie didn't care about the frustrations, the difficulties
or the costs – he just wanted to be a competitor. De Coubertin might have
had him in mind when he defined the Olympic spirit by proclaiming that
the struggle not the success was most important.

The ninth century village of Banyoles, where the regatta was held, was,
unsurprisingly, the scene of an epic celebration. I went looking for Antonie
the following morning and found him, at sun-up, sitting on the banks of
the lake, wet through and looking a touch worse for wear. It had been 'a
lunatic night,' he told me, involving a visit to every bar and disco in the
town and finally a wee-hours swim, from which he had still not dried off.
And then he told me he had arrived at a decision. He was retiring.

Within the next hour, this big – and exclusive – news was rolling off
the presses at home. 'I realise I have been destroying all other aspects
of my life outside rowing and the time has come to do something about
that,' he said for all to read.

But barely had the papers hit the streets than he fronted the obligatory
media conference after the medal presentations, which had been delayed
until the end of the regatta. He had been rapidly overcome by second
thoughts – and unretired himself.

He also revealed that in a rare quiet moment before embarking on the
celebration, he made a brief but poignant phone call. It was to his former
girlfriend in Melbourne. She remained nameless for obvious reasons but
she and Antonie dated for four years until the relationship cracked and
shattered under the strain of his uncompromising devotion to training.

'We just couldn't cope with the pressure of what I was doing,' he said.
'The relationship was totally destroyed and it was destroyed from my
end. We're still close friends and it was good to speak to her after the race,
but it really makes you wonder what sort of a person you have become.

Sometimes I wonder whether I'm just a bastard.'

That's not a sentiment shared by anyone else in the sport, then or ever since. The purity of his devotion to the sport has always been widely admired and for his versatility and longevity he was, after Barcelona, regarded as the greatest rower Australia had produced. Since then, other candidates for that title have emerged, notably Tomkins, McKay and Stewart Ginn, of whom more later. But Antonie is up there with any of them.

Far from retiring, he continued to the Atlanta Olympics in 1996 and narrowly failed to make the team for Sydney 2000, where he was an emergency – and just happy to still be involved in any way.

He was awarded the Order of Australia in 1987, inducted into the Sport Australia Hall of Fame in 1998, awarded the Australian Sports Medal in 2000, and in 2003 the International Rowing Federation awarded him the Thomas Keller Medal. It is the sport's highest honour, acknowledging not only an exceptional career but exemplary sportsmanship.

GILLIAN ROLTON would be the most appropriate winner possible of the Bill Roycroft Medal, if there was one, because she, too, won a gold medal – her second – in very similar circumstances. And she would have a rival for it, too, in team-mate Wendy Schaeffer – the pair of them produced heroic performances under extreme physical stress to enable Australia to win the three-day event in Atlanta in 1996.

Rolton, an Adelaide schoolteacher, became the first Australian woman to win an equestrian gold medal when she partnered Matt Ryan and Andrew Hoy in the three-day event in Barcelona in 1992, with Roycroft watching from the grandstand and his son Wayne coaching the team and Wayne's wife Vicki a specialist show-jumping coach. Rolton and her horse Peppermint Grove were last minute inclusions in the team after an impressive performance in the final selection trial in England three weeks earlier.

She came under extreme pressure when the fourth rider David Green had to withdraw from the show-jumping because his horse was believed – mistakenly, as it turned out – to be lame after a mishap during the cross-country phase. Showing great poise, Rolton and Peppermint improved their individual placings by three to help ensure the team triumph.

Four years later, she was a more established member of the team alongside the perennial Hoy – who went on to compete in seven Olympics, winning three golds and a silver – Phillip Dutton and Wendy Schaeffer.

Not long before the Olympics Schaeffer broke her leg in two places and competed with a screw and a plate in it, fortified by painkillers but still in a lot of discomfort. But sustained by adrenalin, she battled through the three disciplines to share the team gold with the other three. At 21, she was the youngest-ever equestrian gold medallist in company with her horse, Sunburst, a gift from her mother 10 years earlier. She performed so well that if the rules had not been changed since the previous Games, she would have also won the individual gold, the same double Ryan had completed in Barcelona.

Because Schaeffer's injury was pre-existing, as the insurance companies like to say, her courage wasn't as obvious as Rolton's, although certainly no less important to the outcome.

Rolton, still with her beloved Peppermint Grove, or Freddy as she called him, came to grief on a bend during the cross-country phase. The horse came down after treading on a tree root, then skidded along the gravel, taking her with him. She didn't know it then but she had broken her collarbone and two ribs.

The late Harry Gordon, Australia's official Olympic historian, takes up the story: 'A spectator grabbed the horse and she remounted. As she and Freddie began galloping again she became aware it was difficult to breathe and her left arm wasn't working. At the next obstacle, a water jump, horse and rider came down again after the useless arm prevented her from guiding Freddy through a clean jump.

'She somersaulted into the water then waded out and boarded the waiting horse again. She galloped one-handed for another three kilometres, clearing 15 more fences to finish the course. An ambulance took her to hospital, where she refused pain-killing drugs because she felt she might be needed for the show-jumping the next day. She wasn't, but Rolton's gallantry and perseverance served as an inspiration to her fellow riders and the entire Australian team.'

Rolton remained in the sport as a coach and administrator and was awarded the OAM in 1993. She was inducted into the Sport Australia hall of Fame and made a Legend of the South Australian sports Hall of Fame. She lost a battle with cancer in November 2017, aged 61, and a year later was posthumously made a Member of the Order of Australia.

SALVAGING GOLD FROM GRIEF

Olympic gold medals are usually all about the glory, not the grief. They are meant to be symbols of triumph, not tragedy. But for cyclists Scott McGrory and Brett Aitken, who won the two-man Madison on the track at the Sydney 2000 Games, that's precisely how mixed their emotions and memories are, and will always remain.

Both lost their first-born children – in McGrory's case shortly before the Games and for Aitken, a similar ordeal that also began before the biggest assignment of his life took a few more years to reach its heartbreaking conclusion.

The tragedies impacted heavily on their preparations for their most important sporting challenge to the extent that both decided to give up and had to be persuaded by friends and family to keep going.

There has never been a story quite like theirs in the 124 years of Australia's Olympic participation, and while track athlete Cathy Freeman's emotional and very visible heroics have passed into posterity as the signature performance of the same Games, I believe that if the Roycroft Medal did exist the two cyclists would be entitled to share it that year. Their story was, after all, truly a matter of life and death.

McGrory's 11-week-old son Alexander died of a heart condition on July 1, 2000, 75 days before the Games were due to begin, placing his dream under so much pressure he went within a whisker of cracking psychologically.

Aitken's infant daughter Ashli was dangerously ill with Rhett's Syndrome, a development disorder, during the same crucial lead-up period, so he, too, had to cope with extraordinary stress. She was to die at the age of 10, as the tenth anniversary of the Games approached.

That meant both riders, sharing a powerful bond that will last the rest of their lives, were confronting melancholy memories as the rest of the Olympic family prepared to toast those 16 uplifting days.

Happily, McGrory and Aitken have been able to move forward with the passage of time – but not without a lot more pain on various fronts. By the time the 20th anniversary arrived in 2020, each had endured marriage breakdowns, with both their former wives regarding the Olympic story as a thing of the past. Both wives asked for their names and those of their living children – they have two daughters each – not to be mentioned in this retelling, and that has been respected. Of course, both men are as proud of their girls as they hope the girls are of them.

Like many high-achieving sportsman who find themselves confronting the after-life McGrory has had to deal with mental health issues – some of which relate to a problematic childhood – and has spent time in hospital and in the care of a psychiatrist.

But he has never left the sport, spending the past 20 years as a recreational rider, a coach, a TV commentator, a corporate motivational speaker and an administrator, directing Australia's second biggest road stage race, the Herald Sun Tour in Victoria.

For both he and Aitken, the lead-up to Sydney was a roller-coaster from which they were nearly dumped long before it hit top speed.

That happened at the world championships in Berlin in October 1999, where they needed to finish in the top 14 to qualify for the big one almost a year later.

They were doing it easily, in the silver medal position and confident of winning the race, when Aitken crashed heavily at maximum speed, waking up in hospital.

That left McGrory with the herculean task of riding alone for the final 10k, of 50, which was made more difficult when he was docked points and relegated in a sprint for intruding on a rival rider's space.

Against all the odds, he managed to finish 13th so the dream was still alive by a whisker. It did wonders for McGrory's confidence, not so much for Aitken's.

McGrory, who was attempting to make an Olympic comeback 12 years after winning a bronze medal in Seoul as a starry-eyed novice who was just happy to be wearing an Australian tracksuit, told an interviewer that he and Aitken would definitely win in Sydney providing there wasn't another crash. 'I thought I could sound like a twat saying that, but it wasn't arrogance, just pure confidence and belief,' he recalled later.

That confidence was to be sorely tested before the moment of truth arrived.

The catalyst for that was when Alexander arrived five weeks prematurely, needing open-heart surgery and facing the prospect of mental disablement – or even death.

McGrory was persuaded to return to Europe to continue preparing for the Olympics but rushed back when his son suddenly deteriorated. His stopover in Singapore was a nightmare, knowing he might not get back in time to say his goodbyes.

'I was in a very busy airport yet I have never felt more alone or helpless,' he told me. 'I still have a terrible feeling when I take long-haul flights. The dark cabin full of strangers always sparks strong emotions.'

He made it to the hospital – just – and had only 45 minutes with his son before it became too much. 'I couldn't look at him anymore and my wife said it was OK,' he said. That was when – and not until then – that Alexander conceded defeat.

After the funeral cycling suddenly seemed unimportant. 'It hits you how irrelevant and selfish sport is,' McGrory said. So he said he was hanging up his bike. It was over.

He was told vehemently not to quit, that he would regret it forever, that it would be the year he lost twice – his baby and his dream – and that there was at least still something to salvage.

As the Games drew near McGrory still wasn't at peace, far from it. 'There were times when I felt invincible, drawing strength from what had happened, and a day later I'd be absolutely useless,' he said.

'One day I did a five-hour ride to the Dandenongs (a mountainous area on Melbourne's fringe) and as it started to rain. I looked to the heavens and yelled "Bring it on!" The harder it rained and windier and colder it got, the better – nothing was going to touch me that day because I was Superman.

'The next day I got only 20 minutes into the same ride and had to stop on a bridge over the river because I had been crying for several blocks and couldn't see where I was going. I was afraid I'd be hit by a car.'

McGrory knew his training had been compromised and doubts crept in. So did frustrations. At a team camp he was so angry about the poor quality of one workout that he punched a cupboard and thought he had broken his hand.

'I felt like an absolute idiot because if I couldn't do a hand sling (a crucial racing technique in the Madison) with Brett then I couldn't ride.' Luckily his hand was only bruised.

The doubts persisted to the extent that on race morning McGrory looked at Aitken in the next bed and apologised to him under his breath. 'I couldn't bring myself to say it – and never told him until many years later – but while I was never going to give up I had conceded to myself that winning had become unachievable.'

Ninety minutes before the warm-up he gave himself a talking-to. 'Before 6000 people I sat myself down and said, "I don't give a shit that you haven't trained or haven't raced". I had to search for the courage within and get my head straight. There was only one person who could do it – me.'

'It was like I flicked a switch in my head. I was hit by a sense of calm and certainty. I never looked back. I just had to do something to change my mindset, and I am still surprised that you flip mentally just like that and switch on and off – it's extraordinary.'

The result was Australia's first Olympic track cycling gold for 16 years.

Life was so hectic as an Olympic gold medallist – he also got married that year – that plans to simply disappear and grieve in private had to be abandoned.

But months later racing in Germany McGrory returned alone to his apartment one night – and for the first time it all hit home. Hard. 'I was a dribbling mess for three days,' he said. 'I had to pull myself together for a race and won it – but I was an emotional wreck.'

The roller-coaster continued for five years. Trying to train in Australia and race in Europe, McGrory was flattened by glandular fever and then broke five ribs in a racing crash.

At 35 he realised he was no longer firing on all cylinders. It was scarcely surprising. So he retired.

He and Aitken no longer saw each other much – their contact is still sporadic two decades later – but the bond was intact. 'It is indescribable, unique – a connection that no-one else has, and that has been strengthened by tragedy,' McGrory said. 'There is nothing negative you could say to me about Brett Aitken as a person or a cyclist.'

For Aitken, the pre-Olympic script bore distinct similarities, although not quite as tragic at that stage. Like McGrory, he was already an Olympic medallist – twice in fact, winning silver and then bronze in the team pursuit, an Australian speciality, in Barcelona 1992 and Atlanta in 1996. But he desperately wanted gold.

So when he crashed out of the world championships, leaving McGrory to finish the race alone, he did not share his partner's burgeoning optimism. Their survival had been too close for comfort, he thought.

But that was the least of his worries as a year, 1999, he looks back on now as 'incredibly traumatic and difficult' drew to a close, with Christmas soured by the news that his daughter did not have cerebral palsy, as had been originally diagnosed, but Rhett's Syndrome, a more severe affliction.

He decided to put cycling on the back burner, that the golden dream was over. 'I had no choice,' he said. But after a number of 'really tough' weeks to-ing and fro-ing over what to do, dealing with how to manage the situation, he was persuaded to resume training and give it his best shot.

Back in Europe, he printed out a label with a single word – UNBREAKABLE – and attached it to the handlebars of his bike. 'It was a permanent reminder of all the reasons I felt that was what I was, unbreakable, no matter what was thrown at me.

'On top of this being the Olympics and in my home country, I needed an extra edge and the adversity I was dealing with gave it to me – maybe an extra half a percent in my mindset.'

After being told to get back on the bike Aitken made a simple promise to himself – and to Ashli. 'I decided if I was going to do this I might as well make every day worthwhile,' he said. 'Once I made that commitment it changed everything. My determination lifted by 20 per cent and I was already very, very determined. I am a focussed and very goal-driven sort of guy and there wasn't a day when I wasn't 100 per cent committed. I do believe I trained harder than anybody else that year. By nature I'm a bit of a lazy guy but that year was different.'

However, Aitken was painfully aware that McGrory was staring down his own demons and that the interruptions to his training could ultimately cost them both the holy grail.

'Losing just one week in the final few months could be the difference between first and last and it had cost Scott a lot more time than that,' he said. 'I just had to be there for support and to give him space, knowing there was a high possibility he wouldn't be there in the end. It was harder for Scott than for me because I hadn't actually lost a child.'

And if McGrory hadn't made it?

'I wouldn't have liked to try it without him. We are elite athletes and you have to believe you can win and my mindset was that we were going to, no matter what. But the reality was that it was a team event and you have to have the best team – without Scott it wouldn't have been the best.'

Not until a decade later when I told him what McGrory had revealed to me did Aitken discover that his partner had virtually conceded defeat on the morning of the race.

'He kept it well hidden from me,' he said. 'He was compromised and not in his best form but his desire that night was unbelievable – it says a lot about him.'

Aitken said that sharing the triumph with someone was infinitely better than winning an individual event would have been, especially in the circumstances.

'To have achieved it after racing for 22 years I was elated – I then believed I could achieve anything in life,' he said.

His daughter survived to be part of the celebrations but never recovered, dying nine years later, unable to walk or speak but with an 'unbelievable' personality, according to her dad. 'Ashli enjoyed her 10 years and the world enjoyed having her,' he said. 'That time was very fulfilling.'

Like McGrory, Aitken has remained in the sport, working as a coach with the South Australian Institute of Sport.

GRANT HACKETT became the Australian hero of the 2004 Athens Olympics when he won the most demanding event on any swimming program, the 1500m, after a preparation severely compromised by a range of illnesses – culminating in him competing with a collapsed lung which left him on the verge of collapse at the end of the long race. 'He should have been awarded an extra medal for valour,' Olympic historian Harry Gordon wrote in his book *From Athens With Pride*. My sentiments exactly – about Hackett and the others whose feats of bravery and spirit are listed in these pages.

After he retired from the pool with a stunning career behind him, Hackett engaged in a certain amount of dubious behaviour which seriously damaged his personal reputation for several years. For anyone who had watched him become one of the finest distance swimmers the world has seen, one of the brightest stars of a golden era for Australia's favourite and most successful Olympic sport, that was a deeply disappointing development. However, it proved temporary, touch wood. And it should not be allowed to obscure his capacity to provide leadership and inspiration on the pool deck, which is why a year after his Athens drama he became the first person to be officially appointed captain of the Australian swimming team.

Hackett was already a superstar – although perhaps slightly in the shadow of the amazing Ian Thorpe – by the time he got to Athens, having prevented compatriot Kieren Perkins winning a third successive 1500m gold medal in Sydney four years earlier as well as racking up bags of medals at world championships and other events.

Thanks mainly to him, Thorpe and Petria Thomas – who won three golds and a silver after enduring three shoulder reconstructions – the swimmers collected seven golds to spearhead the most successful off-shore performance by any Australian team overall, with the track cyclists also dominating.

Hackett's contribution was special – although just how special, no-one quite knew at the time. Although it was no secret he wasn't well, he didn't tell the media or even the team doctors just how seriously ill he was.

In the lead-up he had been dogged by asthma, glandular fever and pneumonia and then before the final two other afflictions struck – he was running a fever and was pumped full of antibiotics to combat a chest infection, then he suffered a collapsed lung. He kept quiet about the lung problem for fear the doctors wouldn't let him swim. 'My lungs were so blocked and stuffed for so long that it was partially deflated and there was fluid in there – it was fairly serious,' he admitted much later. His coach Dennis Cotterell said the star had lost 25 per cent of lung capacity.

Before the race Hackett simply told himself: 'Whatever it takes.' It took plenty because American Larsen Jensen and Welshman David Davies each sliced more than 10 seconds of their best-ever times to push him right to the line. For Hackett, who had not lost a 1500m final in seven years – but who had been beaten into third place in his qualifying heat – it was the toughest swim of his life. His victory, in Olympic record time, made him only the fourth swimmer in 108 years to win two gold medals over 1500m, behind American Mike Burton, Russian Vladimir Salnikov and Pierkins.

He attempted to make it an unprecedented hat-trick in Beijing four years later but was beaten into second place by Tunisia's Oussama Mellouli.

DREW GINN had a boat – and a partner – to assist him across the finish line in the coxless pairs at Beijing in 2008, which was just as well because he would not have been able to do it on foot, alone.

Ginn won the third Olympic gold medal of arguably the most highly decorated career in the history of Australian rowing in such debilitating pain from a prolapsed disc in his back that he could barely get out of the boat and was then confined to bed for two days, unable to walk.

There have been many such stories of athletes in various sports overcoming severe physical trauma to triumph on the Olympic stage but, as an eye-witness, I have seen none more impressive than Ginn's agonising refusal to give in to his perennially fragile body.

Aware of the nature of the ordeal he was about to put himself through, Ginn – perhaps channelling Grant Hackett's 'whatever it takes' instruction to himself in Athens – wrote a note to himself on the eve of the race. 'What is pain?' it said. 'One great friend once said it is simply a signal that goes to your brain. How you interpret that signal is critical. Back pain is no different to any other pain. Your mind creates an image of your body and with that maps what's going on.'

It wasn't, perhaps, the most eloquent message ever delivered but the meaning was crystal clear – pain is only what you make of it. And that's entirely up to you.

In any case, it wasn't as if this was an unfamiliar experience for the product of the up-market Melbourne school Scotch College, which has a proud sporting tradition.

His back first gave way at the worst possible time, 10 weeks before his home Olympics in Sydney, where he had planned to partner James Tomkins in the pairs, for which they would have been favourite.

Ginn already had a gold medal to his name – in 1996 he replaced Andrew Cooper in the celebrated Oarsome Foursome coxless four, which defended the title that Tomkins, Mike Mckay, Nick Green and Cooper had won in Barcelona – but that didn't lessen the shattering disappointment of having to scratch from Sydney more or less at the last minute.

He spent two years rehabilitating his back before he and Tomkins made up for it by winning in Athens. It had been such a difficult journey that both men wept as they crossed the finish line. But neither was satisfied.

When Beijing rolled around, they had split up – Ginn, 34, was now rowing with an old mate Duncan Free, 35, with whom he had gone to primary school on the Gold Coast, and Tomkins, at 43 and at his sixth and last Olympics, had joined the blue-ribbon eight.

Having won successive world championships, Ginn and Free were favourites – until his back gave way again during the heats before the semi-final. He was in so much trouble that a team-mate was secretly put on standby to take his place.

With intense pain in his left hip – 'just sitting down in the boat was bloody painful,' he said – he made it through the semi. But the pain then got so bad that they couldn't even train on the water. They just had to take their chances, with Ginn promising his mate that he wouldn't let him down.

He didn't. They won the final well from the Canadians and New Zealanders, but Ginn had to be helped out of the boat as his entire right side shut down and put to bed. Days later his right leg was still not working properly. His foot flopped from side to side. Doctors feared the damage might be long term, that surgery might nor repair it, and said he should never row again.

At home in Melbourne, he found himself in the scariest shower scene since Alfred Hitchcock's classic horror movie *Psycho*. He wasn't being attacked by a madman with a knife. Rather, he reached to adjust the tap and felt his back lock up so completely he couldn't move a muscle and was in such extreme agony he burst into tears.

'I screamed for my wife who had to carry me out. I was afraid I was going to lose the use of my leg,' he said. He had surgery the next morning to remove a fragment of disc that was cutting off the nerves in the lower back.

Obviously rowing was a thing of the past. Or was it?

To fill the gap in his life, Ginn took up competitive cycling, proving adept enough at it to win an Oceania time trial championship – but that was never going to get him back to the Olympics.

Only a madman would ignore the advice he had been given by the surgeons, surely. You would have to be especially crazy to take the risk if you were 36, with a wife and two young kids, your status as an authentic sporting hero locked in and nothing to prove.

And yet, little more than a year out from the 2012 Games, he returned to the national championships where, with various partners, he won the pairs and the four and finished second in the eight – and all without a yelp from his back. Amazingly … London, here we come!

There, he returned to where it all began, the coxless four, with three different partners of course. They settled for silver, beaten by just over a second by the British crew. Not for the first time, tears flowed. 'What you have to get your head around is that a silver medal is still a huge achievement,' he said. In his case, that could not have rung any truer.

It meant that from four Olympics he won three golds and a silver, putting him marginally ahead of Tomkins' three golds and a bronze – with the question mark over what might have been in Sydney never to be resolved. Tomkins also won seven world championships to Ginn's five.

ANNA MEARES was an authentic rival for Ginn if any award was being offered in Beijing for the most admirable comeback from severe physical and mental trauma – but she might have been even more worthy of it in London four years later. She was lucky to be alive, let alone competing in either Olympics, especially in a sport as inherently dangerous as track cycling. And yet she won a silver medal at the first one and a gold medal at the second, confirming herself as the best and bravest female cyclist Australia has yet produced.

The 'Coalminer's Daughter' from the Queensland outback town of Middlemount, where Dad was indeed engaged in unearthing the black fuel that has long powered much of the nation, and her sister Kerrie were a double act as they gravitated to the sport as kids, inspired by Olympic and Commonwealth gold medallist Kathy Watt's pioneering performances.

Kerrie was good – she broke numerous national records and won two gold medals and two bronzes at the Commonwealth Games in Melbourne in 2006 – but Anna was better.

Kerrie was a bit too banged-up from racing crashes to make it to the 2004 Olympics, but Anna got there, winning the 500m time trial (a now-defunct Olympic event) by breaking a world record that had been set by another competitor minutes earlier.

Seven months before Beijing, Meares broke her neck in a high-speed racing crash while competing on the World Cup circuit in Los Angeles. She fractured her C2 vertebra, dislocated her right shoulder, tore ligaments and tendons, suffered a heavily bruised right hip and skin abrasions. Witnesses feared she had killed herself. Doctors said if the fracture had been a millimetre or two the other way, she would not have survived.

As she was fitted for a wheelchair, nobody imagined for a moment that she would ever be seen back on a racing bike. Well, nobody but her, that is.

Astonishingly she was back in the saddle after just 10 days, wearing a neck brace and still barely able to walk, conscious that she had accrued enough points before the accident to have a chance of qualifying for the Games in the sprint event – if she could recover in time.

Her first effort at pedalling lasted just two minutes and brought on a dizzy spell but later the same day she tried again. And again. With a modified training drill, every target set for her she met.

But it was still outside her control. If two rivals performed well enough in her absence at the world championships two months later, she would not qualify. They both failed. If she could regain her form, she was back in. And she did.

There, she made it through to the final in slightly controversial circumstances – her semi-final opponent Guo Shuang of China was disqualified from the deciding heat for illegally making contact with her – where she was beaten by the brilliant Englishwoman Victoria Pendleton. Some cynics say the silver medallist is the first of the losers – for Meares, it could hardly have been any more emotionally triumphant after what she had been through.

Meares and Pendleton, arch rivals for most of the time they were racing together, were not finished with each other yet.

In London four years later, Pendleton was on home turf and in front of her own adoring fans – advantages Meares had enjoyed at the world championships in Melbourne earlier that year, where Pendleton prevailed after some fiery interaction between the pair.

At the Olympics they clashed again in the sprint, with Meares – having trained against a male sprinter – winning the three-heat final 2-0 after Pendleton crossed the line first in the opening salvo only to be controversially relegated for moving off her line. Many believed that was the result of Meares riding over aggressively but she responded: 'This is sport – we're not out there to have a cup of tea.'

Regardless of the debate that ensued, the result meant that she had now made it all the way back from her nightmare in LA to the top step of the Olympic podium – a journey that will forever hold a prominent place in posterity for the Australian Olympic family.

CUP RUNNETH OVER – WITH TERROR

Thankfully being a cricket writer is not the same as being a war correspondent – well, not usually. But it could easily have got me killed. Like my father before me, I was lucky to survive a bomb. It was just an accident of timing that I wasn't walking along the waterfront and into the business district of the Sri Lankan capital Colombo when two suicide bombers drove a truck full of explosives into the front door of the National Bank, killing about 90 people and injuring 1400 – and, as a far less tragic side effect, plunging the Australian cricket team into a bitter political upheaval that was partly responsible for costing them one of the game's foremost trophies, the one-day World Cup.

It also led to the Sri Lankan Government more or less ordering me out of the country.

In early 1996, that idyllic little teardrop island off the bottom of the Asian sub-Continent was one of the more dangerous places on earth because it was in the midst of a 25 year civil war between the Singhalese Government and the Tamil ethnic separatists which lasted from the early eighties until peace was declared in 2009. The hostilities didn't do much to dilute the passion for cricket which defined the nation as much as its production of tea and affinity with elephants. So being chosen to co-host the World Cup that year along with its big brothers India and Pakistan as well as Bangladesh was a tremendous coup, elevated in importance by the choice of two of the game's super-powers, Australia and the West Indies, to open their campaigns in Colombo.

But there was a lot of turbulent of water to flow under the bridge before that would happen, with Sri Lanka undertaking a three-Test tour of Australia, which was to become one of the most acrimonious in the game's history. 'Has there ever been a sadder, more damaging summer for the image, spirit and nobility of the game?' I wrote at the time, which was putting it in the same category as the infamous Bodyline tour by England in 1932-33. A big call, yes, given the political fall-out generated by the morally dubious manner in which England captain Douglas Jardine and his fast bowlers attempted to blunt the genius of Don Bradman. But bodyline was a single issue. The 1995-96 season had it all, and it wasn't pretty – match-fixing, chucking, sledging, paranoia about non-existent problems with drugs and, eventually, so much ill-feeling on the field that one captain could not bring himself to shake the other's hand. And the worst, by far, was still yet to come. Australia has never experienced a cricket season quite like it, before or since – and I have never been so relieved to see the end of one.

The Sri Lankans had nothing to do with the match-fixing. That was the burden of the Pakistan team, who toured with former captain Salim Malik, who had been accused of offering bribes to Australian players Shane Warne and Tim May to deliberately manipulate the result of a Test in Pakistan a few months earlier. The International Cricket Council cleared Malik of any wrong-doing but his presence ensured the new series, which Australia won 2-1, would be a tense affair on and off the field, and it was – even though he was injured early and took no part in the Tests.

Sri Lanka followed for three more Tests, the first of which, in Perth, became rancorous when the umpires accused them of tampering with the ball. Compared to the same charge levelled against Australia in South Africa more than two decades later with such explosive consequences, this was smallish beer and was dismissed by the ICC because of an absence of any proof of deliberate sharp practice. But it changed the mood, with the tourists insisting they had been stitched up.

That was nothing, though, compared to the furore that awaited them at their next outing, the showpiece Boxing Day Test at the MCG. There, a simmering controversy surrounding the bowling action of then moderately-known off-spinner Muttiah Muralidaran came to a head

Free at last ... slouch-hatted Bill Reed, second from left middle row, and his fellow prisoners are homeward-bound.

Fat boy, the bomb that destroyed Nagasaki – but couldn't kill 24 Australian prisoners.

We meet again ... Bill Reed and his old captor Kojima Asagoro part on good terms 40 years after the war.

A toast to peace …
Kojima Asagoro's
family welcome Bill
Reed and Murray
Jobling to their home
for an emotional
reunion.

Reflections on years
in hell … Bill Reed
and Murray Jobling
look out over Nagasaki
four decades after the
bomb.

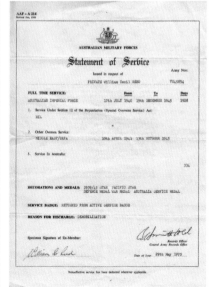

Certificate of discharge and Statement of Service formally end Private Reed's
contribution to the war effort.

On the job as a 17-year-old cadet reporter at the *Warrnambool Standard*, a 50-year career stretching ahead.

Editorial conference … *Sporting Globe* editors Gene Swinstead and Alan Dunn (left), Ron Reed and Greg Hobbs (right) with secretary Nancy Telford and senior writer Ian McDonald (centre) swap old war stories.

Blue heaven with Leigh, helping Carlton celebrate the 1982 premiership.

Flannelled fools … The Plastic XI midweek cricket team boasted some big names, including Carlton footballers Perc Jones, Mark Maclure and Adrian Gallagher, Test fast bowler Ian Callen and foreign correspondent Bruce Wilson.

Cricket HQ ... the 1997 Ashes press corps, Jim and Bruce Wilson, Kim Hagdorn, Jim Tucker, Ken Cassellas, Greg Baum, Ron Reed, Ian Jessup, Malcolm Conn and Gordon Fuad debrief at Lord's.

Packing a punch 1 ... Ghanian boxer Azumah Nelson unburdens his many troubles before destroying Aussie hero Jeff Fenech in Melbourne.

Packing a punch 2 … former heavyweight world champion George Foreman was never short of an opinion.

Big-hitter … flamboyant English batsman Kevin Pietersen gets his eye in at the MCG.

Game on. Fifth from left at the rear and surrounded by the cream of News Ltd's sportswriting and photographic talent at the Barcelona Olympics.

The (very) old dark navy Blues – Carlton multiple premiership heroes Geoff Southby, Perc Jones, Jim Buckley, Syd Jackson, Ken Sheldon and David McKay, plus one ring-in.

Sir Ian — now Lord Botham — and former Australian Test player Ian Callen make up this distinguished trio of fast (and one not nearly so fast) bowlers from the old midweek cricket days.

Proud moment ... with son Adam and wife Leigh after being presented with the Australian Sports Commission's Lifetime Achievement Award.

when umpire Darrell Hair no-balled him seven times. Hair was standing at the bowler's end, not square leg, which meant the first couple of calls were assumed to be for over-stepping and so there was no reaction on the field or off it. But when Hair kept declaring the deliveries illegal it became clear that he had decided the bowling was chucking, and uproar quickly ensued. Bewildered, Sri Lanka's combative captain Arjuna Ranatunga left the field to consult with team management about how to respond. That decision was to bowl Murali from the other end, which drew no further action from Hair or from the other umpire, New Zealander Steve Dunne. With the ball tampering allegations still a source of great angst, the mood now descended into a red mist of anger and dismay.

It was the first time any bowler had been called for throwing in Australia since left-arm paceman Ian Meckiff was called four times in an over by umpire Col Egar – a future chairman of the Australian Cricket Board – against South Africa in Brisbane in 1963. Captain Richie Benaud did not bowl him again and Meckiff immediately announced his retirement, never playing again at any level. Having long been friendly with The Count, the nickname to which the affable, popular Victorian has always answered, I knew he would be at the MCG as this new drama unfolded and quickly located him in the VIP area, where he was almost speechless. 'I have nothing to say, I just can't comprehend it,' he told me.

To digress, the reasons why Egar suddenly decided to take such drastic action have never been revealed, but it wasn't on the spur of the moment. A day or so earlier word had seeped through to the Press Box that something dramatic was in the wind. When it became clear what that was, speculation immediately centred around the most powerful figure in the Australian game, Sir Donald Bradman. Had he, people were asking, decided to ensure that Australia would be at the forefront of eradicating chucking, which had been a highly contentious issue in world cricket since the England tour of Australia in 1958-59 when several Australian fast bowlers, including Meckiff, were condemned by the English media and, by association, the Lord's Establishment? To this day, that question has never been satisfactorily answered and given that Bradman, Egar and Benaud are long dead it probably never will be.

Meckiff is still going strong in his eighties but has rarely spoken about it publicly and when he does it is only to say he has no idea what really happened. He adds that as the years rolled by it distressed his family much more than it did him whenever the topic arose in the media. Despite being a professional journalist and broadcaster all his life, Benaud also was never forthcoming except to insist that he believed he had no option but to take the ball out of Meckiff's hands for the duration of the match because the umpire's decision was final. Egar, too, kept his counsel.

One evening in 1993, in a bar in Hobart waiting for a Test to begin, I was having a drink with Meckiff and several other cricket luminaries – including the then Australian team manager Ian McDonald, who was a journalist working on the fateful match and later Meckiff's biographer, as well as Ian Chappell, Tony Grieg and others – and we were all, The Count included, wondering aloud whether the forthcoming 30th anniversary of the event might shed any light on the mystery. We agreed that only Benaud might have the knowledge and the inclination to finally do that. No sooner had those words been spoken than the lift door opened and out stepped the great man, keen for a white wine himself. I immediately told him what the group had been discussing. He arched his eyebrows, swallowed the rest of the drink and walked straight back to the lift without another word other than 'have a nice evening, chaps.' Make of that what you will. A few years later, I was given access to the cricket board's archives, including the minutes of all board meetings going back decades, to research an official history they wanted written, a task eventually undertaken by two fine writers, Gideon Haigh and David Frith. I couldn't wait to get to the records from the early sixties, believing here, surely, would be the answer to the Meckiff conundrum. Amazingly, it was barely mentioned at the board meeting in Melbourne 23 days after the Brisbane Test.

It was revealed that one board member, the controversial and colourful Queenslander Alderman Clem Jones had said before the match he considered Meckiff 'did not play in accordance with the rules of the game' and should not be selected. He was told he had no right to make such an objection and the matter was closed. Otherwise, a letter was tabled from a member of the public, L McCauley of East Sydney, expressing his disapproval of Egar's action. The letter was 'received' with no discussion. The board contented itself with noting that Meckiff had disqualified himself from further selection that season by writing about the incident in the Press. A motion that no public statement be made on the no-balling was carried.

Many years later, Jones claimed that Bradman always was careful that if something did not immediately bear on a decision but might cause trouble later, it would be scrapped from the minutes. Jones, who was chairman of the umpires selection committee, was convinced the calling of Meckiff was premeditated. 'They had decided to do it a week before the game, so the poor bloke had no hope,' he said. He was convinced Bradman had told the umpires he wanted it done. 'See, Bradman was of the opinion Meckiff was throwing a long time before it happened.'

The Meckiff affair is still the greatest unsolved mystery in Australian cricket history – and it is unfortunate for posterity's sake that the key participants decided to keep it that way for so long, without any coherent explanation. The only one still alive to tell the tale is the unfortunate bowler himself, and even he doesn't know what really happened.

There was no such confusion 32 years later – Hair was simply a strong-willed individual who believed the laws of the game were there to be interpreted, enforced and obeyed and that the ICC was wimping it by taking no action of its own. It is highly unlikely he was told what to do by anybody. And before long he wasn't the only one. Days later, in a one-day match, another umpire, Ross Emerson, also called Muralidaran, which went a long way towards convincing the tourists they were being stitched up, the victims of a conspiracy. At that stage, the 23-year-old was not the megastar he was to become – before Melbourne, he had played 22 Tests for 73 wickets, a far cry from his eventual 800 from 133 Tests, still the all-time record, along with his 534 one-day scalps. And Sri Lanka were still regarded as little more than minnows – a status that was about to change in a big way in a very short time – so it was no great surprise that they sensed they were being victimised and bullied. A certain amount of paranoia set in to the extent that when young batsman Roshan Mahanama, later to become an ICC referee, suffered a hand injury the team management became extremely nervous about using a recommended steroid-based medication for fear they would end up being accused of being drug cheats as well.

Relations deteriorated further during the World Series Cup one-dayers when Glenn McGrath shouldered batsman Sanath Jayasuriya mid-pitch and Ian Healy needled Ranatunga about his request for a runner, saying he was not injured, just too fat. At the conclusion of the last game, Ranatunga declined to shake opposing captain Mark Taylor's hand and his deputy Aravinda da Silva said he had seen no sign that Taylor was remotely sorry for his team's 'rampant boorishness.' By this time, Healy, McGrath, Shane Warne and Craig McDermott had all received death threats if they went to Colombo, adding to the general unease. Muralidaran, meanwhile, did not play again on tour. To nobody's surprise the Sri Lankans had no qualms about picking him to play in the World Cup and his astonishing career was never seriously interrupted again.

The scene was set for another extremely volatile third and final Test in Adelaide, with the Australians scheduled to leave for Colombo shortly afterwards to begin their World Cup preparations. What sort of welcome could they expect there? Astutely, the Herald Sun's Sports Editor Phil Gardner decided I should give the Adelaide match a miss and go straight to Colombo to answer that question. On arrival, I was told by the police chief that the team would be safe because security would be at the level normally reserved for visits by heads of state. The Australian High Commissioner Bill Tweddle and the under-secretary Brian Pullen assured me that despite the many armed soldiers on every street it was 'sometimes hard to believe there is a war going on.' But the problem, they said, was that you never knew when the next suicide bomber would strike – they were a common occurrence. 'But they are never aimed at foreigners or tourists. The biggest worry is being in the wrong place at the wrong time.' Amen to that.

For the first three days I left my room at the elegant old Taj Samudra Hotel – where security was being ramped up to the nth degree in anticipation of the team's arrival – and made the 15-20 minute walk each lunchtime along the beachfront road that led to the business district, passing the Central Bank. Each time, I was accosted by a raggedy but polite boy of about 12 standing outside the bank, asking me to contribute towards his school's sports equipment. He was, of course, begging, but too proud to say as much. I gave him a few coins each time I passed, engaged him in a conversation about his own cricket and decided he was the best mate I had in this town.

On day four, about 11am, just as I was getting ready to do the walk again, an enormous explosion shattered the sunny ambience. Immediately, the house-boy who had been tidying up the room dived under the bed – he knew what had just happened. I had a fair idea too when I looked out of the fourth-floor window and saw a huge mushroom cloud of billowing black smoke just up the road. I was soon to learn that two Tamil extremists had driven a truck carrying 4000kg of explosives up to the main door of the bank I would have been walking past in another half an hour or so, inflicting huge damage on that building and every other one within 100m or so, and killing or injuring everyone in the vicinity. The eventual toll was about 90 dead and 1400 injured, making it the worst such atrocity of many that the island had experienced over a long period of time.

After a short and eerie silence, the street was suddenly swarming with troop carriers and ambulances, sirens blaring. The hotel PA implored all guests to stay in their rooms but I decided, probably foolhardily, to try to get to the scene, reasoning that the bomb had now done its worst and I was unlikely to walk into a second one. Thousands of people were streaming towards the hotel, hot-footing it out of the CBD, many stopping to plead with me to turn around. Eventually I had no choice but to do so, being confronted by several soldiers all pointing rifles at me and ordering me to back off.

Back in the hotel, I made three hurried phone calls to people in Australia who had not yet heard any news of this. The explosion was only 20 minutes old. One was to my wife, telling her not to panic when she did turn the TV on. One was to my editor, telling him … yes, hold the front page! The third was to the Chief Executive of the cricket board, Graham Halbish, telling him that if the team turned up as planned in a few days' time they would be entering a war zone adjacent to their hotel, where nobody's safety could be guaranteed. An emergency phone hook-up of the board directors followed within the hour.

The next morning, I returned to the epicentre of the blast and the armed soldiers allowed me to pass through the barriers on production of a cricket media card. I half wished they hadn't. Barely recognisable bodies burned to charcoal were stacked one on top of the other, small groups of soldiers, most aged no more than 20, staring blankly and silently at the carnage. It dawned on me that my schoolboy mate was almost certainly one of the victims. That realisation seemed to bring the full horror of it home more than the grim sights I was sharing with the rookie soldiers.

The locals were not unaccustomed to such horrific spectacles, apparently. Days later, somebody gave me a copy of The Island Sunday newspaper published the day after two suicide bombers blew themselves and 14 other people up in the same area a few weeks earlier, and there in full colour on the front page were photos of one of them, his decapitated head lying on the road, his leg a metre away, while a third photo showed a bystander's body missing both arms and everything from the waist down. I still have this sickening souvenir, which is unlike anything I have ever seen published in a newspaper anywhere else in the world.

The shockwaves reverberated through Cricket Australia, with some players – especially those who had already been threatened – clearly reluctant to risk going to Colombo. The Sri Lankan board was in damage control, big-time. They knew from experience that this could have drastic consequences. In 1987, a less powerful but still very deadly bomb had been detonated at the military barracks adjoining the Taj Samudra, where the New Zealand team were housed. Several of the Kiwis immediately went home and there were no cricket tours of Sri Lanka for five years. They desperately needed to convince the Australians and the other three teams scheduled to play there, the West Indies, Zimbabwe and Kenya, to not pull the legs out from under the most important sporting event the country had ever hosted, an embarrassment not just for cricket but for the Government and, well, everyone – the bombers possibly excepted. As I was the only international journalist in town, and given that I was making it very clear to a large Australian audience that coming to play there was simply asking for trouble, I was suddenly in high demand. The cricket board president Asa Punchihewa invited me to lunch with his board members, making it abundantly clear that declining was not an option, and after an hour or two of predictable propaganda I was then put in another car, again virtually compulsory, and delivered to a press conference by the Foreign Minister, one Lakshman Kadirgamar. It was put to him that Shane Warne had declared himself unwilling to go to Colombo because you could get blown up while out shopping, to which he replied provocatively that 'shopping was for sissies,' a quote that returned the issue to the front pages back in Australia. Then, at a Friday night drinks party at the Australian High Commission a couple of heavies turned up in a limo and insisted that I and another Australian reporter who had belatedly arrived that day, Lindsay Murdoch of *The Age*, accompany them to an undisclosed destination. This turned out to be the home of the Sports Minister, S. B. Dissanayake, who lived in an enclosed compound out of reach of any passing terrorists. Longneck bottles of beer were produced and Murdoch and I were informed in no uncertain terms that unless the tone of our reporting changed we would not be welcome to remain in Sri Lanka. I told him there were not too many different ways to interpret the carnage that had just happened – Colombo was patently an unsafe place to be – and that message would not be changing. The beer promptly dried up and we were driven back to the Embassy function.

It was time to go anyway because at home the Department of Foreign Affairs had issued the board with confidential advice not to go, adding: 'Please be discreet. This could cost other lives.' The West Indies also pulled out, leaving only the two small African nations willing to take the risk – or perhaps unwilling to offend the powerful Indian powerbrokers who were effectively running the whole tournament and who certainly were capable of threatening to never tour Zimbabwe or Kenya which would have major financial ramifications.

The action shifted to Calcutta, as Kolkata was known then, for a meeting of organisers and participants to sort out how to deal with the loss of two matches in Colombo. India's two most senior heavyweights, World Cup chief organiser Jagmohan Dalmiya and I. S. Bindra more or less took charge even though the West Indies' Clyde Walcott was in the chair. Australia was represented by the urbane Melbourne businessman Malcolm Gray, a vastly experienced administrator who as chairman of the ACB had overseen the organisation of the previous World Cup and who would go on to become chairman of the ICC, and Bob Cowper, a wealthy and unflappable businessman who had called stumps on a successful Test career prematurely in order to make his fortune in business, which he did with even more spectacular success. I found them sitting outside the meeting room mid-afternoon, nursing cups of tea – or it might have been something stronger – and looking shell-shocked. They told me their first mistake had been to turn up wearing open-necked shirts, interpreted as a lack of respect.

The rest of our conversation was pretty much identical to the version that appears in Cricket Australia's official history. The two high-powered Indian administrators 'just shouted at us all morning,' Gray said. 'Called us cowards, called us racists. Threatened us with everything you could think of. After lunch they started again. Bindra had this incredibly loud voice and he just yelled. Finally I said: 'Bindra, I'm sick of you yelling. I can yell too and I'm going to yell now.' So I did. And we broke for afternoon tea.'

With that, the white heat drained out of proceedings but Gray and Cowper were left in no doubt that the Australian team could expect no favours when they arrived the following day.

This proved true when the team got to Mumbai, which was then Bombay, to prepare, for which they had plenty of time seeing they would have to wait until the first round of matches had been completed without them. They found themselves assigned to a third-rate hotel many kilometres from the district in which the elite practice facilities were located in the city's main cricket precinct. It was going to take hours of uncomfortable travel by bus in impenetrable traffic to get there and back each day, an unacceptable situation – but the 'hosts' weren't listening to any complaints. It was only when team manager Ian McDonald, a former sports writing colleague of mine, made contact with another old workmate of us both, Gene Swinstead, that sanity prevailed. Swinstead was general manager of a TV network owned by Rupert Murdoch and was living high on the hog in a luxury hotel near where the cricketers needed to be. He pulled a few strings and, presto, we were all back in the standard of accommodation to which we (well, the team, anyway) had become accustomed. A short distance away was the swanky Bombay Gymkhana Cricket Club, where India played its first Test against England in 1933, which welcomed the team to use its upmarket facilities, practice wickets included. The olde-world colonial ambience of this institution made it seem like stepping back in time a century or two, but it got the job done.

Nonetheless, the Australians were living on the edge because of the massive security precautions put in place. Soldiers with machine guns followed them everywhere, one even insisting on being present when Taylor conducted his captain's press conference in McDonald's room. When they arrived at Visakhapatnam for their first match, against Kenya, a warship and a submarine turned up off-shore and nobody tried to tell us it was a coincidence.

The tournament itself was a bit of a shambles in many ways, coach Bob Simpson later describing it as 'a severe let-down in which the teams were messed around intolerably.' In five frenetic weeks, the Australians worked diligently to shake off the handicap of forfeiting their first match, while Sri Lanka – awarded two lots of points for free from that game and another unplayed one against the Windies – automatically made the quarter-finals. They then played their way through to the decider where, with extreme irony, they were pitted against Australia. In slippery, dewy conditions in Gadaffi Stadium, Lahore, and coached by former Australian Test player Dav Whatmore, they won by seven wickets with more than three overs to spare thanks mainly to a century by Aravinda de Silva. Muralidharan bowled his 10 overs without incident, as he did throughout the tournament.

It was – and remains – the finest sporting feat in the island nation's history. For Australia, it was a heavy and frustrating let-down given the difficulties they had overcome to get to the play-off. There was one more turbulent intervention to come – to his surprise and disappointment,

Simpson was told he was not being held responsible for the defeat but his coaching contract would not be renewed.

The World Cup was not the first or last time the Sub-Continent would prove to be a dangerous place to play cricket. Messing around with guns almost cost a rookie Australian team manager his job almost as soon as he took it on. It might have got me into deep trouble, too, if my instincts had not been in tune.

The 1998 tour of Pakistan followed immediately after the Commonwealth Games in Kuala Lumpur where cricket figured for the first and last time, Australia winning the silver medal. The second of three Tests was played in the northernmost city of Peshawar, a gun-happy town near the Khyber Pass, which is the border with Afghanistan. On a day off from training the team was offered a ride up to a military installation, where a cannon was pointed at a similar installation on the Afghan side. We were assured there was a cannon there, too, pointing straight at us. On the way, the bus stopped several times so players could photograph each other with uniformed soldiers carrying Kalishnakov combat rifles, or posing with the firearms themselves. On the way back, we called into a military base and were taken to a shooting range where the players were invited to try their hand with these weapons, which are manufactured for only one purpose – killing people. Almost all of them did, some very enthusiastically, including the manager, Steve Bernard who was on his first tour in the job. Broadcaster Tim Lane and I were offered the same chance but we both felt uneasy about it and declined.

Next day, the pictures of the players armed with these people-killers were on the front pages all over Australia – and uproar ensued. It wouldn't have gone down well at any time, you suspect, but this was only a little over a year after the Port Arthur massacre in Tasmania, in which 35 people were killed and 23 wounded by a crazed gunman using an assault weapon. And the chairman of the cricket board, Denis Rogers, was a Tasmanian. Unsurprisingly, he was outraged by the photos of his players carrying similar weapons while firearms were being banned by the Australian Government. He delivered a blistering earful to Bernard, stopping just short of ordering him home. Happily for the former NSW fast bowler, it blew over and he kept his job for several years.

Bernard had been in the thick of another major controversy only a week or so earlier when the Salim Malik affair raised its ugly head again with a Pakistani Supreme Court judge Malik Mohammed Qayyum reopening a Government-ordered investigation into match-fixing and issuing subpoenas for Taylor and Mark Waugh to appear. Three years earlier Waugh had been secretly fined along with Shane Warne for taking money from a bookmaker and at this stage it still hadn't become public, so he was extremely reluctant to appear before the judge. Taylor agreed to go after some arm-twisting – he had nothing to hide personally but didn't want team-mates put into invidious positions – and Waugh fell into line. Warne wasn't on the tour because of a medical issue and Tim May, the other player Malik had tried to bribe on the previous tour to Pakistan four years earlier, had retired.

On instructions from Chief Executive Malcolm Speed, who flew to Pakistan to oversee this procedure himself, Bernard did not tell us, the travelling Australia media, of the development, which saw Taylor and Waugh, accompanied by the team's security officer Reg Dickason, who was armed, leave their Rawalpindi hotel under cover of the pre-dawn darkness. But the plans to keep it secret were blown within hours when the Pakistani Cricket Board issued a press release detailing what was about to happen, where and when. By then, it was too late for us to get to Lahore, where the hearing was being held – but dozens of local journalists had no trouble turning up in good time. Naturally, I and the others from Australia were angry about being left totally out of the loop on such a newsworthy development, not even trusted to keep an off-the-record watching brief. Angry words followed with Bernard threatening to bar me from any access to the players if I wrote a word about it, which of course I did – the threat was never carried out.

Speed, Taylor and Waugh were shocked to see another witness turn up midway through the hearing – Malik himself. It was soon obvious he was there only for appearances sake, had never met the lawyer assigned to him and had nothing of any substance to say. It was a provocative ploy designed, for some obscure reason, to prompt the Australians to walk out. They stayed put, repeated the familiar contents of affidavits they had already sworn earlier and were not challenged to say any more. The whole process was a fizzer and ended in faintly comical fashion when the judge asked Taylor and Waugh to pose for a selfie with him and was refused. They were back in Rawalpindi by nightfall and getting on with business.

In Peshawar, the distraction of the combat guns certainly didn't bother Taylor, who batted throughout the first two days for 334 not out, equalling Don Bradman's Australian record Test score that had stood for 68 years. After agonising overnight about whether to go on and claim the record for himself, he declared, stating that it wasn't in the team's interests for him to use up any more time in pursuit of personal glory. It was a typical decision from one of Australia's all-time best Test captains and he was suitably applauded for it.

Having won by an innings and 99 in Rawalpindi, Australia settled for draws in Peshawar and Karachi – and have still never played another game in Pakistan. That's because in March, 2009, 12 gunmen opened fire on a bus carrying the Sri Lankan team to the Lahore stadium. Six players were wounded and six policemen and two civilians killed. For the next 20-odd years Pakistan was forced to play all of its Test matches in the United Arab Emirates, a situation that has only recently begun to resolve itself.

MEDIA AND ME,
BY WARNIE

It's breakfast time on the morning before a Test match at the Gabba in Brisbane back in the nineties. The local paper, the Courier-Mail, is running a column to which, for some trivial reason both of us have long since forgotten, Shane Warne has taken exception.

My phone rings. It's the Australian team's media manager Patrick Keane, inquiring whether I would be coming to training because, if so, 'the leg-spinner would like a word.' The 'word' was unlikely to be all that cordial – Warnie was probably not about to invite me out for lunch (although as later events proved, I could have been wrong there) because at that stage of his stupendous career, and for the majority of it fact, the relationship between him and most of the cricket media was often fragile and rarely stable. There were a handful of exceptions but I wasn't usually one of them.

Keane was unkeen to have this play out in front of every other player, journalist and passer-by so he ushered us both into the unoccupied umpires' dressing room, locked the door and said he would release us when we had sorted each other out. I have never heard of a sportsman-journalist one-on-one Q&A being conducted in this manner before or since. Other than Warne demanding to know why I appeared to be publicly barracking for the opposition at his expense, the exact thrust of the lively conversation that ensued has been well and truly lost in the mists of time, although we both recall the event clearly enough. 'I remember being pissed off but not what it was all about,' he laughed when we got together not long ago to reminisce. After we'd both had our say on that steamy morning, each running out of points to make, I said to him: 'Shane, you're not going to stop playing for Australia any time soon and I'm not going to stop writing about it, so why don't we draw a line in the sand, start over and see where that gets us?' 'Sure,' he said, shaking hands – and banging on the door to signal to Keane that a truce had been established and he needed to get back to the nets.

Some time later, Warne rang me himself. He invited me to join half a dozen other senior cricket writers for lunch at one of Melbourne's best Chinese restaurants. The agenda was simple: why do I get such a hard time in the Press? A full and frank exchange of views followed, constructively and without hostility and it's probably fair to say that from that day on relations improved. It was a smart move on his part, possibly inspired by an expert on such matters. At the height of his dissatisfaction with his public portrayal, he had consulted commentary doyen and former Test captain Richie Benaud, a lifelong professional journalist himself, and was told that if he had an issue with people who mattered to him, and who he respected, he should go and speak to them. If 'they' didn't matter, don't worry about them.

Hopefully that's why we ended up in the umpires' room in Brisbane.

Today, Warne is very much on the other side of the fence, spending much of his working time as a TV commentator – perhaps the best one in Australia, in my view, probably in a dead-heat with his old team-mate Ricky Ponting – as well as a very readable newspaper columnist, and a prolific user of social media, where he has well over a million followers around the world. He is deriving enjoyment and satisfaction from it, knowing that his opinions are well respected and more influential than most.

He appears to be on very good terms with most people who are part of his professional life, or used to be, and from where I sit it is a good example of how time often heals all wounds, and a welcome one.

But it has been a roller-coaster ride.

On one hand, Warne has been dream fodder for sportswriters, probably never surpassed in his capacity to provide good copy. He is, by some margin, the best-performed Australian sportsman of my time, and the one I most enjoyed watching. In any sport, not only cricket. His 705 wickets from 145 Tests and 293 from 194 one-day internationals is evidence enough of his superior status, but there's much more to it than that.

He was just different, a one-off, with a confidence and charisma that would have set him apart even if he had been less successful. The skill he brought to the contest was both physical and psychological. He was a match-winner like no other Australian player of his generation – although he had some extremely influential team-mates who weren't far behind – and everything he did on the field was usually interesting and often exciting, and everything he did off it was controversial, if not always in a good way. Not for him, anyway – but for compilers of news lists he was (and remains, for that matter) manna from heaven.

On the other hand, it wasn't always easy treading the fine line between the on-field genius and the off-field larrikin. Not for him and not for those employed to observe him.

From almost the moment he arrived on the Test scene as a virtual unknown, overweight knockabout from Melbourne's beachside suburbs, who would rather have been playing football for St Kilda, he was made to endure a level of scrutiny with few precedents for a sportsman not long out of his teens.

He readily admits that he made his fair share of mistakes coming to terms with it.

It was the early 1990s – he acquired his first baggy green cap against India in Sydney in 1992 – and attitudes were different, partly because social media wasn't yet a 'thing.' Sportsmen and other celebrities didn't have to worry so much about their public images being, well, quite so 'public.'

There was (and probably still is) also a certain conservatism within what might be termed the Establishment cricket community that did not necessarily approve of some of Warne's more baroque behaviour.

I was at dinner in the Melbourne Cricket Club committee room on one occasion when it was made clear around the table – off the record, of course – that there would be little support for any attempt to install him as Test captain, which was certainly a contingency favoured by a lot of other people.

That venerable old institution does not control cricket but it wields considerable influence among those who do, so that was a clear clue to where any such ambitions were destined to die. Warne never did captain the Test side, despite many believing – with considerable evidence to back them up – that he would have been an unqualified success at it, just as he was on the 11 occasions he was put in charge of the one-day team, winning 10 of them.

Then in 2001 the MCC appointed a panel of selectors to decide who should be immortalised in statue form around the MCG and in a split vote after lengthy argument it was decided to omit Warne.

This was largely my doing. As a member of the panel I suggested that as he was still playing it might be wise to wait until he had retired in case he still had an embarrassing scandal or two left in him. Hey presto – next thing we knew he had tested positive for a drug and been banned from cricket for a year, which made our decision look justified, inspired even.

The statues of Don Bradman, Keith Miller, Dennis Lillee, Bill Ponsford, Ron Barassi, Leigh Matthews, Dick Reynolds, Hadyn Bunton, Betty Cuthbert and Shirley Strickland-Delahunty were installed between 2003 and 2006, and then in 2011 more began to be added – and the first of those was, to unanimous approval, Shane Keith Warne, retired cricketer.

Now a long way into that retirement and having recently turned 50 – a reflective milestone for anybody – Warne comes across as a far more mellow version of the hell-raiser he was during his twenties and probably well into his thirties. Contentedly single and a father of three grown-up kids he adores, he is relaxed and comfortable, which is no surprise given that he continues to earn huge amounts of money just by talking and writing about the game that has always been his passion and because he no longer feels the need to worry about what people might think of him.

He used to, he admits.

While he was always admired and lionised for his ability to play Australia's favourite sport – perhaps only the immortal Bradman did it better – there was always an element who viewed him as a bogan lair with whom they would prefer not to identify. He wasn't a hero to everyone. And he couldn't have not known that.

Asked if his public image was important to him, he pauses thoughtfully before replying: 'I used to worry about it a lot more than I do now. When I was a young player trying to find my way, I did worry about what people thought about me. Not so much now because I am happy with who I am.

'At 22 or 23 you're still trying to find out who you are. You act on instinct, don't think too far ahead. Kids changed me to some extent. If you're a father you're their hero. If I do something wrong, it's like 'my hero, my dad's messed up and it's hurt me.'

'I was slow to mature, to grow up, and I'm still a big kid in a lot of ways. But through all the ups and downs, and luckily I've had a lot more ups than downs, I've become comfortable with who I am. If people say he's a dickhead or a wanker, that's OK. I'm not out to prove them wrong because I know I'm a good bloke. I'm pretty easy to deal with, pretty chilled about most things. Opinionated, yes. But a good father. I've had a pretty amazing life, so I'm lucky.

'I'm not trying to impress anyone. If people like me, great. If they don't, I don't care. I think the more you understand how it works the more you realise that not everyone will like you, even if you're the most likeable person in the world. It took me a long time to realise that before I stopped trying to make people like me.'

Warne says he has many acquaintances but only four or five close mates, people who would drop anything if he needed help and vice versa. One silver lining of his drugs crisis in 2003 was that he found out who those mates were and who were not. There were some surprises in both directions. 'It was an interesting thing to go through,' he says.

When he looks back at the Warnie of old there are ... well, not exactly regrets, perhaps, but certainly elements that he would adjust if he had his time over. That includes the way he sometimes dealt with the media.

He has probably never really admitted this publicly before, but he says he definitely went through a stage where he got a bit too big for his boots. He wasn't the first or the last sportsman guilty of that, of course,

'At some stage during the mid-90s I became a bit of a big-head, a bit arrogant, cocky,' he says. 'I started to get a bit far ahead of myself. I got a bit like, well, fuck you blokes, stop nailing me, I'm just trying to win games for Australia.

'The way I handled the media was a bit ordinary. I think I could have been a bit better than that. It became a bit like me versus them because I felt I was getting nailed all the time and some of the stuff was a bit unfair. Some of the off-field stuff was strictly untrue, just lies.'

He says he was forced to grow up in front of the camera – partly because he was signing lucrative sponsorship deals and had to submit to greater exposure to provide value to the brands – and had to learn to deal with it as he went along.

'I wasn't a pioneer because it was happening long before me but the level of attention on sportsmen in Australia, I think I was a bit ahead of the pack. I know we've always had big sportsmen but not on such a global scale, perhaps, and with all the new-age media there was just so much more stuff.

'Everyone was trying to work out the balance between right and wrong. Is this newsworthy, is that newsworthy, what are we allowed to say?

'I made some mistakes along the way but I think some of those mistakes were magnified. I saw other people doing similar stuff but nothing was ever said. I would get nailed for stuff, get crucified, and I'd go, 'hang on, I don't think I handled that well."

It wasn't necessarily fair on the other side of the fence, either.

'What some people get wrong,' he said, 'is that you bunch everyone in together and say those Press pricks but it's not all of them, sometimes it's just one or two.'

And, he discovered, the problem wasn't always all that big anyway.

'At one stage I decided I would read everything that was written about me and what I found was when family and friends would ring up and say 'have you seen what so and so has written about you, he's nailing you for this and that,' and I'd have a look and it usually was never as bad as your friends thought.

'If it was about cricket and factually wrong, I'd go and have a chat to the journalist and if they took offence or disagreed all I could say was that you've got it wrong.

'If I've done the wrong thing and you nail me, that's fine. But I don't have to like you. If they get something wrong and I take the time to tell them and they say they're standing by their source or just don't believe me, I just move on. Next time they ask for an interview, you just say no.'

Unsurprisingly, Warne didn't enjoy being taken advantage of when he was trying to do the right thing. Case in point: against England at the Gabba in 1994, he took his career-best figures of 8-71 in the second innings to give Australia a 1-0 lead in a series they won easily.

'I spent 45 minutes straight after the game doing the electronic media and all I wanted then was a beer and a fag so I asked the print media to wait for 10 minutes while I did that. But they all had deadlines, so I said I was happy to talk for as long as they wanted while I had the smoke – but I didn't want my picture in the paper smoking.

'Next day, there it was – cigarette in hand. That really pissed me off. I tried to do the right thing and still got shafted.'

Looking back almost wistfully, Warne says: 'They were different times. I think back in the day there was a bit more reporting of the facts and some of the off-field stuff, well, no-one was really interested in that, we just cared about the sport.

'But there became more of a mentality in the magazines and the papers of get it on the front page and get a bit more sensationalism. The thing that started to happen in my time was the off-field stuff started to be just as important as the on-field.

'When I started, it was all about the cricket and some of the stuff that was going on, the journos were doing it with the players, that's why it was never in the papers.'

Well yes, there was a time when journalists and players did drink together – even in the dressing rooms sometimes, which would never happen now – but Warne is correct when he says that largely died out during the '90s, and the developing distrust over the reporting of after-hours activities was largely the reason for that.

No-one was more at the epicentre of that extra-curricular agenda than he was. Was that unfair? He thinks about the question for a long moment and is unable to come up with an answer he's happy with, so he tails off with: 'I don't know...'

But he says: 'I was very young, just 22 or 23 when it all started happening, the Gatting ball and all that (a reference to the famous 'ball of the century' with which he clean-bowled the England captain with his first delivery in an Ashes match in 1993) and there was just so much attention.'

To this day, long after retirement, Warne feels he has to remain wary about where he goes and who he is seen with. Sitting in the loungeroom of his mansion in the upmarket Melbourne suburb of Brighton, which was about go on the market, he tells me he hasn't been to a pub or a nightclub for 18 months.

'If I want to have a drink with people, I bring them here – I've got my own version of a nightclub downstairs,' he says. 'It's a quandary for a lot of modern-day sportsmen. People pretend to talk on their phone but they're actually videoing you, no matter who you talk to or how innocent it is. Then there's this story about Warne flirting with someone, anyone can write it and it ends up in the women's magazines or anywhere at all.

'I don't blame modern sportsmen for being reluctant (to put them themselves on show.) We cry out for characters, not robots, and for people to be themselves and show their emotions and passion. But sometimes if they overstep it we crucify them, absolutely nail them.

'It's not easy.'

It would be an exaggeration to suggest Warne's after-life as a commentator has been as successful as his playing career – nothing could match that – but he has certainly earned more applause for it than most of his contemporaries who have tried their hand.

That's because he not only has a fluent insight into what is, or is not, happening but because he does not settle for sitting on the fence, afraid to say what he really thinks.

'Some people I know are very careful about what they say and don't want to offend or criticise anyone,' he said. 'We don't just sit up there and bag people all the time, we try to be constructive – but it's not enough to just say a player who dropped a catch is having a bad day or a batsman played a bad shot.

'The punter wants to know why – the reason he played a bad shot was that he was scared of the bowler or didn't know which way the spinner was going. Kerry Packer told me not to tell him what he could see, but to take him out to the middle.

'It can be difficult but it's your job to say what you feel and if you feel a player has done something wrong and you don't say so, you're not being true to yourself.

'I'm not saying I'm a great commentator like Richie Benaud but I like to think I give insight and enhance the coverage, and I have had a lot of great feedback about it.

'I'm lucky I'm passionate about the game of cricket so there are a lot of worse things I could be doing for a job.'

Benaud, of course, was always the doyen – the role model – for cricketers looking for media work after they stop playing, and that was largely because he was a professional journalist himself before he became Test captain.

That's why one of his first initiatives when he took over the job in 1958-59 was to invite cricket writers into the dressing room after stumps for a beer with the players so that they could get their stories straight from the horses' mouths and not have to resort to guesswork or gossip.

In those faraway days, of course, it was a completely different environment. There was very little TV coverage and absolutely none of the squadrons of media managers that inhabit every dressing room these days – that was one of the captain's many jobs – so there was much less chance of being fobbed off with artificial answers of the 'it was a great team effort and everyone played their role' genre.

From his current perspective, it is one of Warne's pet dislikes. 'Give us a break! You want someone to say 'I worked my butt off this Test match, I worked on this and that and it really helped because I bowled to so and so and was able to drag him across the crease and got him out, which was really satisfying.' That's what you want rather than the stock standard line.'

Hear, hear!

Benaud's professionalism across all the traditional, mainstream platforms was as impressive as his prodigious output – as well as his year-round TV work, he wrote or edited well over 20 books while working simultaneously for multiple newspapers around the world.

One of them was The Herald afternoon broadsheet when I was the Sports Editor there, and an annual highlight was the Perth Test match because the three-hour time difference meant that in order to meet the first edition deadlines I needed his copy by about 7am – or 4am where he was. So you would have to ring and wake him up, whereupon a sleepy voice would inquire what aspect of the match you were interested in, then ask to be transferred to a copy-taker. Twenty minutes later, you had 500 words of crisp, concise comment straight off the top of his head that needed little or no editing. It was a skill he learned as a junior newspaperman chasing police cars and ambulances around Sydney and getting the information to print ahead of the opposition, if at all possible.

Later, when I stopped editing and started writing about cricket myself, the great man was even more helpful. If you were agonising over which way to tackle an issue or needed informed background, he would always take a phone call, even at night, and you would never hang up without suggestions, advice or wisdom to go on with.

Benaud's own hero, the flamboyant, friendly all-rounder Keith Miller, was just as generous in exactly the same way, if not necessarily as erudite. Miller had a million stories, as you would expect, and was happy to share them, especially if they were about any of his many mates.

The one touchy topic with him was Bradman, but even so when I rang to ask for help with preparing an obituary in advance Miller gave me plenty to consider, most of it strictly off the record – but highly valuable.

Like Warne, and for much the same reasons, Miller never became Test captain, which was a pity. He might not have been the greatest strategist of all time – 'just spread out you blokes,' was one of his field-setting instructions when he was in charge of NSW in the Sheffield Shield – but there would never have been a dull moment.

A romantic old cliché insists that the Test cricket captaincy sits alongside the Prime Ministership as Australia's most important job but let's just settle for saying that the ones I worked with, one way or another, were without exception interesting people to know.

As well as Benaud, they included two others who wrote columns for The Herald in my time, Bob Simpson and Ian Chappell, as well as Ian

Johnson, who did so years before I met him when he was secretary of
the Melbourne Cricket Club. Then there were Bill Lawry, Greg Chappell,
Graham Yallop, Kim Hughes, Allan Border, Mark Taylor, Steve Waugh
and Ricky Ponting in their various on and off-field roles and it is fair to
say they were all a pleasure to deal with – most of the time.

Taylor was the most helpful, never losing his cool or his sense of
perspective no matter how much pressure he was under.

Waugh was the only one who went out of his way to formally spell out
the terms of the relationship. His first series in charge was the tour of the
West Indies in 1999 and on arrival he called a meeting with the half-dozen
writers who were there and told us he would answer the phone or a knock
on the door at any hour, within reason, to respond to legitimate queries.

But he would not be seen fraternising with us in the bar. 'We are not
here to be mates, we all have jobs to do as professionals,' he said. He
was as good as his word, in both respects, then and for the rest of his
tenure, in which he earned unqualified respect from the media. The
bar ban didn't bother us. As far as I could tell it was never his natural
environment anyway, and some team-mates were occasionally known to
amuse themselves – I did see this happen one night – by waiting until he
made an early exit, possibly without having got around to shouting, and
then charging their drinks to his room, making sure they were on hand
at checkout time the next morning to witness his annoyed response.

There was no bar ban when Hughes led the rebel team on a sanctions-
busting tour of South Africa in 1985. One night, after a typically cavalier
hundred that afternoon, the white wine was flowing copiously when
he declared himself to be 'the best white batsman in the world.' The
reference to white was an acknowledgement that the West Indies' Viv
Richards had no equal, but it was also a shot in the direction of Border,
who had inherited the official Test captaincy after Hughes had resigned
in tears, and who was at that moment preparing to lead his team into
battle against India at the MCG.

I was well aware, of course, that quoting in print what players might
say while relaxing over a few beers was a sure way to burn your contact
book irretrievably, but in the context of the unspoken rivalry between

the two Australian teams, official and unofficial, this was irresistible grist for the mill. So I asked Hughes if I could use it, and he not only gave permission, he encouraged it. He clearly enjoyed the thought of the response it would get. Within an hour or two of it being printed in Melbourne, a clipping had been pinned to the dressing room wall at the MCG and studied with intense interest by all occupants.

Some of those rebel players made it back into Test cricket – but the outspoken Hughes never did, or even attempted to. The sad way his captaincy and his career finished at Test level – mentally shot and literally unable to score a run to save himself – is one of the game's more melancholy stories.

SINKING ANOTHER FOSTERS

Nobody died – but that doesn't mean it wasn't one of the most unforgettable disasters in the history of Australian sport, expensive, embarrassing and ultimately the death knell for an unlikely source of fascination for the nation's sports fans for a dozen or so years. Now, it is a distant memory, one they couldn't care less about – and probably never will again.

But while it lasted Australia's interest in the America's Cup – a boat race for boys with multi-million dollar high-tech toys – was an amazing ride, until the day it literally sunk without trace in the Pacific Ocean off San Diego in California on March 5, 1995.

No-one knew it at the time but when oneAustralia, considered – optimistically, as it turned out – to be the last word in racing yacht design, snapped in half mid-race and plummeted straight to Davy Jones' Locker with master sailor John Bertrand, his skipper Rod Davis and 17 crew forced to swim for their lives, one of the great Australian sports stories was over.

Bertrand — who famously snapped the New York Yacht Club's 132-year-stranglehold on the most unwinnable trophy in world sport in 1983 when his wing-keeled Australia II defeated Dennis Connor's Liberty in Newport, Rhode Island – never campaigned again after San Diego. And nor did any other Australian.

Bertrand is a charismatic and confident character, successful in most things he has done in life, especially competitive sailing but also in business, who doesn't necessarily wear his emotions on his sleeve. But as the only Australian journalist in the sunny American seaport both before and after the sinking – although not on the day, regrettably – I spent a lot of time observing just how much this project meant to him, and how hard he struggled to keep his own and other people's morale intact while refusing to declare the battle lost even though the odds were stacked hugely against them.

It was a very impressive performance – in its own way, not much less admirable than the timeless triumph a dozen years earlier.

In recent years I have kept in fairly close contact with Bertrand in his role as chairman of the Sport Australia Hall of Fame, of which he is one of more than 30 official Legends of Australian Sport. That accolade was conferred during his chairmanship, a potentially contentious move but one that has never attracted any criticism – which probably speaks for itself in terms of the genuine esteem in which he is held.

The historic, euphoric victory in 1983 – who can forget Prime Minister Bob Hawke gleefully declaring an unofficial public holiday after a long night of celebrations? – would qualify him in itself, but he was also an Olympic bronze medallist and was still winning world championships in his beloved Etchells class until he was almost 70. He has also served as president of another major Olympic sport, swimming, while charitable work also has guaranteed that his public profile, especially in Melbourne, has remained extremely strong.

Bertrand wasn't involved in the defence of the Cup in Fremantle in 1987 because Newport had been his fourth campaign, he had achieved what he set out to do and was totally lacking in the motivation to go again. So Alan Bond, the controversial businessman who had bankrolled the big win as well as three previous forays, found a new crew and soldiered on with a new boat and new crew without much success. Another wealthy Perth businessman named Kevin Parry snapped up Bertrand's former helmsman, the vastly experienced Iain Murray, to steer Kookaburra III which made it through to the final only to be crushed 4-0 by Connor's Stars & Stripes representing the San Diego yacht Club. The feisty American not only revelled in his revenge over Australia but gave the bird to the New York Yacht Club which had more or less disowned him after the 1983 embarrassment.

Fremantle was a surreal experience for an America's Cup debutant like me and even more so for the overawed locals – the population was only 25,000 – who found their sleepy little, rundown seaport overrun with international celebrities and awash with a champagne lifestyle as one big party raged for weeks. You never knew who you were going to meet. Bertrand strolled around like royalty, holding court. There was no shortage of real royalty. The Aga Khan threw parties, so did Prince Albert of Monaco, Princess Anne dropped in for a look. Not everybody was somebody – yet. I was invited to have breakfast with an unknown (to me, anyway) shy young Canadian athlete in town for a sports carnival associated with the yachting extravaganza and then watched him break the 100m world record (unofficially, because of an overly-helpful breeze behind him) on an old suburban track that had hardly ever seen top-class athletics since it hosted the 1954 Commonwealth Games. Up to that stage, this might have been the most high-powered sporting moment ever to have occurred in Perth, it arrived completely out of the blue and there were only maybe a couple of hundred people there to witness it. His name was Ben Johnson, later to become officially the world's fastest man – and its most famous drug cheat, at least until cyclist Lance Armstrong came along.

The whole regatta was like Melbourne's spring racing carnival multiplied by a factor of maybe 10 and perhaps only Sydney's Olympic Games has since matched it for atmosphere. Fremantle has never been the same again – which is a very good thing because until the big boats and the even bigger spenders descended, it was a complete backwater where the many pubs sold one beer, the local Swan Lager, and very little else. The American satirist J. P O'Rourke lamented that he couldn't even procure an acceptable version of 'that vital piece of sailing equipment, the gin and tonic.' These days Fremantle is one of the most sophisticated places to visit in the land, a transformation it owes almost completely to the yachties..

For we denizens of the media, it was a wonderful story to cover. The racing, which was conducted on a stretch of wild and windy water known as Gage Roads between the mainland and Rottnest Island was spectacular, the larger than life personalities participating in it, or watching from party central, were always up for a chat, and it wasn't unheard of to discover Connor and his crewmen playing football in the street at midnight if there was no race the next day – or maybe even if there was. You didn't have to know much about the arcane rules and strategies that governed the racing because they would be explained in fine detail at the nightly press conferences.

I thought work couldn't get any more enjoyable than that. But I was wrong, as it turned out. San Diego, being in California, was a bit more blasé about the celeb count but it was still an extremely pleasant place to be while the event was on. How hard was the work this time? Well, it helped that the time difference meant that the races would start at lunchtime, which was late-ish at night in Australia, and finish about 1am back in Melbourne and Sydney, which meant the result was too late for the morning editions – and because there was no internet to speak of back then, too late to necessitate any story being filed for at least 12 hours.

So the race-day routine was this: arise at your leisure, drop by the media centre which was very conveniently located in the grounds of the hotel where the media were all staying, check if anything had happened overnight, go for a run along the adjoining beachfront, find a like-minded soul to join you for lunch – oysters, prawns, catch of the day and a crisp Californian chardonnay – at one of the many excellent seafood restaurant/bars nearby, and watch the race the only way it was possible to do so – on TV. Return to your room for a short nap, then repair again to the media centre where the boat skippers and anyone else who might be in the news would present themselves sharp on 5pm and talk their heads off about what had transpired out on the waves.

Write your report. Go out to dinner. Get up at your leisure, check the local papers and with the media centre to make sure you haven't missed anything – and, at last, file your story. Rinse and repeat! For the most part there wasn't even anyone there from the other Australian news outlets to complicate matters by providing competition. And just to make it easier, Bertrand's communications chief was one of Melbourne's best and most experienced PR men, John Fitzgerald, who had also once been my editor at the by-then defunct *Herald* evening newspaper, and a long-time friend and mentor. I certainly wasn't going to miss anything while he was on the job.

It was such a soft gig that I probably should have been paying News Ltd for the privilege of being there.

Actually, it wasn't News footing the bill when I arrived for the start of Bertrand's new campaign. It was one of his sponsors, the Phillip Morris tobacco giant, who became worried that nobody was paying attention – Newport and Fremantle were both in the distant past by now and the America's Cup was a fading memory for those who compile the news agendas – and so their PR people parachuted me in for a week or so to stir up some interest.

As usual, Bertrand was not doing this by half measures. But why was he back in the fray at all, having declared himself done and dusted years earlier, admitting that if he had not succeeded in 1983 and then kept going it would probably have cost him his marriage?

'I guess the answer lies in that old but true saying: never say never again,' he wrote in his autobiography Born To Win. 'After 83 I decided I couldn't go back. And for nearly a decade I barely set foot on a racing boat. I'd go on cruising holidays with Rasa and the kids, but they did all the sailing. My spot was up at the bow with a book, in charge of nothing more demanding than the anchor. I had charted my course and put my life on a new heading.

'I had conquered a short period of uncertainty, then boldly set sail for new challenges and new ventures in Australia and across the globe. And best of all, I had reconnected in a meaningful way with my wonderful family. I couldn't have been more content.'

Then he had his arm twisted – and it turned out that it didn't need all that much manipulation.

In 1992, he was approached by Bruce Siney, the marketing chief for the Foster's brewery, who said the company needed a sports success story to hang their hat on but couldn't afford the Olympics. What about the America's Cup? That plunged Bertrand deep in thought, to the extent that his wife had to take over all the driving because he was running red lights with his mind otherwise occupied. Eventually he agreed to go again – with one important difference from all previous campaigns. This time, he would be in charge, the head of the syndicate – and not the racing skipper, although he would sail as crew. He would build it from scratch. Other sponsors were recruited and $26 million was committed to the challenge, with Victorian Premier Jeff Kennett also an important supporter.

He had gone to San Diego to research the latest developments and noted that the old 12 metre class yachts were now obsolete, replaced by a new model that was 23.8 metres long and built of cutting edge carbon fibre with masts 11 storeys high. Everything was bigger but they were half the weight with twice the horsepower. Rasa Bertrand described them – perfectly, in her husband's opinion – as 'elegant swans.' His own analogy: 'It was like getting out of a Model T Ford and into a Ferrari — very exciting.'

With three years of hard work and planning ahead, Bertrand formed a company called Fluid Thinking to bring the new dream to reality and named the syndicate oneAustralia – a challenge to unite the nation, as the 1983 version had done.

Some months out from San Diego, I attended the official launch of the project on the Gold Coast and watched as the unfinished but distinctive new craft in its pure white livery was unveiled to sponsors, supporters and the media and you couldn't help but be struck by the pure passion and pride that glinted in Bertrand's eyes as he silently embraced Rasa and admired the fruits of his past two years of work. Here, truly, was a man on a mission.

When I got to San Diego, that much hadn't changed. When I found Bertrand in his base camp, a compound on one of the city's many waterfronts, it was like entering a wartime military installation. The staff, numbering nearly 50, were all in uniform and all accustomed to being dragged out of bed at dawn for strategy meetings. No strangers were admitted. The high-tech computer room with its satellite links to the world's most sophisticated meteorological systems was swept regularly for bugs.

So I was surprised to say the least when, one evening, the boss took me behind a locked fence into a large shed draped with green tarpaulins and 'no admittance' signage. Inside was his precious baby, oneAustralia, in the final stages of being prepared for combat. This was the most top secret asset in the entire Cup fleet, or so Bertrand told me, but he had no qualms about permitting me to clamber aboard and stand on the deck. That's because, of course, he knew I wouldn't have any idea about what I was actually looking at – and I didn't have a camera. He stood there beside me, the same rapt expression on his face that I had observed on the Gold Coast. He explained that the conveyance was made of the same carbon fibre technology as the Stealth Bomber that was the last world in combat planes back then, and that it had taken 12,000 man hours to construct, not counting design time. 'It is the most advanced piece of machinery ever built in the world, I believe,' he said. 'Time will tell.' As famous last words go, those last three were to prove pretty much 24 carat.

The moment of truth was at hand and excitement was at fever pitch.

The plan was to contest the qualifying races with his older B Grade boat, also named oneAustralia, bringing out his big gun when the whips started cracking seriously. That was still two or three weeks away and the entire campaign had months to go so I went home, detouring via Las Vegas to watch former Russian boxer Kostya Tszyu, now fighting under the Australian flag, win his first world title by demolishing a Puerto Rican slugger named Jake 'The Snake' Rodriguez.

The fight was on January 28. Fast forward five weeks to Monday, March 5 – Sunday in America – and I turned on the breakfast news at home in Melbourne to see oneAustralia – the new one – sinking rapidly and ingloriously to the bottom of the Pacific, with crewmen diving for their lives. It took just two minutes and 15 seconds to disappear from view.

Stunned, I went to work, where I immediately got a call from head office in Sydney telling me there was a flight leaving for California in five hours – be on it! I didn't even have time to see my wife and son, who were at work and school, just a phone call saying I was off again and had no idea how long I would be away. I very nearly wasn't away long. The immigration guy at Los Angeles saw journalist in my passport and demanded to see the appropriate visa, which I hadn't been asked for a month earlier and didn't know I needed. This could mean being put on the next plane back. But he also guessed where I was headed and why – the sinking was big news – and after a few stern words from his superiors I was allowed in as long as I left within a month.

Back at the Bertrand compound, the atmosphere could best be described as defiant – the power of positive thinking was being employed as hard as the boss could deliver it, which had always been one of his specialties. The message was that they still had the spare boat, everyone was still alive – and Australia would be expecting them to get on with it and not just lie down and cry. Interest might have been minimal in the lead-up but now their plight was captivating the nation. It was a massive news story, in its own way not far short of the original win.

War veterans will confirm that in such situations, morale is a crucial factor, more important, perhaps, than professional ability, sporting talent or physical strength – and Bertrand, who did not employ a sports shrink because he is so well equipped in that arcane art himself – knew it. But, looking haggard, he had to come to terms with it himself. Had he ever contemplated anything like it? 'Not in my wildest nightmares,' he told me. 'It was an unbelievable experience, something you would never visualise or practice in your mindset.'

There was never, for him, a moment of utter despair. But some others did lose it psychologically, he admitted. 'There was self-doubt in the organisation.'

Bertrand's message to them, and to the audience at home was that 'Australians have a history of overcoming adversity. We do not give up.' It hit a nerve – hard. The fax machine in the compound blew a fuse, and had to be replaced, because so many messages were flowing in from every conceivable source – politicians, schoolkids, businessmen and even opposition syndicates. They papered the walls of the gym.

Outside, the souvenir shop was doing its best-ever business. One Spanish sailor from a rival syndicate paid $1500 for a weather jacket just to show solidarity. To no-one's surprise, the Kiwis – not necessarily the two racing syndicates, but certainly the nation in general – were having a field day with it, with the infamous cricket underarm ball furore still only two years old. 'There go the Aussies, sinking another Fosters,' they crowed, referring to the sponsor's logo on the mast that was the last thing anyone saw of the boat.

A ditty hit the airwaves from out of Auckland:

'When the bow breaks, the challenge will fall
And into the ocean jumps the crew one and all
Rock oneAustralia your hull was too thin
But thank God almighty your crewmen can swim.'
There were another 14 verses of that.

Bertrand took it all in good humour but did not deviate from his mission to renew his crew's motivation, telling them: 'We are all world-class professionals. We are all moving in the same direction and when you do that you can move mountains.

'I believe this team can do it now. We know about adversity. We have been to hell and back with this project and I don't want to hear anything that's not relevant to moving forward. People say it's impossible now, but that's not on our agenda. It's amazing how if you don't give up and you keep trying, how the game breaks in your direction. It's quite staggering.

'I also know that when the heat gets turned up in the kitchen, rational people start making irrational decisions. Anything goes then. The psyche of boat speed, all those things, becomes less and less relevant and the pressure of decision making goes on. Assuming the equipment is pretty equal, that could be the difference at the 11th hour between winning and losing, which I have seen many times in the past.'

This proved not to be mere whistling in the dark. Back in the old boat, which had been rapidly and extensively refurbished, the crew resumed where they had left off, not exactly seamlessly, but successfully. Having already qualified for the second stage of competition, they went on to beat boats from Italy, France, Spain, the other outclassed Australian boat under the command of Sydney veteran Syd Fischer and one of the two New Zealand entries. But they met more than their match in the Team New Zealand outfit, representing the Royal NZ Yacht Squadron. who beat them in the semi-finals and went on to whitewash Connor, in Young America on behalf of the San Diego Yacht Club, 5-0 in the final. In every way, the Kiwis had the last laugh.

Bertrand departed America's Cup racing forever, not with his tail between his legs – far from it. He wrote to the editors of every major Australian newspaper insisting that as a nation we should not be apologising for pushing the envelope. 'At the top of every sport, you leave nothing on the table. In F1 motor racing we see this all the time,' he wrote. 'Sometimes engines do blow up. That's the game we're in.'

So what did actually go wrong? For starters, neither Bertrand's team, nor the other syndicates wanted to race that day because winds of 22 knots were forecast – and eventuated – where the average had been between six and 12. But it was eventually discovered the boat itself, for all its technological excellence, was flawed. 'We later discovered we had a 'hot spot' in the deck area immediately behind the main genoa drums, meaning an area of highly concentrated stress,' Bertrand says. 'When you're pushing beyond the leading edge to the bleeding edge, sometimes you pay the price. With perhaps 10kg of additional carbon fibre reinforcement, the deck probably would not have buckled. All well and good in hindsight.'

No attempt was ever made to salvage the dream machine. 'The carbon hull and gear was in 200m of water and would have been completely crushed, so little salvageable value,' he says.

There was never any chance of another comeback. 'After 95, there was no desire,' he says now. 'Although we didn't win, I very much enjoyed the challenge and the project – as chairman, not skippering the boat. But by then I had had 25 years of the America's Cup and it was time to get on with my other business career. I had various offers to go again but none was of any interest. It's full commitment or don't even think about it.

'I have no regrets. We gave it our best shot. Sometimes you win, most times you lose. That's the nature of high-end sport.'

OH BROTHER, JEZZA'S JOY

Like most supporters of the Carlton Football Club during the high-flying but turbulent latter half of the 20th century, I occasionally wished there were two of Alex Jesaulenko, that the club's most gifted player of a glorious era could be cloned. One day I was astonished – although not half as much as he was – to learn that there was, indeed, a second Jezza. And he could play football a bit too.

Football, like most sports, has always been full of human interest stories but there haven't been many to match the arrival in Jesaulenko's life of the brother he had never met and never really knew whether he still had, the older son his mother had given up for dead before Alex was born.

Of the thousands of stories I wrote across more than half a century in sports journalism, none gave me more pleasure than the one that appeared, exclusively, on the front page of the Herald Sun on August 13, 1994.

It was headlined MY JOY – it referred to Jezza's joy, not mine.

It stayed exclusive for a few days because after hearing a rumour at a footy funeral I had been able to confirm it with him only when he rang in to provide his weekly column in our Sunday edition and then disappeared back into the NSW bush where he was fishing with mates, unreachable by phone. The day it was published, I flew off to Canada for the Commonwealth Games, leaving the rest of the media tearing their hair out in frustration at being unable to speak to him until he returned to Melbourne.

The report told of how a letter had arrived from the international Red Cross tracing service, the night before Jesaulenko's 49th birthday, informing him that a relative of his mother was seeking information about her and permission needed to be given for that to be provided.

The inquirer was named Aleksander Loj, who said he was born with the surname Altuchowa, his Russian-born mother's maiden name. He had all the right information about the family history so Jesaulenko had no reason to doubt that he was who he claimed to be – his own mother's first-born son. 'This is just unbelievable,' he said – but that's just a figure of speech, of course.

Wera Jesaulenko – that's the English version of the family name, which is actually Esavlenko – was then a frail 71-year-old living in Noosa, Queensland, to be closer to her other two off-spring, Viktor and Larisa and she could scarcely believe her ears either.

Exactly 50 years earlier, in 1944, pregnant with Jezza, she had been interned in Camp Annahof in Germany by the Gestapo for six months for buying a blouse that she did not know had been stolen.

There, her infant son became ill, apparently with pneumonia and was taken away by a nurse who knew that children were no more than nuisances in prison camps and were likely to be exterminated. Sick children were sure to be killed.

The nurse took him to a special children's camp, where the commandant invited local people to take young inmates home. Only 10 of 1240 were adopted. The rest were almost certainly killed, according to the Red Cross. There is now a monument to them nearby.

Mrs Jesaulenko was never told why the baby was taken away or where he went but spent many years trying to find out, unaware that he was simultaneously trying to find her. On release, she found herself in the Austrian city of music, Salzburg, where her second son was born. If you Google Salzburg now, as I did when I was last there in 2018, you will find a list of its most famous people and even though he lived there only very briefly as a small child before coming to Australia, Alex Jesaulenko's sporting eminence in a faraway country has been enough to get him on it.

Mrs Jesaulenko named him Alex 'because it made it easier for me' after losing Aleksander, she told me.

Aleksander Loj grew up wondering about his real family and spent 25 years searching for them from his home in a tiny Polish village, where he had become a father of four, a farmer and a former soccer goalkeeper of roughly international standard

They eventually found each other through the Red Cross tracing service only after a sophisticated computer system enabled the agency to match up the myriad names 'lost' deep in decades of paperwork.

A Red Cross official escorted Loj to Melbourne four months after contact was initially established. Aleks and Alex did not speak each other's languages but that didn't stop them having a Christmas celebration to remember.

'I am numb, ' Mrs Jesaulenko said. 'It's a dream you couldn't even think about. But it was always in my heart that I would see him again. I was sick a couple of weeks ago but I never stopped praying. I thought I have to see him before I die. Now my prayers have come true.' She had another 14 years to live before succumbing in 2008, having well and truly earned her happy ending.

By 1994 she and the boys' Ukrainian father Wasil, also known as Bill, who was a German policeman during the war, had been separated for some years but remained friends until he died about a year earlier. Even before experiencing the atrocities of a prison camp, Wera knew all about the horrors of war. She was in her early teens when she saw her Russian father shot dead by German soldiers. She also lost two brothers in the war.

Perhaps sadly, the brotherly reunion, joyous fairytale though it was, had a limited lifespan.

Aleksander Loj returned to Poland and they never saw each other again, or even kept in touch, although Jesaulenko's eldest daughter Sally says they parted on good terms. 'My grandmother stayed in touch until she died,' Sally said. Does her Dad care? Sally is the one you have to ask about that these days because he prefers to leave all discussion about his life and affairs, past and present, to her. 'I think so,' she says. 'But he was raised to look forward, not backwards. He's very much like that.' She has been trying to research her family history to find out more about her grandparents' background but has found it difficult to get access to relevant documentation from Ukraine, her grandfather's home. 'We have a lot of questions,' she says.

It will come as no surprise to anyone who had much to do with the brilliant Blue in his playing and coaching days that it is difficult now to discover what he is really thinking about his brother or anything else. It always has been.

On the field, he was a flamboyant figure at least in terms of what he could do physically, playing 256 games for the Blues and another 23 for St Kilda. He coached both cubs, twice in Carlton's case. He was the last captain-coach to win a League premiership when he led Carlton to the 1979 flag and also played starring roles in the 1968, 1970 and 1972 triumphs. He kicked 115 goals in 1970 and was a regular selection for Victoria.

Off the field, there was little or no showmanship. Rarely did he get outwardly excited about anything, always believing that actions spoke far more loudly than words.

Former team-mate Wayne Johnston used to delight in telling a story that Jesaulenko's coach's address before the '79 decider consisted of just one sentence: Get out there and win, or words to that effect.

All his friends and long-time acquaintances – and I have known him professionally and socially for nearly half a century – always wondered what really made him tick, because one thing was always certain: he wouldn't tell you.

In team-mate Percy Jones's pub in the heart of Carlton one night, Jones and I tried at length to get him to tell us about his and his family's background and how they had fled from the ravages of war. He stared at us over his beer and insisted that he didn't care what had happened then.

Of course, that was highly unlikely to have been the truth and it eventually became clear that there was much he simply did not know, had never been told and did not understand.

But the day did come when he was forced to make a profound statement about who he was and what he stood for, and it had nothing to do with his personal life.

This was a football crisis, at that stage – and probably still – the biggest ever to engulf the Carlton Football Club, which has never been short of political drama in a history dating back to the beginning of football time.

It erupted just a few short weeks after Jesaulenko had masterminded the

1979 premiership, dramatically disappearing into the dressing rooms with an ankle injury minutes before his charges prevailed over Collingwood by five points in one of the most controversial finishes in Grand Final history, when on-baller Wayne Harmes set up the winning goal from a play almost certainly from the wrong side of the boundary line.

'What's better than beating Collingwood by 10 goals? Beating them by five points!' gloated Carlton's combative president George Harris.

The tough-talking Harris, who had been a prisoner of war, was a polarising figure inside and outside the club, serving two terms as president, 1965 to 1974 and 1977 to 1979, overseeing four premierships, the most of any Carlton president. In his second term he became the club's first paid president, earning more than any of the star players, as much as $80,000.

Jesaulenko was a fan, perhaps even a disciple.

When the euphoria of the premiership started to dissipate it became clear that Harris was on a collision course with his own committee over his insistence that the club invest in a range of dubious business deals involving such esoteric – and ultimately highly unprofitable – products as spring-loaded chopsticks, wobble boards, foot powder, plastic irons, kiss-of-life masks and a sports medicine centre across the road from its Princes Park headquarters.

This came to a head – for the first time – at the annual general meeting in Brunswick on Monday, December 3, when Harris unexpectedly read a letter of resignation, claiming the committee was 'obviously divided, where disloyalty, distrust, suspicion and constant petty bickering have become the normal atmosphere.'

This, remember, was the aftermath of a famous triumph when the club should have been basking in the glory, not engaging in an ugly civil war.

But worse was to come – especially for the successful captain-coach.

Four days later, Jesaulenko stunned the club – and the football world in general – by also formally quitting, putting his support for Harris in writing and asking for the members to vote to see who they wanted running the club and the team.

Many years later Jesaulenko told author Dan Eddy, whose 2018 book

Larrikins & Legends is an excellent reference point for this bitter drama: 'I could have gone neutral and stayed right out of it but I didn't want to be sitting on the fence. I wasn't against the Carlton footy club because both sides were trying to do the best thing for it. They just wanted to decide who was boss.'

The bosses were already changing. Businessman and political identity Ian Rice had reluctantly agreed, at the behest of Prime Minister Malcolm Fraser, who was a Blues supporter, to become interim chairman until the mess could be sorted out. The popular 'Percy' Jones, the veteran ruckman, was asked, to his great surprise, to step in as coach and oversee pre-season training and for the season proper.

Harris was convinced that while his resignation was a massive gamble he would eventually prevail in the power struggle because the members would not want to lose their favourite – and best – player.

A showdown was called for Tuesday, February 19, at Festival Hall, an appropriate venue as it had long been known as the 'House of Stoush' because it was the city's main boxing venue as well as a music hall that hosted the Beatles among other headline acts.

The lead-up was like a Parliamentary election campaign, only sometimes uglier and more sinister. Jesaulenko's wife Anne received a call at her suburban dress shop saying: 'Tell Alex to keep out of it. If he doesn't you'll have an axe through your head. If that does not worry him the kids will be next.' Bricks were thrown through the window of the family house. 'I can't describe what the past two weeks have been like,' Anne said just before the meeting. 'Hell isn't the word. There must be something worse. You don't really sleep when you're going through something like this.'

Harris campaigned relentlessly, phoning me as Sports Editor of *The Herald* – and no doubt repeating the calls to editors and reporters at other outlets – almost every day to ensure we knew where and when he and Alex would be having something to say. As often as not it would be on the front page because Melbourne had never seen a footy yarn quite like this.

It even got to the Supreme Court, which ruled on the eve of the meeting that any outcomes in favour of Harris would not be legally binding, but refused a request from the club to prevent it being held.

It promised to be manna from heaven for we, the footy media, as we took our seats one floor above the action on a sweltering summer's night, and we weren't disappointed.

As one passionate speech followed another, it descended – or perhaps ascended – into vaudeville when 74-year-old Harold 'Soapy' Vallence, a crusty old character who had been a star goal-kicker in his day, got up and danced a jig on the stage, and told the former president: 'George, there's something shifty about all this.' He pointed at one wobbly leg and shouted 'Carlton!' and then the other leg, ditto. The crowd loved it and as an endorsement of the ethos that the club had to come before any individuals, it was a winner.

When his turn came to speak, Jesaulenko got a standing ovation. But the mood changed when he made the mistake of saying: 'Greetings to everybody but not to the current membership holders.' In Eddy's book, Rice says: 'They booed him. Jezza was stunned. It was the silliest thing he could have said and he couldn't believe that a Carlton audience was booing the king. That really ripped through him.'

By the time he sat down, Rice said, 'Jezza had devalued himself so fast, going from a brand who was valued, plus a wonderful bloke, team man, family man, to suddenly losing a lot of respect.'

When the time came to vote, it was a no-contest, 480 for Harris and 1241 against. The two biggest losers walked off into the night, one never to return. Jones and some of 'his' players, as they now were, repaired back to the Social Club for a post-mortem, with me in tow. There was no sense of victory, certainly no jubilation. They had lost more than a coach and an asset to the team, they had seen a mate, with whom they had been through so much thick and thin, and it did not sit well.

Jesaulenko was snapped up by St Kilda, first as a player and then as playing coach when club president, trucking tycoon Lindsay Fox, decided to dispense with the incumbent coach, former Richmond star Mike Patterson, after just two games. Harris went on to make a fast fortune developing supermarkets.

Fast forward almost a decade to a warm autumn night at Princes Park just before the first game of the 1989 season. It's a typically high-flying, flamboyant Carlton Football Club night out, the men in dinner suits, the women in formal finery as they wined and dined grandly in a huge marquee erected on the field of combat in front of the new John D. Elliott grandstand. They listened to the coach, a favourite son of the Blues, Robert Walls, promise better things to come than the disappointing (by Carlton's lofty standards) third placing the previous year.

Elliott, the business and sometimes political heavyweight who had succeeded Rice as president six years earlier, as big, blunt and impossible to ignore as the luxurious new edifice named after him, warned the coach and the players that anything less than a distinct improvement would not be tolerated.

In those days, Elliott always meant what he said as all present were soon to discover – but on the night the message may have been allowed to drift away in the euphoria of the highlight of the party.

That was the naming of a composite Carlton team, selected from the many distinguished champions who had worn the famous dark navy blue in the preceding 50 years. The greats had flown in from all over Australia to acknowledge the accolade, standing one by one as the applause rocked the canvas room.

But the biggest and most spontaneous ovation of all was reserved for one familiar figure, a little balder, the trademark moustache still in place, moving with an easy, lithe grace that defied the extra kilograms around the midriff, who extracted himself from a tableful of cronies as his name was read out on the half-forward flank.

Jezza was back home.

It was a poignant moment, one that nobody was prepared to let slip before they had to – least of all Alex Jesaulenko himself. Dawn had well and truly passed into full-blown morning before the last toasts were drunk, the tall tales and true finally laid to rest at Perc Jones's pub.

And then Jezza was gone again, back to serve another year, to complete a decade of what was, by then, universally regarded as the silliest, saddest, most futile exile in the history of Australian football.

Crystal-ball gazers abound in football but no-one who left that marquee would have dreamed how prophetic the night would turn out to be. Certainly not Jesaulenko. But just ten weeks into the season, less than two years after he had overseen a premiership, Walls was sacked true to Carlton's unforgiving administrative style in those days, and Jesaulenko was invited back to resume where he had left off in such dire circumstances a decade earlier.

'I never thought for a minute I would get a second chance, in football not many do,' he told me. Buoyed by his presence, the Blues immediately won three games in a row against Sydney, North Melbourne and the West Coast Eagles, prompting supporters to start referring to him as The Messiah. After accounting for arch-rivals Collingwood by a goal, even Jezza entered into the spirit of that. Beaming hugely as he walked into the dressing rooms, he said: 'It was a dry day today so I walked on land.'

His return was good for the club in every way. When the resurgence gathered pace, chief executive Ian Collins took out newspaper advertisements asking supporters to register their commitment. He got 10,000 replies, only one per cent of which were from people already on the mailing list. 'That's 10,000 supporters we didn't know we had,' he said. Similar ads exhorting people to join 'Jezza's Army' became the norm as the following season approached.

He might have been a long time out of sight but clearly to the fans their old hero was never out of mind.

For him, the scars took a long time to heal. 'It was a pretty traumatic time,' he said. 'It has to be when you put nearly all your physical and emotional energy into one place, call it home … and then it isn't there.' But he said the concept of being in exile never occurred to him.

As uplifting as the homecoming was for all concerned, it turned out that the great man was not The Messiah after all. In the 12 games he was in charge in 1989 he won seven, drew one and lost four – giving him at that stage a highly impressive overall coaching record at Carlton (leaving out St Kilda) of 42 wins and a draw from 54 matches – but the tardy start under Walls meant the Blues finished only eighth. The next season they won 11 and lost 11 and were eighth again, which was never going to be enough for Elliott and his born-to-rule cohort. They replaced Jesaulenko with David Parkin, who had already had a five-year stint for two premierships. This time, he was there for a decade, winning one more – in 1995. Carlton have never won again since.

So in the time it took Carlton to win the last four of their equal-record 16 flags, three coaches – Jesaulenko, Parkin and Walls – were all successful. The only one who wasn't was Jones, which is, perhaps, not surprising but there are definitely grounds for feeling a tad sorry for the jovial ruckman.

He was given only one opportunity, a single year in problematic circumstances. An amiable giant of a man who had the same outlook on footy as he did on life – it's there to be enjoyed – was never really anybody's idea of a strategic genius or a leader of men, unless perhaps he was leading them to the pub and devising tactics for not being sprung having a drink the night before a game.

But at the height of the Harris drama, somebody had to be put in charge and it needed, in the judgement of powerbrokers Rice and Wes Lofts, a calming influence, somebody who was popular with players and supporters alike, who would not 'scare the horses.' There is little doubt it was a temporary appointment from the word go.

Indeed, after the smoke had cleared, I got one more phone call from Harris not long before the first match. He was out to throw one more cat amongst the pigeons. 'Tell your mate,' he barked, 'that it has already been decided that he will be sacked at the end of the season unless he happens to win the premiership.' Harris was correct that Jones was my mate – still is – and so I decided to pass on the message, believing that forewarned is forearmed. Of course, there was an alternative course of action – say nothing and allow him to proceed without a distraction he probably didn't need. Decades later I'm still not sure I did the right thing, but one certainty about Jones has always been that if he's got something to say to someone else – whether it's an uncomfortable truth or a jibe in jest – he'll say it himself, regardless of any embarrassing overtones. Sure enough, back in his pub the night of the first game, in which he oversaw an impressive, morale-boosting win over Collingwood at their Victoria Park fortress, he asked me to repeat what I had told him to Lofts, who was drinking with us. So I did, asking Lofts to tell us both whether or not it was true. Needless to say, no straight answer was forthcoming, so that was enough confirmation for me – and, deep down, probably for Jones too.

Jones did not win the flag – and he was sacked, making way for Parkin's first incarnation at Carlton, where he promptly won the next two premierships.

Jones had one thing going for him, of course – he had inherited a premiership team, one good enough to go on and win another two. So it was no huge surprise that they finished equal top of the ladder behind Geelong, only on percentage, and ahead of the two eventual grand finalists, Richmond and Collingwood in terms of games won. But both those rivals beat them as the Blues exited the finals in straight sets, sealing the coach's fate.

Ever since then, and he's well into his seventies now, people have taken great delight in reminding Jones that he was the coach responsible for Carlton not equalling Collingwood's all-time record of four flags in a row. They're just having a lend of him, of course, just as he is happy to bait anyone else when he gets a chance, and he takes it all in his good-humoured stride. But he wouldn't be human if it didn't sit in the pit of his stomach just a little bit.

For the record, that gives him a coaching win-loss percentage of 77%, compared to the high fifties or mid-sixties of all the greats, such as Barassi, Clarkson, Hafey, Sheedy, Jeans, Smith, Parkin, Matthews, McHale and Malthouse, all of whom, of course, enjoyed much longer careers in the box.

More pertinently, Jones was a significant player, reaching 249 games, playing in four premierships – in one of which he might have been a candidate for the Norm Smith medal for best afield in the Grand Final if it had existed then – and won a best and fairest. He is in Carlton's Hall of Fame and also the Tasmanian football Hall of Fame and as well as coaching Carlton he did a stint on the committee. It's a record to be proud of, not always fully acknowledged because of his richly-earned reputation as a larrikin.

He would have cracked the 250 games easily but for him being the first to discover, to his dismay, the unpalatable truth about life under Jezza the coach. Perc was at least a stone overweight, which wasn't uncommon for him. The previous coaches had let him get away with it.

Jezza sentenced him immediately to a long spell in the Reserves until the excess avoirdupois was removed. The easiest way for Jones to have achieved that probably would have been to stop or cut back on drinking beer, but there was one problem with that. He was still one of the coach's drinking mates. It took him an inordinately long time to realise that merely shouting first – an unfamiliar procedure for him in any case – was not enough to get him back in the team.

Jones was responsible for me committing an act of sacrilege. In footy-mad Melbourne, it is simply not done to change your football allegiance. You learn to barrack for a team as a kid and you're not allowed to change. Because my grandmother's brother was Percy Beames, a legendary footballer with Melbourne – and a good first-class cricketer – I grew up as a fan of the Demons, as did Jones for that matter. We both idolised the great Ron Barassi, who was coach of Carlton when Jones realised he had a future in the big league, meaning the Blues had his signature in the bag.

I became so involved with Jones in the early seventies that it made more sense to spend time watching him, and quite a few others with whom I became friendly, playing for Carlton whenever my weekend working hours allowed, than watching the Demons, where I knew no-one. So I switched. It turned out to be a good move. Having enjoyed Melbourne's run of six premierships between 1954 and 1964, which was destined to be their last, I then got to watch from much closer quarters as the Blues also won six under my newly-acquired patronage.

I met Jones through mutual mates after returning from a couple of years doing the rounds of London and Europe and was surprised one day to see him walking, unannounced, through the door of a Toorak flat I was sharing with one of those mates, carrying a suitcase in either hand. His grandmother had kicked him out, he said, and my other mate – Peter Coster, also a journalist at The Herald – had said, without consulting me, that he could move in with us even though we only had two bedrooms.

That proved to be an interesting arrangement.

It wasn't long before the doorbell rang at dawn one morning, and there was an agitated Barassi demanding to know where his ruckman was, storming into the bedroom shouting: 'Get up you loafer!' and dragging him off to a training session at a nearby park.

The coach wasn't the only one to come knocking.

One night Jones and Coster decided a party on a balcony at the next block of flats was a bit loud for their liking – an irony lost on them both – and pelted them with potatoes, breaking several glasses and creating chaos.

Within an hour, the cops were at the door and they knew exactly who they were looking for – Jones hadn't bothered going to the trouble of hiding as he launched the missiles with the highly-suspect bowling action he utilised when we played cricket together. When optimistically asked if they had a warrant, I was unceremoniously shoved aside as they stormed through to the same bedroom on the same mission as the coach had done. The matter ended up in Prahran Court, where the irascible ruckman was fined and admonished, but without attracting any media attention of significance. Imagine the headlines if that happened these days.

When a shotgun was discharged over the heads of a party on the other side of our place one night, eliciting another angry visit from the gendarmerie – they searched in vain for the weaponry, which had been carefully hidden under a bed not belonging to the culprit – and then, one Sunday morning, I awoke to find the back door had been shouldered open because one or maybe both of the others had come home sans door key, we had just about worn out our welcome in Melbourne's toffiest neighbourhood.

Coster left the country, Jones and I went our separate ways until I decided to follow his modus operandi and gatecrashed my way into his new pad in Albert Park. That turned out to be a good move because he soon worked out that there were two young wenches living next door, to whom he decided we should introduce ourselves. I ended up marrying one of them and 40-odd years later we are still together.

Jones and I also shared a mutual love of cricket and so, together with his Carlton team-mate and business partner in a couple of pubs, Adrian Gallagher, and another sportswriter, Trevor Grant, we formed a team to play in what was then a thriving Midweek Cricket Association, which brought together teams of policemen, firemen, high school and university students and random assorted like-minded people to play 40 over matches on Wednesday afternoons.

We called it the Plastic Eleven – when asked why, we'd say because we cracked easily under pressure – and it lasted for more than 20 years, populated by journalists, footballers, club cricketers of every conceivable standard and quite a few elite cricketers.

In all we had 15 former or future Test players from five countries who played either briefly or regularly, including two future captains of England, Ian Botham and John Emburey, as well as Australians Dean Jones, Rodney Hogg, Gary Cosier, Ian Callen and others. These luminaries, along with a dozen or two first class players, came and went so we were hard to beat for a while and won two or three premierships – and, yes, cracked under pressure just as often.

Jones captained us to one flag – but only one. That was because during one match, he took umbrage at being bounced by a bloke who had played a few matches as a fast bowler for Victoria, and shirt-fronted him from behind, knocking him over, as he walked back to his mark. I was president of the association at the time and we had no tribunal, but the professional umpire in charge of the match wrote me an angry letter suggesting Jones be suspended anyway for appalling sportsmanship. I replied that he wouldn't captain the team the following season, and nor did he.

The team also cost Gallagher a leadership position. Once a good opening bat for Carlton at District level – in 1970 he became the first person to play in premierships in the VFL and the VCA in the same year – he was working as an assistant coach at Carlton, footy that is. But on one stinking hot Wednesday arvo, he decided that staying back for a few after-match beers with the newly-recruited Emburey was preferable to turning up to a scheduled training session, so he got the sack.

We still supplied Carlton with a proper coach eventually because Denis Pagan, an enthusiastic medium-pacer and middle-order batsman, was one of our keener participants before he made his name as a dual premiership coach at North Melbourne, later taking over the Blues for an unsuccessful stint.

Two other star Blues, Wayne Johnston and Mark Maclure, and North's
Sam Kekovich, were also among the many footballers who enjoyed time
with the Plastic Eleven because their summer training didn't allow them
to commit to weekend club cricket. Eventually, that led to me ghost-
writing Johnston's life story, titled *The Dominator*. Johnno was a truly
great footballer, especially in the four Grand Finals in which he starred,
but he was a wild man off the field. I was well aware of that so before
agreeing to write the book I insisted that it had to be the unvarnished
truth, no matter how confronting some of that might be. Sure thing, he
promised. So we proceeded, with plenty of lurid tales about nights on the
town and a few in hospitals, with drugs involved. When the manuscript
was complete, it was so replete with this sort of stuff that I figured it
might be smart to run it by Carlton's CEO Ian Collins before publication
just to make sure it was on the money. Collo took me to lunch to discuss
it, and laughed. 'It's all accurate,' he said, 'but he hasn't told you the half
of it.' That made me wonder. But it wasn't the last time Johnston was to
do my head in.

Nearly 30 years later, in late 2019, I ran into him for the first time in
ages at a wine and food show in a park and he looked fit and well and
declined my offer to buy him a drink, saying he was trying to clean up
his life. That he certainly needed to do. Now in his sixties, he had recently
been inducted into the AFL Hall of Fame, by far the highlight of his post-
playing days, which had included far more lows than highs, including
the death of his son Matt, at 11, from an asthma attack while playing in a
school footy match in Brisbane.

Now, he told me, he was on the way back from a living hell that
had involved drugs, alcohol and gambling, the break-up of his second
marriage, and mental and physical health problems that included an
infection that almost saw the amputation of one of the legs that had
carried him to starring roles in four premierships. In an interview with
the AFL Players' Association's Courageous Conversations website, he said
he was so zonked out at one stage that when his sons arrived to rescue
him he did not even recognise one of them for four hours.

It had all been his own fault, he told me, and then asked if I would be prepared to write a second book, detailing this descent into self-loathing – and his determination to recover. Why would he want to make all that public? His motivation, he said, was to counsel young men embarking on their own careers in the cut-throat world of professional sport so that they would be aware of the many potential pitfalls. In other words, he wanted his experiences to help others, however unflattering the exercise might be.

It sounded like a noble enough ambition and, after insisting that this time it be the truth, the whole truth and nothing but the truth, I agreed to write it for him. I also enlisted the help of his old coach, Parkin, who had once said he found the first book almost impossible to read because he never realised how much carry-on, involving so many players, had been going on behind his back. So not surprisingly he had misgivings this time about becoming involved again but agreed that the premise of the new project had a lot of potential upside and came on board with his customary whole-heartedness.

Three months of hard work later, I had 50,000 words done – about 90 per cent of the planned total – and while there were a lot of positive observations to make and insights to glean about the golden era Johnston (and Parkin) lived through at Carlton, the confessions about what ensued in later years made for pretty depressing reading. Suddenly, the subject stopped answering the phone or replying to emails, which set my alarm bells ringing. Sure enough, a message – not a phone call and certainly not a knock on my door for a face to face meeting – eventually lobbed, saying simply that his family didn't want the book to go ahead and he wished me all the best. Just like that, the project was in the bin. I can easily understand why his sons would be uncomfortable with it, and I am not hostile about it, but perhaps he should have consulted them at the outset, which would have saved both of us a lot of time, effort and heart-ache. At the time of writing this, several months later, I have never heard from him again, which has been a disappointing way to end what had been a friendly relationship going back a very long way. I can only hope that he has, indeed, got his act together because the alternative would have little future.

There is always a silver lining. In this case, Parkin provided me
with the written feedback he circulated to Johnston and every other
player after the winning Grand Finals in 1981 and 1982. These reports,
which he called 'Retrospectives,' make great reading if you're an old
Blues supporter like me – and not for just us. Collingwood fans with
long memories – and there's a lot of them about – would be intensely
interested in one part of Parkin's essay after beating them in '81, which
I don't recall ever having been made public at the time. It would cause
uproar these days.

He revealed that he had a long post-match conversation with his
opposite number Tom Hafey, who he admired greatly as a coach.
'He has achieved much with a limited bunch of footballers over the
past few years,' Parkin wrote. 'At the risk of being a little unethical or
unprofessional, I want to pass on a couple of points he made.'

The points were:

> **1:** His five top salary earners are his worst trainers.
>
> **2:** His five top salary earners are his greatest whingers and excuse
> men.
>
> **3:** His five top salary earners hardly touched the ball in Saturday's
> last quarter.
>
> **4:** His five top salary earners lack the courage which is found in men
> with real strength of character.
>
> **5:** His five top salary earners cost Collingwood the chance to win its
> first premiership in 23 years.

It was unclear whether Hafey, who has since died, named the culprits
and if he did Parkin did not identify them – but he said 'it's not too
difficult to work out who those players are,' adding that he wouldn't
know who Carlton's best-paid players were and wasn't really interested
in finding out. 'From each according to his ability, and not according to
his salary,' he wrote. 'There were very few stars in our team but no non-
contributors either.'

So who might the Collingwood whingers and non-goers have been?

This is the team that lined up:

B: Ian Cooper,   Peter McCormack,   Ray Byrne.
HB: David Twomey,   Bill Picken,   Graeme Allan.
C: Rick Barham,   Mark Williams,   Warwick Irwin.
HF: Peter Daicos,   Craig Davis,   Rene Kink.
F: Ray Shaw,   Ian Brewer,   Craig Stewart.
Rucks: Peter Moore (c),   Michael Taylor,   Tony Shaw.
Inter: Stuart Atkin,   Noel Lovell.

Presumably exempt from the coach's withering accusations would be the best players, who are listed in the AFL guide as Picken, Williams, Twomey, McCormack, Taylor and Stewart.

Here are the rudimentary match stats, disposals and, in brackets, kicks, marks and handballs.

Allen 6 (3, 0, 3),
Atkin 11 (6, 3, 5 and 11 hit-outs),
Barham 13 (9, 5, 4 and two goals),
Brewer none listed,
Byrne 10 (1, 3, 10),
Cooper 7 (4, 4, 3),
Daicos 18 (14, 1, 4 and one goal),
Davis 11 (9, 5, 2),
Irwin 15 (12, 1, 3),
Kink 15 (9, 2, 6 and two goals),
Lovell 8 (4, 1, 4),
McCormack 11 (9, 3, 2),
Moore 9 (5, 4, 4 and one goal and eight hit-outs),
Picken 21 (17, 5, 4),
Ray Shaw 11 (10, 0, 1 and one goal),
Tony Shaw 25 (12, 1, 13 and one goal),
Stewart 15 (10, 4, 5 and one goal and four hit-outs),
Taylor 27 (19, 2, 8 and one goal),
Twomey 16 (10, 1, 6),
Williams 17 (14, 1, 3 and two goals).

The fall-out was dramatic. The following year, Collingwood did not make the finals, plunging to 10th, Hafey was sacked mid-season, and Moore, the captain, a Brownlow medallist and dual best and fairest, left the club and finished his career at Melbourne.

Carlton, meanwhile, sailed on like the good team that they were. The premise of Eddy's book is that this group – *The Dominator* and his many like-minded mates – probably should be recognised as the protagonists of the greatest era in the famous old club's history. He gets no argument from me. Certainly, it was a memorable time to be a Carlton supporter – even if you had just adopted them for convenience's sake, as I had.

IN SEARCH OF
PHAR LAP'S GHOST

For nine decades it has been the biggest mystery in Australian sport – for longevity, perhaps in any sphere of Australian life – and it is safe to suggest it will never be solved. Who, or what, was responsible for the death of Phar Lap? And why?

I once met an old man who was one of the last living souls who witnessed the mighty galloper's final race and he was adamant that he knew the answers to most of these burning questions. There was no good reason for me to disbelieve him and at the very least, his story belongs among the many hundreds of thousands of speculative words that have been written down the years about this heroic horse's sad fate.

It is certainly one of the most colourful – and he would have died himself by now, taking his memories to the grave with him.

Phar Lap died – apparently from arsenic poisoning, according to latter-day experts – in circumstances that have never been fully explained in Atherton, California, on April 5, 1932.

In most countries, the death of a racehorse – even a very good one – would have been long forgotten almost 90 years later. In many, it would never have been regarded as particularly important in the first place. It certainly wouldn't have provoked a potent mix of national grief, outrage, suspicion, curiosity and a form of hero-worship.

But this isn't most countries – this is Australia, where the horse has always been a revered animal. And still is in many ways.

That was made obvious to the world during the opening ceremony of the Sydney Olympic Games in 2000 which exploded into life with the thunderous arrival of a whip-cracking cavalry in the form of 120 stockhorses and their riders.

Few sports have contributed as much to Australia's proud Olympic history as equestrian, with six gold medals, three silvers and three bronzes in team and individual three-day eventing across eight different Games.

Banjo Paterson's iconic poem The Man From Snowy River, with its stirring tale of the hunt for the colt that had joined the wild bush horses, is as well-known as any item of Australian literature.

Thousands of horses saw active duty during the first World War, none more famously than another of Paterson's heroes, the indestructible and incredibly brave Bill the Bastard.

Pony clubs have always thrived. Draught horses pulling beer wagons and milk carts, mounted policemen patrolling city streets, drovers on horseback rounding up cattle – all have been a prominent part of public life almost since the year dot.

But of course, the thoroughbred racehorse has always been the head of the equine family – royalty, if you like.

Horse racing is a massive industry and a major reason why Australia identifies so passionately as a nation obsessed by sports of all sorts. Nothing else brings the entire nation to a halt as the Melbourne Cup does for three minutes on the first Tuesday of November every year, for which a public holiday is observed in Melbourne and every Tom, Dick and Harry, and Julie, Joan and Jenny, indulge themselves in a bet of some sort regardless of whether they would normally know one end of a horse from the other end of a sheep.

Nothing is more Australian than the Melbourne Cup, and now it is also a prominent international event.

All of which goes a long way to explaining the mystique that has always surrounded Phar lap and the reverence in which he is held, to the point where his mounted hide is displayed in a museum in Melbourne, his heart in another museum in Canberra and his skeleton in a third such establishment in New Zealand, where he was bred. It is why a film of his astonishing career was called Phar Lap: Heart of a Nation.

Phar Lap won the Cup in 1930 carrying a massive weight of 9 stone 12 pound, or 63 kg, which is six or seven kilos, or at least a stone, more than the winner ever lumps these days. The next year, they asked him to carry even more, 68kg, and naturally it proved impossible; he finished eighth.

In all, he won 37 of his 51 races over four years, including 20 at weight-for-age, and was placed in five others, a record that has allowed him to reign unchallenged as Australia's greatest galloper – until recently.

The conversation changed with the unexceptional arrival but unprecedented progress of the amazing Sydney mare Winx, who won 37 of 43 races, including a record 33 in a row, 25 of them Group 1, before being retired in 2019. While it is virtually impossible to compare eras almost a century apart, Winx had plenty of admirers who believed that she had displaced Phar Lap as Australia's greatest-ever horse.

It remains a moot point and probably always will be.

Phar Lap's last race, and last win, was in the Agua Caliente Handicap at a course by that name in Tijuana, Mexico, on March 20, 1932, two weeks before he died.

The Agua Caliente racetrack had been opened only a bit over two years earlier, a multi-million dollar object of defiance in the face of the Great Depression, a monument to opulence and extravagance that quickly became a favourite playground of the Hollywood set with celebrities such as Charlie Chaplin, Bing Crosby, Buster Keaton and Al Jolson regular attendees – as well as Mafia mobsters.

In 1995, while working at the America's Cup yachting in San Diego, California, a short drive from the Mexican border, I decided to make a pilgrimage to Tijuana to investigate whether it might be possible to locate any surviving clues to the mystery, or whether the big red galloper had any lingering presence at all, whether anyone remembered him. This is the account of what – and who – I found:

Each night the wizened old man arrives at the racetrack that has always been his second home.

He brings with him memories of more than 60 years ago when sinister men in dark suits and a big red horse from a faraway land were the central figures in a mysterious drama that still haunts the people of three nations.

Bobby Topete, now 78, was just a teenage peanut seller – 'peanuts,

peanuts, five cents a bag, that's what I would yell out,' he says, his ancient Mexican face creaking with laughter – at the Agua Caliente track on Sunday, March 20, 1932, a date embedded in Australian sporting legend.

It was the day the chestnut champion Phar Lap – Australia's most famous four-legged national hero – raced for the last time. Carrying the considerable impost of 9 st 3 lb and stand-in jockey Billy Elliot and starting favourite, he blitzed a field of 10 quality opponents to win the Agua Caliente handicap and the world's biggest stake – $100,000.

A fortnight later, he was dead – and to this day nobody has been able to prove how or why.

But Bobby Topete is in no doubt. 'Everybody knows the Mafia killed him,' he told me. 'They would always come here, even Al Capone himself, and they would sit and drink late at night. They would talk about Phar Lap. They did not want him to go to California, and so they had to kill him. The barman heard them saying this, and he told me.'

Hearsay, rumour, speculation. These are the only clues history has to the tragedy, and what Topete offers is more of it. He is and was no more than a bystander. But there are precious few, if any, other witnesses left alive and so his recollections must be added to the archives, for what they're worth.

Certainly, there is not the slightest reason to disbelieve him. His faculties are intact and he speaks with passion of the days of grandeur when horse racing was one of the most dominant aspects of life in his home town of Tijuana, first stop south of the Mexican border.

Alas, those days are as dead as Phar Lap. The ghost of the great galloper would not recognise his last old stamping ground now, and, sadly, it is doubtful if most of the desperates who frequent it now would recognise him.

There is almost nothing left of his memory, except for a seldom-used bar named after him. Not even a photograph.

It's not even a proper racetrack any more. Only the dogs race there. The pilgrimage there involves a 30-minute drive from San Diego, where the America's Cup yachting is being held. In itself this is a depressing experience.

As you near the border the freeway is marked with silhouette signs depicting a fleeing mother and her children. And sure enough, 3km out, there is the amazing sight of an entire family, including an infant in arms, dodging between the speeding traffic with an American security guard in hot pursuit.

Illegal immigration is something of an art form here, which explains the clanging, spiked one-way gates through which pedestrian access to Mexico is gained. It has the sound and the feel of going to jail. There is no passport control but there certainly is on the way back.

On the other side, beggars, many of them children, line the walkways. You cannot help notice that nobody smiles. Drivers of decrepit taxis, mostly without meters, vie for custom. This is not only the third world but a step back in time.

So is Agua Caliente – the name means hot water and is derived from the thermal springs of the area. The racetrack boasts an imposing art deco edifice guarded by statues of six prancing white horses and other more formidable animal life.

On either side of the main entrance are enclosures containing brown bears and a white leopard. Further inspection reveals that the entire place is a zoo, containing lions, tigers, lynxes, giraffes – and several kangaroos. 'They like it here. They breed very well,' a worker says.

The place has seen much better days. The original buildings burned down in 1971 in suspicious circumstances, as the arson police like to say. As a business, horse racing was struggling to compete with fierce opposition from the more glamorous Californian tracks.

Where once 10,000 Americans would cross the border for each meeting, now there were hardly any.

The facilities were rebuilt in 1974 but in 1989 the staff went on a prolonged strike. It was a death sentence. Racing never resumed, and a dog track which once occupied the infield was moved to intrude on the course proper.

Now every night, twice on Saturdays and Sundays, the dish-lickers are led out to the strains of Colonel Bogey and the Mexican national anthem and sent after the lure while bored wolves peer morosely through their bars on the sidelines and jungle cats prowl where the run to the back straight curves past them.

Only two or three hundred of the needy and the greedy are in attendance and most never leave the main centre of what little desultory activity there is –- the Sportsbook betting shop, a windowless, dingy room in which you can drink at the bar and punt on anything. Even, when we were there on a Wednesday night, the races in Mornington, Victoria, Australia.

Waiting for the first dogs to make an appearance we watched in some astonishment as one swarthy customer suddenly approached another sitting on a bar stool and with a right cross that would have made Carlos Monzon proud knocked him flying.

The victim picked himself up, rubbed his jaw and shook his head, resumed his seat and returned his attention to his form guide. The assailant continued to lurk menacingly behind him. And not a word was spoken by either man, before, during or afterwards. Nor did anybody else appear to pay the slightest heed.

One floor above, via a window riddled with six bullet holes, is the Phar Lap bar, the name picked out in neon light above the door. You search in vain for any other sign of the horse. There are photographs on the walls but they are of old-time movie stars such as Johnny Weissmuller and Clark Gable, although none are captioned.

The bar is used only when it is booked for functions and that is not often – although one of yachtsman John Bertrand's syndicate executives has noted its possibilities as an evocatively appropriate venue for a get-together if the Australians manage to challenge for the Cup they seek.

But wait, says the track's marketing man Jorge de Buen, there is a photograph of the horse in a disused office. He and a security guard lead the way through musty back passages to a locked room. Inside, there is no light –- and after a torchlight inspection, no photo of Phar Lap either.

On the walls there are many other faded images of races of long ago, and a space where one once was. But the last remaining memory of Big Red has disappeared. Jorge shrugs and says he is sorry.

Bobby Topete remembers that in the old grandstand, before the fire, there were huge photographs of the seven best horses ever to race at Agua Caliente, including the great American galloper Sea Biscuit – and Phar

Lap. Just old ashes now.

Phar Lap was a five-year-old when he came here against the wishes of trainer Harry Telford. The autocratic owner David Davis had done a deal for the horse to be used as the major drawcard for the annual race and Telford's assistant Tommy Woodcock took over the training.

The Americans and Mexicans were unimpressed with Woodcock's methods, but when Phar Lap won in brilliant fashion Davis was swamped with lucrative offers for the horse to make special appearances at tracks around the US as well as an invitation to compete in match races in England.

The Melbourne Herald's racing writer Bert Wolfe watched the triumph and reported: 'Phar Lap made all dreams come true to the shouts of 50,000 racing fans when he won the Agua Caliente Handicap. He did more to advertise Australia and New Zealand in the US and Mexico than $1 million.

'Today he is big news. Every newspaper of any consequence is printing stories of the success of the Big Train from the Antipodes. They are saying that Phar Lap and his connections made American trainers and jockeys look like suckers.'

The international world of racing now had a lot more respect for racehorses from Australia.

Soon afterwards Phar Lap injured a heel in training and was returned to his base, a stud farm outside San Francisco. There he suddenly became ill and while a vet diagnosed a mild case of colic, his stomach kept swelling until the pain became so intense that he was returned to his box.

With Woodcock in a state of shock, Phar lap haemorrhaged and died. Woodcock, covered with blood, knelt with his arms around his beloved horse's neck and cried.

When vet Bill Neilsen and others arrived back, they had to prise him from the horse and forcibly lead him away. There was no knowing whether Phar Lap had been poisoned deliberately or accidentally, although Woodcock maintained up to his own death that it was not deliberate.

But perhaps he just wouldn't or couldn't believe that anyone would perpetrate such bastardry.

There was outrage in Australia and the horse's real home, New Zealand, embarrassment in the USA and dismay in Mexico. The entire racing world was stunned.

The New York Sun published a poem which began:

When the thoroughbreds immortal
Graze in pastures ever green
And steeds of song and glory
Feel the touch of hands unseen
There's a whinny in the distance
And a pawing at the gate
As the big stout-hearted Phar Lap
Joins the legions of the great.

Australians took a long time to forgive America, if they ever did. The popular theory was that the mafia – The Mob – controlled American racing and there was no room for a champion horse which they could not manipulate and so he had to go.

That is what Roberto Topete believes. A shy man who would not allow his face to be photographed, he has worked at Agua Caliente all his life and he remembers when 1200 horses were trained on the track and 20,000 punters would attend each race meeting.

'The barmen and the waiters were my friends and they told me what they would hear,' he said. 'There are a lot of rumours, like at the fights. Nobody really knows.

'But the Mafia killed him, it's what they all say. They told the owner the horse should not win but he was a good man, an honest man. If people bet on his horse he liked them to get their money.

'Phar Lap was a very nice horse, very docile, very popular.'

Despite its storied history and strong status in Australian culture, racing can be an acquired taste. It was for me. But unlike many at least I was introduced to it profitably, if in a roundabout way. The first honest dollar I ever earned was as a 16-year-old schoolboy doing a shift pulling beers in the outdoor bar at the Warrnambool racecourse during the famous three-day May carnival, the biggest and best rural race meeting in the land. And as soon as I started work as a cadet journalist at the local paper, I was assigned to accompany the crusty old racing writer Don Burnett to the races to help compile the betting information.

This led to a fascination with the old seaside club's signature event, the Grand Annual Steeplechase, which is one of the most captivating – and sometimes controversial – spectacles in the entire Australian sporting calendar. Dating back to 1872 and always on the third day of the carnival, it is run over 5500 metres, including two sections in paddocks adjacent to the course proper, and demands the gallant gallopers negotiate more fences, 33, than any other race in the world.

I have lost count how many times I have attended and how many wonderful stories have materialised but it has formed the basis of my gradual immersion into the so-called sport of kings and these days it would be almost unthinkable to not make the three-hour journey from Melbourne with a bunch of mates every year, with the rare exception of 2020 when the COVID crisis meant no spectators were allowed. We hardly ever back the winner of it – it's a very difficult race for all concerned, horses, jockeys, trainers and punters – but that's half the fun of it.

In any case, it's not about the punt for me, not at the Bool and not anywhere else. I do enjoy a small bet when I'm at the races but it's more about the people because you find characters of every ilk at the racetrack. The term 'colourful racing identities' was coined for a reason. It has always had a certain negative connotation but that doesn't mean that they're all rogues, ratbags or snake-oil salesmen. Some are, most aren't and trying to tell them apart is also what helps make the whole caper so interesting.

Sometimes, for the rank and file racegoer, and for professional observers such as specialist racing journalists for that matter, the truth can sometimes hove into sight, unseen and unexpected, and explode like a bomb, loudly and with widespread fall-out and damage.

Even the Melbourne Cup, for all its glamour and prestige, is not immune.

In my hands-on experience over the past 25 to 30 years, there probably hasn't been a more popular result than the 2015 win by the 100-1 rank outsider Prince of Penzance, ridden by Michelle Payne – the first female jockey to win the great race – and trained by the 'punters' pal,' the prolific Darren Weir.

It was such a feel-good fairytale that they made a movie about it – only for one of the heroes, Weir, to end up three years later being thrown out of the industry for four years, perhaps effectively forever, after being found guilty of behaviour prejudicial to racing, namely being in possession of electric devices known as jiggers used to shock horses into performing better.

Weir was an ambiguous character, a self-made knockabout from the bush who started from scratch and built possibly the most successful training empire ever seen in Australia despite having little or nothing in the way of formal education in managing big businesses. Although immensely popular with punters for obvious reasons – 'back Weir, drink beer' became a catch-cry on racecourses all over Australia as his strike-rate soared year after year – I found him a hard man to get to know or to warm to, even after he joined the same sportsmen's lunch club, Vingt Cinq, as I had many years earlier.

Whether he will ever be seen on a racecourse again is anyone's guess. So is the warmth of his welcome back if he ever does return.

It must be said there has never been any suggestion that Prince of Penzance owed its win to anything untoward but nevertheless the trainer's descent into disgrace means there will always be an invisible, informal asterisk in the record books.

While that is a great pity, it doesn't detract from Payne's historic feat, or the many other elements of what was otherwise one of the most uplifting stories in the great race's long history.

For me, though, there was one even more emotionally triumphant edition.

That was in 2002 when Damien Oliver, who has always been one of Australia's best and most admired jockeys, rode the Irish horse Media Puzzle to victory in 2002 a week after his jockey brother Jason, 33, had been killed in a trackwork accident in their home town of Perth.

They made a movie of that one, too, and rightly so. Having known Oliver off and on since he first came to Melbourne as a starry-eyed apprentice in the eighties, I was riveted by the way he was able to channel his grief into steely professionalism, shedding tears either side of working hours but not during them. I hadn't witnessed anything quite like it in any other sport. Nor have I ever, before or since, had to follow up on a day of towering triumph by going straight to a funeral, having been instructed by an editor to catch the same plane as Oliver to Perth the next morning and watch him and his mother, Pat Rudland, bury their brother and son. That could have been an awkward, difficult intrusion but again Oliver's professionalism shone through as he welcomed me to the church – the same one where the Perth racing fraternity had gathered 27 years earlier to farewell his father Ray, also a jockey who died in the same tragic way – and the wake at a suburban pub where he admitted he was 'a bit dusty' from having joined in the raucous celebrations with the Irish owners the previous night, but overwhelmed by the outpouring of support from the racing fraternity.

For me, writing the race-day 'match report' of how the Cup unfolded has sometimes been a challenging task in that there are often multiple stories to be linked together on a tight deadline, an obligation to do justice to them all. Not this time. There was only one tale to tell and in racing I have never had a better one to work with. Here it is:

Jason Oliver goes to his grave today having achieved every jockey's ultimate ambition – he won the Melbourne Cup yesterday.

Certainly he had some expert assistance from his younger brother and best mate, Damien, who actually guided Irish stayer Media Puzzle around Flemington.

But everybody knew that Damien, 30, was sharing the saddle and that this win was for Jason, 33, who was killed when a young horse fell and rolled on him during a barrier trial in Perth early last week.

Damien, wearing Jason's riding breeches as he did throughout Derby Day on Saturday, looked to the heavens as he realised with 200m to go that he had the race in his keeping.

As he flashed past the post, he had just one poignant message in mind: 'This one's for you, mate!'

For Australia's finest rider and one of the most popular people in racing it has been a long and harrowing eight days of grieving and searching. But it ended with perhaps the most emotional climax in the 142-year history of the great race.

Many in the crowd of 102,533 and in the massive international TV audience were unable to hold back the tears and certainly not the cheers.

The old racecourse has echoed to some outstanding ovations in its time, but few, if any, to match Oliver's reception as he returned to scale.

The champ himself managed to remain dry-eyed, although it was a near thing on more than one occasion as he was swamped by well-wishers.

It might be different at Jason's funeral in Perth today when he walks at the arm of his mother, who lost the boys' father, Ray, also a jockey in a racing accident 27 years ago.

He will be surrounded there by colleagues from the jockeys' room who flew across the country last night to offer their support, all of them acutely aware that they are brothers in arms in a dangerous and sometimes deadly business.

Maybe it will sink in then with an even more crushing impact than he has felt so far.

But the sheer thrill of winning the Cup – his second – in such circumstances allows Damien to move forward on a much-needed high note.

Some wondered whether the tragedy might prove too much, that he might feel unable to fulfil his most important engagement of the year – or, indeed, see the need to put himself at similar risk again. Certainly, there was no preventing such melancholy thoughts intruding.

'It was a difficult week, to say the least,' he said, 'and for the first few days racing was not important to me.

'It brings you back to reality. Life is much more important and racing came to seem insignificant.'

But not for nothing has Oliver been the best in his demanding business for some years now – he is the ultimate professional. And, as the cliché goes, when the going gets tough, the tough get going.

Although uncertain whether he could cope, he returned to work on Saturday and endured a long and luckless afternoon, failing to ride a winner but fielding plenty of commiserations from well-meaning acquaintances who really only made the day even harder.

'It meant I had to keep dealing with it again,' he said.

Not riding at all was a definite option, but he discussed it with his mother and others close to the family and everyone agreed Jason would want him to keep going.

'He was my biggest supporter and he taught me everything I know,' Damien said.

'He was my best mate, so you can imagine what it would be like to lose him. It was very tough.'

His mother had more reason than anyone to not want to see him get back on a horse, but she, too, gave her blessing.

'Mum's always given us kids great support in whatever we wanted to do,' Oliver said. 'It would have been hard for her, but she knew what my brother would have wanted me to do and she wouldn't have got in the way.'

For his last words to his mother, Oliver made a simple promise he was determined to keep. 'I told her I'd win it,' he said.

To the pro that he is, there was also the considerable matter of keeping faith with the horse's connections and all the punters – many of them putting their money where their sympathy was – who had kept Media Puzzle at or near the top of the betting charts.

Trainer Dermot Weld didn't arrive in Australia until late last week, well after the accident, but his son Mark had taken all the pressure off Oliver, telling him to take his time making up his mind.

'This is only a horse race,' he said, putting precisely the right perspective on matters. His father said he was proud to read the remark in the papers.

The Welds operate one of Europe's most successful stables and produced the winner of the 1993 Cup, Vintage Crop, and Oliver knows them well, having ridden horses for them a couple of years ago.

He was in Ireland for the experience and one of the things he learned, he said yesterday, was that European horses can sustain a run more easily than their Australian counterparts.

It was to prove a crucial piece of intelligence.

Oliver is a good judge, too.

He knew he was on a good thing when he rode Media Puzzle to a highly impressive victory in course record time in the Geelong Cup a couple of weeks ago and scoffed at suggestions the horse was a B-grader in Europe and would be out of its depth.

'Dermot is an intelligent man and I knew he wouldn't have brought the horse here for the scenery or to make up the numbers,' he said.

All of Oliver's skill was on display as he positioned Media Puzzle beautifully behind highly-regarded stablemate and race favourite Vinnie Roe, until he found himself needing to make a run for the post slightly earlier than he wanted, trying to avoid getting caught up in the crush.

But he had no qualms about doing so because of what he had learned back in Ireland – the horse wouldn't knock up.

In the end, the margin was so emphatic that Oliver was able to spend the final, dramatic moments looking to the heavens. The applause that would surely be coming from there drowned out – in his ears, anyway – the wave after wave of sound from the packed grandstands.

It was a moment nobody wanted to miss and which will never be forgotten by anyone who witnessed it.

The invaders might have made off with the Cup, just as everyone feared they would, but this was still a victory to inspire pride in every sports fan in Australia.

There are a lot of formalities in the wake of a Melbourne Cup win, and Oliver's emotions were stretched to the limit throughout it all.

But the theme never changed. On the official dais, he dutifully thanked the sponsors, the club and then said: 'Lastly, to my brother Jason – I know you're there, mate.

'I couldn't have done it without you, Buddy. Thanks again.'

On and off the track, he was sheer class – but that shouldn't have surprised anyone.

Everyone knows he's a champion – but the day he won the Cup with another man in the saddle will take its place as one of the great legends of Australian racing history.

WINNING AGAINST ALL ODDS

So the deadliest of men is not he with a gun
But the one that tells you it can't be done
For that taken by burglars can be got again
But what can replace your will to win?

Or in other words, never give up.

The last four lines of a motivational poem, author unknown, called ROBBED, was taped to the wall of Darby McCarthy's modest Housing Commission home in Toowoomba, Queensland, when I visited him in June 2004.

There have been a lot of rags to riches and then riches back to rags stories in Australian sport, or life in general, over the years but very few have had quite such a roller-coaster ride as the legendary McCarthy, one of most talented, charismatic and popular indigenous sportsmen Australia has ever seen.

Some experts consider him to have been, in his time and perhaps still, the best jockey to throw a leg over a racehorse in this country.

But he was forced to spend 31 years fighting for justice after being accused of conspiring to rig a race at a nondescript bush meeting in country Victoria, which triggered the longest official inquiry Victorian racing had ever seen.

The highly controversial scandal irreparably damaged his colourful and hugely successful career, sent him broke and almost cost him his sanity, despite widely-held opinion in high places that he was innocent of any wrong-doing – and his own vehement insistence that he had been made a scapegoat.

That's why the poem was on his wall – 'I was robbed,' he told me.

Was he? Well, he managed to convince a Melbourne policewoman, Lauren Callaway, that he was and the book she wrote entitled Darby McCarthy: Against All Odds convinced me – and between us, we eventually persuaded the racing authorities to restore his pride and reputation, inasmuch as that can ever be properly achieved after such a long period of notoriety.

The pen may or may not be mightier than the sword, as the old saying goes, but the media does sometimes have the power to get wrongs put right and this is one example that made me proud.

McCarthy's story is best told from the beginning.

Richard Laurance McCarthy was born in a squalid station camp in the dusty south-western Queensland outback town of Cunnamulla in 1944, one of 13 children to parents Albert and Kate who had married, perhaps not altogether legally, at 13.

He had only three years of formal education and was working on the station by the age of seven, learning to ride horses with the stockmen – and displaying an uncanny affinity with the animals, which is a gift many indigenous people share.

He was 10 when he rode in a race for the first time, borrowing a pair of boots three sizes too big and weighing just 6 st 7 lb, or 41.2kg, and requiring extra lead bags to make the weight allocated to a horse called Rusty at an unregistered amateur meeting at a speck on the map called Thargomindah.

Rusty scored by six lengths – and the boy was on his way to a career that would see him ride more than 1000 winners in several countries and earn more than a million dollars in prizemoney, an enormous sum at the time.

Back then, young Richard had left school early – the teachers didn't think much of his carefree attitude, apparently – to work at the Yakara station for a character named 'Cocky' Easton, who decided to call him Darby after a great Aboriginal jockey of the era, Darby Munro.

He moved to Brisbane at 14, lied about his age, got an apprenticeship with trainer Jim Hennessy at Eagle Farm and the winners started to pile up, especially on horses regarded as difficult to ride. In those days, they put this special element of his enormous talent down to 'black magic' but to McCarthy it was just a matter of understanding the different natures of individual horses.

From there, the world was soon his oyster. He won many of Australia's biggest races, including the AJC Derby on Divide And Rule and the Epsom on Broker's Tip at Randwick on the same day in 1969, for which the famous club rewarded him with a presentation of a gold-plated whip which was his proudest possession – until it disappeared one day.

Years later, he got it back – from me. It had been offered for sale, for a pittance, to a Melbourne sports memorabilia expert, John Holmes, a fan of McCarthy's, who recognised the value, both monetary and sentimental, and feared it would end up in a pawnshop if he did not 'rescue' it. Knowing I had been in contact with the original owner he gave it to me for safe-keeping. The next time I saw McCarthy, Holmes and I returned it to him – and he promptly donated it to the racing section of the National Sports Museum at the Melbourne Cricket Ground. McCarthy suspected what had happened to the whip – it had been stolen by someone close to him to fund a drug habit, but he wasn't interested in making an issue out of that. 'I'm just glad to see it again,' he said. 'I thought it had gone walkabout.'

As his career flourished and fame and fortune accrued, McCarthy grew extremely fond of the bright lights and the playboy lifestyle – wine, women and song. He rode in Paris, where he lived in a mansion with a butler and a maid written into his contract, but enjoyed little success, winning only one race.

That was perhaps partly because of his off-track mateship with fellow Australian hoop Billy Pyers, who was an expert when it came to lurid lifestyles, living it up with champagne and playgirls. McCarthy was a very willing accomplice and had a very good time but it didn't do his career any favours. 'It was great while it lasted,' he said later.

The booze got him again, big-time, less than two months after the greatest day of his career, the Randwick double. After a day spent arguing with his girlfriend Kathy, partaking of a long, long lunch with another jockey, and then Kathy refusing to let him in when he got home, he drunkenly punched through a big plate-glass window, inflicting massive damage to his left arm. At the hospital surgeons were contemplating amputating the arm until Kathy pleaded: 'Don't cut off his arm, he's a jockey. You may as well slit his throat.' They patched him up but with little feeling in his arm and hand there was every chance he would never be able to ride again. But after a lengthy rehabilitation, he made it back, this time after moving to Melbourne.

He didn't know the biggest threat to his career was yet to come.

Nothing changed his life more than the day, March 31, 1976, when he caught a light plane from Melbourne's Moorabbin airport with a racing associate, Ray Effron, to fulfil two engagements on the first day of the Hamilton Cup meeting.

They were joined, to McCarthy's unease, by a man he had not met before but recognised as a punter referred to only as Mr X, or 'the mystery witness' in the many newspaper accounts of what followed. He is named in Callaway's book.

In the last race, the Black and White Scotch Whiskey Handicap over 1600m, McCarthy rode veteran Rickshaw's Luck, which drifted in the betting from 3-1 to 6-1, into fifth place behind the place-getters, an outsider named Matrium, firming favourite Blue Bubble and another firmer, Flash Future.

Immediately after the race stewards reprimanded McCarthy for causing 'run of the mill interference' to Blue Bubble 800m from home.

Blue Bubble's trainer, well-known Warrnambool mentor George Rantall, incensed at what he believed to be a good thing knocked out of contention, told stewards that Flash Future's trainer, Bob Smerdon, had tried to bribe him to put a 'slow' on his horse.

Uproar ensued, and during a lengthy investigation Smerdon admitted making the approach to Rantall – who angrily refused to have anything to do with it – on behalf of the mystery punter, who believed Flash Future was a good thing and Blue Bubble the danger.

But when racing crosses over to the dark side, nothing is ever what it seems. And so Smerdon admitted to stewards he disliked Mr X and had told him Flash Future could win when in fact he gave it no chance. He wanted to see the punter lose as much as possible, he said.

Meanwhile, because he had travelled to the races with Mr X and had, deliberately or not, compromised the chances of Rantall's horse, McCarthy found himself in the hottest seat of his life.

The ordeal seemed to last forever – the inquiry dragged on for three months – and the book devotes several chapters to edited transcripts of the 200 pages of evidence.

It is true McCarthy trips over certain facts and recollections, but it is difficult – if not impossible – to read those passages years later and arrive at the conclusion that he was definitely guilty of 'fixing' the race.

As the lawyers were to tell the authorities, there was too much hearsay and conjecture for 'any reasonable tribunal' to convict McCarthy.

Nonetheless, they disqualified him for seven years, meaning he could have nothing whatsoever to do with racing – he couldn't set foot on a racetrack or a stable, work in the industry in any form or associate with people involved in it.

At 31, it was a virtual career death sentence.

They also banned the punter from entering racecourses, a call later overturned by a court. Smerdon surrendered his licence while police considered whether to book him for conspiracy, which never happened.

A strange sequel awaited.

McCarthy appealed and the sentence was reduced to two years but without any suggestion he was any less guilty.

The case had become an embarrassment for the Victoria Racing Club, which then controlled the sport, with the newspapers and a future Premier, John Cain, then an Opposition MP, campaigning on McCarthy's behalf.

One day, several months later, the VRC committee mysteriously simply gave McCarthy his licence back – without saying why.

'To this day, there has never been an explanation,' McCarthy said when I took the matter up with him in 2004. 'I've had to carry the stigma, but there is no doubt whatsoever in my mind that the VRC stuffed it up.'

He claimed reliable sources told him later he had been in the wrong place at the wrong time when certain important people in racing had the

WINNING AGAINST THE ODDS

punter in their crosshairs. 'I was the bunny,' he said.

Eminent racing journalist Les Carlyon agreed. He said soon after the saga reached its puzzling conclusion: 'I think Darby was just in the way … he just got knocked over.'

Asked how the truth could be established, Carlyon said: 'They'll never say he was innocent because he could sue them, even now. What you can say is that simply the sentence was removed. I've never heard of a sentence being removed from a jockey – even in criminal cases it happens about twice a century. You can go on to say that the only conclusion anyone can come to is that it was removed because it should never have been there in the first place.'

Cain said: 'Darby was railroaded and treated very badly. My sense of natural justice was outraged by what they'd done to him.' When he later became Premier, Cain changed the way racing was administered in Victoria, setting up an appeals tribunal to deal with such disputes.

McCarthy resumed riding in 1977, but by then he had spent time in a Melbourne home for alcoholics and drug addicts after suffering a nervous breakdown, and a further period living in a convent.

He enjoyed intermittent success, especially with the great galloper Hyperno, but with his left hand little more than a claw the magic was gone. He retired and returned several times and eventually got out of the saddle for good in 1991.

There was no fairytale finish, just a flat and frustrating end to a career of remarkable highs and lows.

'He was one of the most beautiful horsemen I've ever seen,' Carlyon said. 'You would see him with young horses at the training track and he was an absolute master. There was something placid and kind about him that seemed to come across to the horses.'

The lows are almost too depressing to list. His grandfather, he says, was shot dead by white settlers in full view of his son in 1912. After a day at the races in 1965, his father, an alcoholic, died mysteriously – probably of a heart attack – in a police cell. His brother Ian died of a drug overdose in McCarthy's home. A coroner found it to have been suicide and McCarthy blamed himself for not looking after Ian properly, as he had promised their mother he would do. An aunt was jailed for murder. A sister lost a stillborn son. 'I've buried a lot of family,' he says.

His first marriage was only ever consummated twice, he says in the book, and his third wife Glennis suffered strokes which made her totally dependent on him.

He has lost a lot of money and is now broke, he tells me when I meet him and Glennis at their home for coffee and later for a couple of beers at the pub, where he apologises for not being able to return the shout. He doesn't have the necessary few dollars.

He is a pensioner and lends his name to a punters' club, which does no more than make ends meet – just. 'I'm breathing,' is all he says.

Even that was no more than the basic truth. His health was not good. He had been through a triple heart bypass and suffered from asthma and diabetes.

Asked how many children he has, he says: 'Many.' Pressed, he says: 'About two handfuls – to seven different mothers.' (When he died in 2020, seven offspring were listed in death notices.)

He tells you all this with a clear-eyed articulateness – he is clearly a proud, dignified and intelligent man – lacing his conversation with bushmen's lingo. He refers to his house as 'not a bad camp' and says he hopes to earn enough from the book 'to buy a bit of damper.'

His easy charm is perhaps partly due to his Irish ancestry, which he says dates back eight generations to the First Fleet, and a disarming candour about his own failings, which makes his protestations of innocence all the more believable.

He has been, and probably always will be, a hero to his own people.

In a foreword to his story, legendary Olympic athlete Cathy Freeman says she used to stay with his family when she was at boarding school in Toowoomba 'I learned some precious lessons from Darby, who taught me in his own charismatic, crazy way what it takes to be a real contender,' she wrote. 'Darby influenced me to strive for excellence in all that I do and to persevere against all the odds. I will be forever thankful.'

Callahan writes: '... Darby does his part in advancing the breakdown of barriers between Aboriginal people and white Australians. He either changes people's attitudes by simply being himself – or gives them something positive to remember about a great bloke they met who happens to be an Aboriginal.'

He says: 'It's the blackfella culture – I've got two bob so here's a shilling for you – and a very old culture it is. Money was never important to me. I just loved working with animals. I loved my chosen sport. My horses took me around the world. They say this country got where it is on the sheep's back – I went on a horse. And I worked hard at it.'

Although Aboriginal jockeys were in plentiful supply in those days, many hid their identity, claiming to be Indian, Jewish, Portuguese or Maori for fear of being victimised. Not McCarthy, though.

Callaway again: 'His Aboriginality was a badge of honour long before Cathy Freeman carried the Aboriginal flag down the home straight of the running track at the Commonwealth Games in Canada in 1994. He embraced his heritage at a time in society when there was nothing to be gained from cultural pride.

'I would love to say that Darby was the poor little black kid who made good, but like most true accounts it is not that simple. He has never seen himself as a victim because he is black – he does not identify with the rhetoric. He is a battler, that's for certain.'

McCarthy has never suggested that racism was responsible for what he was put through, but the campaign to clear his name was driven by past injustices to his own family and Aboriginal people in general.

'Two of my fathers died before we were even recognised as citizens in our own country,' he said. He made several unsuccessful attempts to enter local politics to address discrimination issues.

When the conversation returned to faraway, long-ago Hamilton, the lingering pain was obvious. McCarthy said the trauma of the ordeal cost him not only his career but almost his sanity, as well as sending him broke.

'It was a physical, mental, emotional and financial kick in the guts,' he said. Suicidal thoughts sometimes had to be repelled.

Days before our meeting, he had written to Racing Victoria chairman Graham Duff and chief steward Des Gleeson requesting an 'act of grace' to clear his name.

'I find that time does not diminish the feelings of devastation I suffered when my career was effectively destroyed,' he said in his letter. 'The disqualification permanently scarred my reputation and has ever since been a source of embarrassment.'

Elaborating later, he told me he was not prepared to live out his life with the stigma hanging over him.

'If I'm guilty give me life, if I'm innocent give me nothing.

'They've been very naughty to me. They've got to fix it up and I won't let them go until they do. I'll go to my dreamtime when I get justice. I've waited a long time for it and I know I'll get it. When I do it will be for my father and grandfather.'

They say everything comes to he who waits – but McCarthy still had some waiting to do.

It took just on three years after the publication of Callaway's book and my interviews with him for Duff to announce in May, 2007, that Racing Victoria had reviewed the case and now agreed that he had been the victim of a serious miscarriage of justice. He was offered an official pardon on condition that he did not pursue a speculative request years earlier for a million-dollar compensation pay-out.

'It stinks, frankly,' Duff said. 'Our review indicates that he was not guilty.' Much later, he told me he had made the call on the pardon despite considerable pressure from a party he would not name. When I asked if that was the VRC he did not reply.

Duff gave his daughter Lisa, then teaching filmmaking at an Aboriginal TAFE in Sydney, the book to read, suspecting it would fascinate her. It did. She planned to make a movie of the story, which has been in mothballs ever since – but not abandoned.

Although he remained indignant about his treatment and the accompanying stigma, McCarthy gladly accepted the peace offering, saying the time had come to stop fighting and get on with the twilight years of his remarkable life.

'I've had a terrible time in my life and it has left scars,' he said. 'I'm getting ready to go to dreamtime but I'm alive to see this. I's a very proud moment.'

The atonement did not stop there.

In July 2015, Racing Victoria flew him to Melbourne to announce that in conjunction with the Koori Academy of Excellence the Darby McCarthy Indigenous Scholarship would be instituted to help young horsemen with ambitions to follow him.

It amounted to an informal apology – or at least an admission of deep regret.

The announcement was made at the MCG museum as he handed over the lost whip. It was the first time he had ever been to Australia's greatest sports venue and he was moved to see how many Aboriginals – including Freeman – featured in the Australian sports Hall of Fame, which is also housed there.

The ceremony was followed, in the company of 10 teenagers from the Koori Academy, by an afternoon at the Geelong races, where one event was named after him. The 1000m helter-skelter was won by the favourite Howdee, ridden by a journeyman jockey named Dale Smith, which quickly revealed itself as a highly appropriate outcome.

Until he was given a copy of a newspaper previewing McCarthy's visit to speed-read before the presentation, Smith had no idea who the old man handing him the trophy was. Then he revealed that his own grandmother, Carmel Moore, was a full-blooded Aborigine and he, according to his own estimate, was one-tenth indigenous.

'I grew up in an environment where it was pretty much spot the white kid,' Smith said. 'Our family is proud of our heritage and we hold our heads high. So this is a great honour.'

The scholarship continues to help racing-minded youngsters but the Koori Academy of Excellence's role has been taken over by Anglicare Victoria who have created a Big Dreams leadership Academy, which inspires Aboriginal and Torres Strait Islander people to make good decisions about health, development and leadership.

Finally at peace with his past, McCarthy went to his Dreamtime at 76 in May 2020.

LORDS OF THE RING

Boxing is populated by more colourful characters than any other sport – and that's before you even start counting the fighters themselves. Well, maybe that's a slight exaggeration – but go to any fight night in Melbourne for the last couple of decades or so and the chances are you will have been rubbing shoulders at ringside with plenty of people described in the newspapers as 'underworld identities' or bikie gangsters. At the most popular – and, it should be stressed, best-organised – venue, The Pavilion in Kensington, one night in early 2019 one patron was shot dead and another wounded by gun-toting criminals who had paid at the door to get in. Getting hit at the fights is an occupational hazard, of course, but it's normally only the guys inside the ring and the weapons of choice are gloved fists, not bullets. You might end up in hospital, but not usually in the morgue.

When I used to go there, and elsewhere, to write about the so-called 'sweet science', which was about once a month on average, I would more often than not be greeted cordially by Mr Mick Gatto, probably Melbourne's most famous – infamous? – 'underworld identity,' and a man who had beaten a murder rap by insisting he had acted in self-defence when he shot another shady figure dead in a restaurant a few years back. If you owe money to the wrong people in this town, you do not want to learn that big Mick has taken an interest in the collection of the debt, which he frequently does.

Fortunately, Mick, money and me have never been in the same conversation – well, not legitimately. However, not long before I left newspapers I got an email from an anonymous contact who I had never met but who often sent me snippets of gossip about what was going on behind the scenes in the fight game, and they nearly always proved to be accurate. This one informed me that the subject of the rumours was now … moi. The word around the traps apparently was that I was taking slings from Gatto and the wealthy promoter who owned The Pavilion, Brian Amatruda, to publicise certain boxers ahead of others and that this would be made known to the editors of the *Herald Sun* with a view to having me sacked. It was nonsense, of course, and laughed off as such by the paper without any questions being asked. I never did find out what the purpose of this little hatchet job was and perhaps the best way of finding out might have been to ask Gatto himself to look into it – he's good at that sort of thing and it would probably have taken him 10 minutes to find out. But I wasn't going to be around much longer anyway so there was no point in turning a non-issue into a real one.

Gatto did buy me a glass of wine once, if that counts as corruption. When I heard in 2013 the scuttlebutt that he was planning to promote fights himself, I arranged to meet him at one of his favoured lunch haunts in the city to ask whether he had cleared that with the State Government's watchdog, the Professional Boxing and Combat Sports Board, which issues licences for any such involvement – but only to 'fit and proper persons.' He had done no such thing of course but airily and pleasantly assured me that there was not the slightest reason why he would not be granted a permit when he got around to asking for one. After all, he said, as the waiter delivered a couple of full glasses without having had to be asked, the notorious American Don King had enjoyed a long and highly successful career as a promoter despite killing two men and doing time for one after a charge of second degree murder was reduced to manslaughter. He was later pardoned.

'He was actually convicted of murder and still became a promoter. If that's the case I don't see why I can't be,' said Gatto, who was behind bars on remand for 18 months before being acquitted of his own murder charge.

Perhaps only Gatto would consider comparing himself to Don King to be a good reference point for a career in a sport with more than its fair share of image problems.

Was he just another of those image problems himself?

Well, that depended on your perspective. The fight game in general wouldn't worry too much – by definition, it is no place for shrinking violets, in or out of the ring.

Many remembered that he was an old pug himself, having had nine professional fights, for five wins, as a heavyweight in his long-gone youth. At the time of his foray into management he was in his late 50s and living in a fortified mansion on the outskirts of Melbourne, where he had installed a ring so that he could keep fit by sparring. I went there one Saturday morning for a media call for the sport's other most controversial figure, Anthony Mundine, and Gatto spent more time prancing around inside the ropes than Mundine did. Anyone with more courage than sense might have been indiscreet enough to suggest that he was showing off, but you wouldn't catch me saying that. 'I can handle myself, I hit pretty hard,' he had told me at our first meeting. 'But look, I don't want to hit anyone – and I don't want anyone to hit me. If someone had a crack, obviously I'd retaliate but I hope that doesn't happen. I'm always worried if I hit someone I'd kill 'em because they'd hit their head on the ground or something, and 'see ya later."

Gatto, who can be disarmingly charming to meet, has always loved mixing with the fighters and has always been popular with them. In that environment, he is a celebrity. 'He is an asset to the sport,' said former world champion Barry Michael, a latter-day promoter himself, as well as a prominent media commentator. 'Mick Gatto's a good man,' said legendary American heavy-hitter Mike Tyson, who once did three years in jail for rape.

And perhaps unsurprisingly, there have been a lot of fight fans in town who do not hesitate to find the price of an expensive table when invited by Gatto to attend any of the promotions with which he associates himself, usually those officially promoted by Amatruda, an extremely smart operator without whom the sport would have been well and truly on struggle street in recent years.

Even the then chairman of the professional boxing board, prominent lawyer Bernie Balmer, saw no reason – at first – to deny Gatto his wish. 'He has grand ideas and might be good for boxing – we'll wait and see,'

Balmer told me. But when it emerged that 'Bernie the Attorney' had previously represented Gatto in court, he absented himself from the board hearing to consider the licence application, which was duly approved.

Gatto's new status didn't last long, however. The Premier at the time, Denis Napthine, was having none of it and changed the law so that a 'prohibited person' – anyone banned from casinos and racetracks – could not obtain a licence. 'It's important that people who run these events continue to hold the highest standards of integrity,' said sports minister Hugh Delahunty.

It made little difference. Gatto has been a prominent and influential presence at ringside ever since and no-one is made more welcome by the rest of the crowd.

Boxing has long had an ambiguous status, especially in Melbourne, where it thrived in the sixties and seventies thanks largely to the heroics of two popular champions, Lionel Rose and Johnny Famechon, and a weekly television show called TV Ringside, which had a cult following. But the sport has long since forfeited its mainstream media presence. For quite a few years I was pretty much the only newspaper sportswriter with a regular presence at ringside, which was odd because it wasn't as if there weren't enough good stories on offer, or any shortage of people with plenty to say.

To name just some who figure prominently in my scrapbook: Jeff Fenech, Kostya Tszyu, Joe Bugner, Jeff Harding, Anthony Mundine, Barry Michael, Danny Green, Sam Soliman, Lester Ellis and Will Tomlinson, all of whom fought for or won world titles of varying authenticity as home-grown or imported Australians, while being trained, managed or promoted by the likes of Bill Mordey, Johnny Lewis, Tony Mundine and Max Markson, as well as a number of other identities not entirely unacquainted with law enforcement authorities. No other sport I have been involved in, with the possible exception of horse racing, has provided quite such a memorable cast of characters – most of them likeable, helpful and eminently quotable.

Despite setting foot in the ring himself only once as an amateur, Mordey contributed more to modern boxing history than most – in fact, he is credited with resurrecting it during the eighties when it was almost out on its feet.

He did that by 'discovering' Fenech and then turning him into a three-time world champion and then doing the same for Tszyu, before acrimonious splits with both boxers. Mordey staged 24 world title fights. Bugner – the English heavyweight who twice went the distance with Muhammad Ali before basing himself in Australia – Harding and Ellis were other prominent names in his stable.

He was one of a kind: a knockabout sportswriter with the Sydney *Daily Mirror* evening newspaper where he specialised in rugby league, tennis, boxing and his great passion racing, Mordey was described at his funeral in 2004 as 'a unique character – a villain, knave and rascal of warmth and generosity who enriched life immensely.'

I'm happy to second that slightly double-sided sentiment having met him early in his new life as a boxing promoter not long after I watched from ringside as Fenech was, without a doubt, robbed blind of a medal at the 1984 Los Angeles Olympic Games by judges who were either incompetent or corrupt (and it could easily have been either in those days). I found him in tears outside the venue, promising anyone in earshot that he would now turn pro and win a world title. With Mordey's astute management and Lewis's down-to-earth training techniques he was as good as his word within seven months, and one of the great Australian sporting careers was up and running all the way to the International Boxing Hall of Fame.

Even though Mordey, Fenech and Lewis were all from Sydney, they fought almost exclusively in Melbourne – the spiritual home of the fight game – for the second half of Fenech's career, and mostly successfully. But not entirely.

This was where Fenech met his match – in spades.

In 1991, he fought the accomplished Ghanian Azumah Nelson in Las Vegas for the WBC super-featherweight title and was again almost certainly robbed when the judges returned a split decision draw even though the Australian looked to have had far the better of the contest, especially in the closing rounds.

Nelson came to Melbourne a year later for a rematch, staged by Mordey at the unlikely venue of the Carlton footy ground in front of 30,000 people – perhaps the biggest fight in Australian boxing history, then and for many more years.

In his hotel room a week before the fight, the affable African broke down in tears while telling me, in one of the more intriguingly emotional interviews I ever conducted, that Don King had sold him into virtual slavery with a group of his countrymen who took most of his earnings from every fight, and this one would be no different, and also that at one stage earlier in his career he had a vision about his ill wife and when he arrived at the hospital to check on her, the love of his life had died.

It all came completely out of the blue, without prompting, and given how much expensive gold bling he was wearing, the slavery claim seemed a bit far-fetched. But his distress about his lost wife was so clearly genuine that I accepted the whole story as gospel, and never found out any differently even though it later became apparent that the so-called slave had become a very wealthy individual.

He told me one other thing – and this certainly proved true enough. Namely, that he would knock out Fenech no later than the seventh round – he did it in eight, comprehensively, claiming that he had merely miscounted. Perhaps he had been looking at the ring girls instead of the numbered cards they carried at each break.

It was Fenech's first defeat in 28 fights and he was never quite the same again, losing another two of four more bouts before retiring in May 1996, with his record standing at 29 wins from 32 fights.

He accepted it with dignity and class on the day but also claimed he had engineered his own downfall by being over-confident and taking liberties with his preparation, including bedding three girls a day – no wonder his legs went from under him.

He never got over it. It rankled. He refused to accept that Nelson was a better boxer and that, in turn, rankled with the pride of Ghana, who also recognised it as a potential earner. And so, 16 years later, in June 2004, the pair decided to come out of retirement and go at it a third time, again in Melbourne. Nelson was 49, Fenech 43. It had all the makings of a travesty, an insult to the reputations of two superb warriors, and a body-blow for the sport's fragile credibility.

But there was no talking them out of it – maybe Mordey could have done so, but he had been dead for four years and he and Fenech had finished up not on speaking terms anyway, which was sad.

Lewis agreed to take his customary place in Fenech's corner after convincing himself that it would be a respectable spectacle – but making it clear that once it was over, nothing like it should ever happen again.

A couple of weeks out, I visited Fenech at his Sydney mansion to satisfy myself that he was fair dinkum about it, that it wasn't just some elaborate, futile con job and found him going flat out in a lengthy training session in his private gym, looking as fit as a flea. He was well on the way to losing 20kg to meet the agreed weight of 70kg. He took obvious pleasure in showing me his impressive collection of Grange Hermitage red wine and French champagne – it wasn't there for show, but evidence of the good life he had enjoyed since finishing up the first time – but, alas, he offered me only what he was drinking himself, water.

Nelson, too, seemed to be hell-bent on making sure his pride wasn't hurt.

The public scepticism knew no bounds – 'if people buy this, gullibility has plumbed new depths,' one letter to the editor said, capturing the mood accurately. And yet, there was an undeniable curiosity, too, especially as Fenech's 'I love youse all' schtick had made him extremely popular in his heyday.

From where I sat, the trick was to decide how to straddle the fine line between taking it too seriously and not seriously enough, made no easier by the arrival of flamboyant Sydney marketing entrepreneur Max Markson to oversee the promotion.

There has never been anything Markson won't do to sell a ticket and this, his first – but far from last – foray into the fight game was no exception. 'Anything you want them to do – if you want a photo of them changing nappies, that can be arranged,' he cheerfully assured me.

I was on my guard with the likeable but devious spruiker, but not guarded enough. A couple of days before the fight, he called a press conference at the casino where he introduced an American named James

Smith, who claimed to be Nelson's biggest fan to the point where he had always flown around the world to watch him every time he ever fought – and to back him to win. Whereupon, he produced $250,000 in crisp cash for a bet with Fenech's manager Joey Melham, with both boxers participating in the photo call.

It seemed feasible enough – the money was on the table, after all – so we reported it in good faith. It didn't register that we were in a casino where that amount of cash might not be hard to procure for an hour or so, or, for that matter, to inquire whether Melham had the wherewithal to participate.

The next time I saw Smith, if indeed that was his name, was in a nightclub on fight night when he walked up, admitted he had never heard of Nelson until he met Markson in the bar the night before the stunt, and apologised for lying to me, the rest of the media and by extension the public. I angrily confronted Markson, who was utterly unfazed. 'It's just publicity,' he laughed, rejecting my suggestion that he apologise for conning the public.

It came as no great surprise, then, that when Gatto announced himself as a promoter, the publicity for that was being handled by Markson, who had become a regular at ringside in Melbourne. One night at The Pavilion, he tapped me on the shoulder and said there was someone in a private bar upstairs I might want to meet. So there was – Ben Johnson, the infamous Canadian sprinter who was thrown out of athletics after winning the 100m gold medal in world record time at the Seoul Olympics in 1992 and then testing positive for steroids, had slipped secretly into Melbourne on some unspecified business assignment – and Max had brought him to the fights for a night out. I ended up with an unexpected, exclusive interview – probably Markson's idea of a belated apology – and walked away thinking they were a good pair: both very good at what they did but neither to be taken entirely on face value.

But we digress. Credit where it's due, Markson made sure Fenech and Nelson, already wealthy men, got a big pay-day, with a fair bit left over for charity. It was part sporting event, part business deal, part charity effort, part showbiz promotion and part social occasion, but a lot of people spent up big to either be there – about 8000 – or to watch on pay TV. It was a multi-million-dollar production.

For their money, the punters got the full 10 rounds of whatever it was they came to see. A few found it unwatchable and I agreed that it wasn't pretty but nor was it the embarrassment many had feared. Fenech, despite fighting with a broken rib he had not declared beforehand and with his fragile hands giving him trouble as they always had, got a clear points verdict from two judges while a third found a way to declare it a draw. In due course, Nelson complained that he had been dudded because the arrangement had always been that the result would be a draw. True or false? That's anybody's guess from this distance.

So what did it prove?

For Fenech, nothing much – but at least it is on his official record as a win, squaring the ledger with his nemesis, for whatever that's worth.

For everyone else – that the concept of seniors boxing, no matter how big the names might be, should be consigned to history, never to return.

That said, I have always had great admiration for Melbourne boxer Sam Soliman, who had the last of his 62 professional fights in April, 2019, at the age of 45, a year older than Fenech was for the comeback. Well, not 'always' – almost a decade earlier, it seemed to me that 'King' Soliman was pushing his luck by defying Father Time, the implacable enemy of all boxers. Bernie the Attorney agreed that he and his board were watching closely, ready to insist that he quit if it became apparent he was endangering himself.

Bernie and I were both wrong. Soliman not only pushed on successfully, but he won the highly-regarded IBF middleweight world title in 2014, by far the most important of his 46 victories.

The most impressive thing about Soliman – a fanatic in the gym – is that he might have been Australia's fittest and most likeable sportsman, a God-fearing family man who was never into drink or drugs and who spent much of his down time helping disadvantaged kids. As every birthday rolled by it seemed incredible that he could fight on and on, but he was always a reminder that the great American heavyweight George Foreman – another agreeable, God-fearing indestructible veteran, as I discovered when he made an entertaining visit to Melbourne during the 2006 Commonwealth Games to promote his business interests, mainly a portable meat griller – was able to reclaim the world championship after a long absence at 45 and fought on for three more years.

Soliman signed off by defeating the anonymous Mark Lucas for the WBF middleweight title, a lightly-regarded 'world title' but still a satisfying way to take his leave from a sport for which he was nothing but a very good advertisement for 23 years.

Danny Green was 43 when he narrowly beat Anthony Mundine, 41, in Adelaide in February, 2017, and that wasn't a particularly edifying spectacle, either, although at least both were still active, if only just in Green's case. And there was a genuine grudge element to their rivalry which kept people interested enough to guarantee both a million-dollar pay-day.

Green, who was a popular winner because of his public campaign against 'coward punch' street violence, had the good sense to call it quits but Mundine's over-developed ego wouldn't allow him to admit defeat let alone walk away forever, which resulted in him being humiliated in a matter of seconds by Jeff Horn two fights later. That made it five defeats from his last nine fights, which – together with the reality that the three world titles he claimed all had asterisks attached because the men he beat were not undisputed world-beaters themselves – means that he is not entitled to keep pumping himself up as the best Australian fighter of the modern era.

Following the Rose-Famechon era, which is now ancient history, that title probably belongs to Fenech – if not, who?

The best I saw was a kid I clapped eyes on for the first time the day Fenech came to grief against Nelson. Actually, I didn't. Just as an unknown Kostya Tszyu was climbing into the ring for his first professional fight, against one Darrel Hiles, I paused on my way to my seat to buy a hamburger – and by the time I turned around, the undercard fight was over in a brief flurry of powerful punches lasting only a minute.

Another of Bill Mordey's discoveries had been unveiled to the world.

The canny Mordey had recognised the young Russian's immense potential at an amateur world championship in Sydney in 1991 and persuaded him to move to Sydney to turn professional.

His progress wasn't as rapid as Fenech's but after 13 undefeated outings in just under three years, Mordey had him challenging the accomplished Puerto Rican Jake 'The Snake' Rodriguez for the IBF super-lightweight title in Las Vegas on January 28, 1995, conveniently for me just up the road, really, from San Diego where I had been watching a very different sport, the America's Cup yachting.

Mordey knew he had a winner in the ring but what he didn't see coming were the massive ramifications outside it.

The first clue was the presence in the gym of an apparently uninvited character with a Russian accent, a Sydney car dealer who introduced himself as Vlad Warton and inquired with an oily smile who each and everyone present was, including me.

He obviously wasn't there just as a fight fan. There had to be another agenda.

With Lewis in his corner, Tszyu destroyed Rodriguez in six rounds, landing an incredible 401 punches in 21 minutes.

After the fight I found Mordey drinking alone in one of the MGM Grand Casino's many bars at 2.30am with Tszyu, Warton and other family members and supporters, many of them Russian, celebrating elsewhere.

Fenech materialised and whispered something to Mordey, who then told me that some jewellery had gone missing from Tszyu's room. I decided to go and see what the story was. The fighter and his entourage weren't in the room, but the door was open so I walked in only to be confronted by a burly, hostile off-duty cop from Sydney who was moonlighting as a security guard, probably hired by Warton and certainly not by Mordey.

This thug was threatening to break my head until Fenech materialised again, told him I was a friend and to back off – and then told me to piss off too, in no uncertain terms.

Next morning I visited Mordey in his room and found him clad only in his underpants sucking on a fag and a can of beer, a very Mordey-esque scenario.

'Bill,' I said, 'you've found another star here, and another cash cow –

but I reckon you're going to hear more from the mysterious Mr Wharton.'

'You're not wrong,' he replied.

Sure enough, not long after we all got back to Australia Tszyu announced that he was leaving the Mordey camp to be managed by you know who.

After a protracted and very bitter wrangle the matter ended up in court with several other parties including Fenech involved and Tszyu was ordered to pay Mordey a multi-million-dollar settlement for breach of contract.

'Break-even Bill,' as he was universally known, had finished well ahead – permanently.

During this time feelings ran so high that Mordey raced a moderately successful racehorse named Kostya, which won $80,000 – but he never called it by that name, referring to it only as 'the horse.'

Happily, the two made their peace before Mordey lost his battle with cancer.

Eventually Tzsyu and Warton fell out over money, too, and when he died mysteriously in China in 2018 Warton also owed a small fortune to Fenech, who said he didn't care because he considered him a friend.

Tszyu, who grew up in Siberia and also had Korean and Mongol blood, often said that he enjoyed living in Australia because he considered it the best country in the world, but he nonetheless eventually returned to Russia, apparently permanently, leaving his family behind.

He was an intriguing character who was pleasant enough to deal with and who seemed to enjoy engaging with people while also cultivating an understated air of latent menace.

During a dawn training session in a Sydney park one day, he warned Australia's best sports photographer Wayne Ludbey that if he came any closer in search of a close-up of the sweat pouring off his face, he would 'be in a dangerous place' … in other words, the diligent snappper might cop one for his trouble.

He didn't sound like he was joking – and Ludbey wasn't about to find out by disobeying.

Later, over breakfast at his Sydney mansion, Tszyu took delight in showing Ludbey and me his pets – a couple of poisonous snakes – in the presence of his then eight-year-old son Timophey, who has since grown up and demonstrated that he can go a bit inside the ropes too, demolishing former world champion – and one-time conqueror of the legendary Filipino Manny Pacquaio – Jeff Horn in August 2020.

Tszyu soldiered on through the legal distractions, assembling a record – 31 wins with 25 knockouts and two defeats – that had some experts declaring him to be the best pound-for-pound fighter in the world, whatever that hackneyed expression means exactly.

It was enough to get him entry to the International Boxing hall of Fame and the Sports Australia Hall of Fame, alongside Fenech in both cases.

It remains a matter of opinion who was the best but there is no disputing that the two of them were without peer in Australia during their respective eras, which overlapped only briefly as Fenech was on the way down and Tszyu passed him on the way up.

ONE FALSE
STEP HAUNTS
A CHAMPION

Cycling, both on the road and the track, has been an acquired taste for many Australian sports fans – but it has been an impressive success story in the past 20 years or so, despite being its own worst enemy at times. In Australia, it has suffered from questionable administration for decades, almost crippled by financial instability despite churning out a steady stream of Olympic gold medals, producing a winner of the Tour de France for the first time, establishing a race capable of bringing the big professional teams to this country for serious competition and generally making an important impact on the peloton worldwide.

Internationally, an entrenched doping culture that had been in place for eons – personified by the disgraced American Lance Armstrong – almost brought the sport to its knees, and might have done so if not for a tendency among the European nations that dominate it, France, Spain and Italy mainly, to shrug dismissively because of a cynical view that if everybody is doing it, then there are no victims – just more superhuman performances. That might have something to do with why Armstrong, who won the Tour de France seven years running, was able to get away with it for so long.

But of course, there were victims - and probably still are, despite the sport making a largely successful, although far from flawless, attempt to clean up its act across the second decade of the 21st century. Those who paid the price were the riders who opted out of the dark side and tried to compete cleanly, soon realising that this was next to impossible to do. One of the few who succeeded was Australia's Cadel Evans, whose breakthrough win in the 2011 Tour de France – after having twice been runner-up – was, in my opinion, the single greatest feat by an Australian sportsman for at least half a century, quite possibly ever. Evans never failed any of the countless drug tests he took and had never been remotely suspected of having anything to hide, which makes his defining performance all the more memorable, even heroic. It is a toss-up whether Australia is more proud of Evans for winning the Tour drug-free or winning it at all. Certainly, those in the sport should bow to him every time he walks past because of the respect he has generated on their behalf as well as his own.

And then there were the riders starting out in the sport, young, ambitious, talented – and naive. As the millennium hoved into sight and ticked over, there were waves of them coming through in Australia. They might have been babes in the wood but they knew the score. They had crucially important decisions to make about morality, integrity and self-esteem, and the wrong answers had the potential to wreck their lives – or at least their pathway to fame and fortune – or make it hard for them to look at themselves in the mirror forevermore. Seeking advice and guidance was a tricky business at home, where even a respected vice-president of the Cycling Australia board of directors, one Stephen Hodge, owned up to having been a doper in his competitive days. So did a leading coach, Matt White, who was suspended from his job with the fledgling GreenEDGE team, the only Australian outfit competing at the elite level, the World Tour, in Europe. Sure, there were plenty of honest coaches and advisors around but it was no easy task to differentiate and once an L-plate rider had moved overseas, one step in the wrong direction could prove disastrous – even if it didn't become immediately obvious.

And that's what eventually transpired, not just for any moderately talented young wanna-be-if-he-could-be, but an immensely gifted, ambitious, brave and proud young South Australian named Stuart O'Grady. Looking back, the term 'all-time great' fits him like a glove – one of the four or five best road racers Australia has produced and an Olympic gold medallist on the track – and for a long while so did that other cliche, 'an ornament to the sport.' That was until the dark day arrived when one fateful act from the distant past came back to haunt him and brought his decorated career to a premature and painful end, leaving him with a stigma that could not be completely unloaded for years to come – possibly never.

To appreciate the magnitude of his fall from grace, it is necessary to set it against both his achievements and his personality. To take the second one first, one of the words that best defines him is courage. All racing cyclists are brave, or at least well aware that it is no sport for wusses. Coming off the bike at high speed, wearing only a Lycra body-suit and lightweight head-gear can cause serious injury and it happened to O'Grady often, resulting in extended stints in hospital and rehab but he was always back in the saddle at the first opportunity, sometimes still in debilitating pain. The worst incident was when he had to abandon stage 8 of the 2007 Tour de France after crashing on a descent, fracturing eight – yes, eight – ribs, his right shoulder blade, right collarbone and three vertebrae and punctured his right lung. By the time he finally walked away altogether, he had lost count of the broken bones — and if he ever complained or looked for sympathy, the public never heard about it.

His career could not have been much more lavishly adorned with accolades and achievements but unfortunately there is a self-inflicted asterisk. He won an Olympic gold medal on the track, teaming with Graeme Brown in the Madison in Athens in 2004, and a silver and two bronze from six Olympics altogether. There were also four gold and three minor medals at the Commonwealth Games and two gold and two bronze at the world championships. He rode the Tour de France 17 times between 1997 and 2013, equalling the record held by American George Hincapie. He won stages in 1998 and 2004 and spent several days in the famous Maillot Jaune, the leader's yellow jersey, on two occasions and was runner-up in the points classification, the green jersey, four times. In 2007 he became the first Australian to win a major one-day Classic, one of the so-called Monuments, when he saluted in the Paris-Roubaix, a race so demanding that it is colloquially known as the Hell of the North. It was his greatest triumph, among many.

So what was the problem? Why the Asterisk?

It exists because O'Grady has confessed to experimenting with doping. Put as bluntly as that, it is a damning self-condemnation, and constitutes all the ammunition some people need to relegate his achievements and credibility to a file marked 'never to be forgiven,' which has, sadly and unreasonably, been the case for him. But life is rarely that simple. In my opinion, it is far too harsh to label him a drug cheat and leave it at that, in perpetuity, with no allowances for circumstance.

This is one of the problems with the scourge of drugs in sport generally, in that the hard-liners see it as only a black and white issue – either you're a remorseless, calculating villain (hello Lance Armstrong) or you're a squeaky clean paragon of all that is good about sport (welcome, Cadel!) with no room in between for human fallibility, especially in people with little experience of life, no willingness to concede that everybody makes mistakes, sometimes quickly and sincerely corrected, sometimes not.

O'Grady has been the perfect example of this unfortunate dichotomy and no matter how sceptical you might be about the extent and duration of his sin, there is no convincing evidence that he belongs in the same Hall of Shame as Armstrong and his ilk. In my opinion, which is not universally shared, it is not, by a long way, the normal cynical, sorry tale of unrepentant, selfish cheating of which Armstrong and his cohort were guilty.

O'Grady's story is a cautionary tale for all young sportsmen who might be dazzled, confused and intimidated by finding themselves being thrown in at the deep end to sink or swim.

So what actually happened?

That's best explained by revisiting *Green Gold & Bold*, the book I co-wrote about the 100th edition of the Tour de France in 2013 with John Trevorrow, who is a former international rider and modern-day commentator and administrator. He is a close mate of O'Grady's, which made our involvement in the unfolding drama a painful exercise both for him and for me given that over a decade of dealing with O'Grady I, too, had come to admire him and regard him as a friend. But the story had to be written, of course – and seven years later, it still resonated as strongly as any other I have ever written.

This is it as it appeared in the book:

Stuart O'grady's wonderful cycling career ended badly and sadly with a confession that he had once succumbed to the temptation to use performance enhancing drugs.

The eye of any sports doping storm is an unforgiving place for an athlete to be, and the 39-year-old veteran – widely regarded as Australia's greatest all-round cyclist and one of the most admired international performers in any sport – certainly discovered the truth of that very quickly.

But for all the opprobrium that engulfed him, time will probably tell that this was one case where a certain amount of sympathy would not be out of place. Indeed, in his home town of Adelaide – and in the cycling community generally –-that was already happening within a month of his shock revelation.

The teak-tough South Australian spent the overwhelming majority of a long and extremely successful career as a passionate ambassador for cycling and is entitled to have that taken into account when posterity balances the books on his life and times.

And while there is no escaping the reality that he made one very bad decision when he experimented with the banned blood booster EPO before the infamous 2008 Tour de France, he was a young athlete a long way from home, with little in the way of the advice and support systems that exist these days, and was under intense competitive pressure. As he readily admits himself, that does not add up to an excuse — but it is an explanation that should not be dismissed as meaningless or insincere either.

Cycling lived in a much murkier world in those days and has now moved on immeasurably with the 100th Tour de France arriving at the finish line in Paris without any suggestion that doping was still the problem it once was. Indeed, the organisers reported that not one of 622 blood and urine tests turned up positive.

The Tour was an uplifting experience for Australian cycling in general and Orica-GreenEDGE, the nation's only elite level pro team, in particular, but O'Grady's plight provided a painful sequel.

The popular veteran rode his 17th and final Tour knowing he was going to have to confront the consequences at the end of it, and that his superb career was over before he intended it to be.

He didn't have far to look for a friend in need. The team's sports director Matt White had been through this same ordeal only a matter of months earlier, but with a happier ending. To say the least, to have your inaugural head coach and your first captain under a drugs cloud, one after the other, is not an acceptable situation for any team, let alone one as committed to the fight for clean sport as Orica-GreenEDGE had been from its launch two years earlier. But the fall-out extended well beyond GreenEDGE – this was Australian cycling's nightmare in broad daylight.

As a daily newspaper sports columnist I have often written in praise of the golden era that Australian road cyclists such as Evans, O'Grady, Robbie McEwen, Brad McGee, Simon Gerrans, Matt Goss and many others have created throughout the 21st century.

It has, rightly, been a point of enormous pride for the sport, enabling it to achieve unprecedented popularity among recreational participants and to greatly magnify its presence in the mainstream sports media.

But I have also suggested often that if one of these high-profile champions were ever to test positive, the damage could be enormous in terms of credibility and respect.

That's why O'Grady's stunning mea culpa constituted a crisis, with no real way of predicting where the ramifications would end.

Certainly, anyone labouring under the naive assumption that Australian cyclists were, without exception, squeaky-clean in an obviously tainted environment over a long period of time – something that had never seemed remotely realistic – have now had their delusions rudely revealed.

The unravelling of the age of innocence began in October 2012, when White confessed to having doped in the years before his guilty conscience got the better of him and he retired, swapping his black hat for a white one and joining the fight against the drugs scourge. That temporarily cost him his job at GreenEDGE and, permanently, his other role as director of Cycling Australia's road program. He served a six-months ban – greatly discounted because of his co-operation with the authorities

– but was back holding the reins at GreenEDGE in time for the next Tour de France after anti-doping expert Nikki Vance recommended that he had done all he could to atone for his sins and should be reinstated.

Vance had been asked by GreenEDGE owner Gerry Ryan to investigate the team's doping protocols and ethics. She gave it the thumbs up but told me later: 'I'm not so naive to think there may not be someone with a past, but I'm not concerned with current riders.' She added that if someone other than White was to admit something they could expect to be sacked.

At the same time as White's past was revealed, Cycling Australia's vice-president Stephen Hodge, an accomplished rider in his day who had ridden the Tour de France regularly, also fessed up. He had no choice but to abandon his influential role, which was the correct thing to do, but unfortunate, because Cycling Australia has never been so blessed with good administrators that it could afford to lose one of its best ones.

And then along came O'Grady, by far the biggest fish of the three.

In the professional peloton White and Hodge were average performers with very limited public profiles, but O'Grady was an all-time great both on the track and the road, a figure of international importance and respect.

So the impact of his fall from grace was more severe – and the response more savage. He knew he was in trouble when, just before the Tour began, he read that the French Senate had investigated the 1998 edition of the race, notorious for the French team Festina having been caught red-handed with a car-load of drugs.

The French Press reported that the Government would be releasing the names of dozens of riders whose urine samples from back then had retrospectively tested positive to EPO, for which there had been no test at the time.

Four Australians – O'Grady, McEwen, Patrick Jonker and another of GreenEDGE's sports directors, Neil Stephens – contested that Tour, Stephens with Festina.

Knowing he could be on the list put O'Grady in a deeply uncomfortable place for the duration of what had quickly become a triumphant campaign for everybody around him. Weeks earlier, O'Grady had extended his contract until the end of the 2014 season, giving him the opportunity now to ride an 18th Tour, more than anyone else had ever done. It would break the tie with retired American George Hincapie, who also rode 17. (Since then, three of Hincapie's rides have been removed from the record for his part in Armstrong's cheating.)Perhaps presciently, O'Grady said at the time: 'Obviously you never know what's around the corner in terms of any plan we've put together. Hopefully it all works out.' Famous last words!

About a week out from the end of the Tour O'Grady declined to confirm those plans when asked by an Australian journalist. Sounding very weary, he said it wasn't a good time to discuss his future.

This was the first faint sound of alarm bells ringing.

There was no sound at all emanating from the GreenEDGE camp.

O'Grady attended the team party on the Sunday night the race ended, as did I, but seemed to be in a more subdued mood than the rest of the riders, who had much to celebrate between them, having won two stages and put two riders into the famed yellow jersey worn by the race leader.

The next afternoon the team issued an email press release stating that O'Grady had retired. This, too, was most unusual — indeed, in the eyes of the media anyway, highly inappropriate. One of the great Australian sporting champions of this or any other era was either being asked or permitted to walk off into the night without even a press conference to enable the media to pay proper tribute.

Thinking their month-long assignments had been completed, journalists returned from their own wind-down lunches in Paris — in at least one case in the company of White and other GreenEDGE personnel — to find that was far from the case.

Another big story had broken — ostensibly a good news one — and yet the central figure was unavailable for interview.

The alarm bells grew louder.

And then, two days later the Senate report was released, naming 30 riders. Eighteen of them had returned positive tests, including the three place getters, Italian Mario Pantani, who had since died, Germany's Jan Ullrich and America's Bobby Julich.

O'Grady's name was missing from the list of positives but was included among another 12 deemed to be 'suspicious'.

That didn't prove anything – and it provided the option of standing his ground and denying he had any case to answer.

But to his considerable credit, he decided to get it off his chest, which he did in an emotional and explosive interview with Reece Homfray, a News Ltd journalist from Adelaide who had been spending months preparing to write O'Grady's autobiography – a story now destined to take a very different tack.

O'Grady told Homfray he had administered the EPO during a two-week period before that Tour, but not during it, and having been alarmed by the fall-out from the Festina scandal he decided never to cheat again. And did not.

He kept his guilty secret for 15 years.

'That's the hardest thing to swallow out of all this – it was such a long time ago and one very bad judgement is going to taint a lot of things and people will have a lot of questions,' he said.

With drugs in sport having been one of the most volatile news issues in the media for months, and the Essendon AFL club under the spotlight fiercely at the same time as O'Grady came clean, his confession created uproar.

The first ramification was already in place – he and GreenEDGE were no longer an item and his career was finished. GreenEDGE never used the word 'sack' or any synonym of it – as had been the case with White, they preferred to enable the culprit to dismiss himself.

They did, however, issue a statement signed by general manager Shayne Bannan, which read: 'Orica-Green-EDGE supports Stuart O'Grady's decision to step forward and place the finding of the French Senate Report of today into perspective regarding his own past.

'The team would also like to express its support of Stuart as a person and as an advocate for a clean sport. Like the majority of the riders in his generation, he was also exposed to the issues and wrongdoings of the sport and made some wrong choices in that environment.

'We would like to underline that in all of our interactions with Stuart, he has always been extremely clear about the right path for the sport and we believe that certain mistakes in the past shouldn't be allowed to tarnish his entire career and his integrity as a person.

'Orica-GreenEDGE is proud to work in a sport that is at the forefront of the fight against doping and that we compete and win as a 100% clean team. The sport has undergone a revolution in setting up the right future for cycling and we consider ourselves one of the strongest advocates for this.'

Cycling Australia admitted the fears that any such revelation would be hugely harmful were well founded.

'This is a real disappointment to us as a custodian of the sport,' chief executive Graham Fredericks said.

It was, he said, now O'Grady's responsibility to help rebuild the public trust in the sport.

'Stuart and a number of other riders in recent decades have kept coming out with constant streams of disclaimers. Now Stuart and those riders have to turn around and really put back that trust into the community and into the public. I think that is going to take a long time.'

Fredericks said great gains had been made to restore the trust of the cycling community but he conceded O'Grady's admission would stall the recovery.

'It's going to take a long time particularly at the men's road elite level,' he said. 'Where there is money there is going to be people trying to cheat and that is where it is going to take a long time to restore public confidence.'

Elsewhere, the reaction was more savage.

The Australian Olympic Committee, which has a zero-tolerance policy to doping, gave O'Grady 24 hours to resign from its Athletes Commission, and when he didn't, they sacked him.

O'Grady competed at six Olympics – only horseman Chris Hoy has done more – and won four medals on the track, including gold in the Madison in Athens in 2004. The AOC said it was possible they could be stripped from him. (That never happened.) President John Coates said athletes who elected him as one of their representatives to the AOC were 'entitled to be angry knowing they supported an athlete who cheated.' He would no longer be regarded as a champion.

O'Grady was particularly dismayed by this, pointing out that he had always aspired to represent Australia at what he regarded as the pinnacle of sport and had never considered going down the doping path there.

The South Australian Government, who sent Sports Minister, Leon Bignell and three staff on a junket to France during the Tour so they could applaud O'Grady, was now wondering whether it could make him pay back money he was paid to promote the state in Europe.

At a function in the grounds of the GreenEDGE hotel, Bignell dispensed South Australian wines and meat pies and presented O'Grady with a Port Adelaide AFL guernsey, which the lifelong supporter proudly donned. But as the fall-out continued, the club sacked him as its ambassador.

The onslaught, from official sources and on social media, was so relentless that his family — led by his father, Brian, a former competitive cyclist himself — felt compelled to release a statement pleading for the public to realise that their son was 'not superhuman.'

He needed people to understand why he made a bad decision as a vulnerable young man trying to survive in a difficult era, they said.

'To us, his honesty now has proven his integrity. To us that is what counts.'

Should there be any sympathy?

In my view, the answer is yes – absolutely. And I would certainly get no argument about that from John Trevorrow, who has known the O'Grady family since he competed against Brian more than 30 years ago and who is one of Stuey's closest mates and confidantes. Trevorrow's admiration for O'Grady is encapsulated in our book in his list of Australia's all-time 50 greatest road racers, where he is placed fourth, a whisker behind third-placed Robbie McEwen.

That's where he remains. That is recognition that O'Grady's life's work, more than two decades of it, surely outweighs one mistake made long ago.

Even serious crimes do not necessarily cost 15 years of your life.

In fact, the maximum suspension for a one-off sports doping offence is two years, and if that had applied to O'Grady in 1998 he would have been back on his bike by 2000 and everything he achieved after that would be legitimate and worthy of high praise, not endless recrimination.

He would have lost his stage win in that Tour de France but his two greatest triumphs, the Paris-Roubaix victory in 2007 and the Olympic gold medal in 2004, would be safe, along with many other victories.

His record would still be enough to place him high on any list.

And he would not have been prevented from carrying out his late-life role as an inspiration and mentor to young riders, putting back into the sport that had given him so much.

Of course, for this charitable view to be valid, one has to accept his assurances that his offence was a one-off and that he rode the vast majority of his career clean. The sceptics have been thick on the ground about that and who could blame them? However, my instincts – developed over more than a decade of dealing with him, which has always been a pleasure – are that he is an honest, proud and reliable man with a deep and enduring passion for his sport.

I am prepared to believe him and I think most of the cycling media agree. As much as his confession hurt him personally – his reputation might never recover and the financial price will be high given he is unlikely to work in the sport for some considerable time – the realisation that he has damaged cycling will pain him even more. He has said he will spend the rest of his life trying to undo that damage.

He had no-one to blame for his predicament – not even his French team at the time, GAN, because he says he sourced and took the EPO entirely off his own bat – and he did not seek to blame anyone.

Nor should it be forgotten what a tough brave athlete he was. He has broken virtually every bone in his body, sometimes several at the same time, in numerous high-speed crashes but has always come back for more. In the end, it wasn't falling off the bike that left him a broken man – it was one bad decision when he was a much younger and less worldly character blinded by the same burning ambitions as hundreds of others around him.

If nothing else, his sorry plight will act as a stark reminder to the new generation of cyclists who, it is universally agreed, are rapidly obliterating the old cultures and breathing new life into a sport that is now nothing like it was 15 years ago.

This has been one of the more difficult, depressing stories I have witnessed in nearly 50 years writing about sport. 'I wish it could be changed but it can't,' OGrady said. So did I.

****

O'Grady's own version of events is also worth recalling in detail, especially as the sceptics have never been able to provide any evidence that he is not telling the truth.

In interviews with Homfray and Trevorrow he guaranteed the doping offence was strictly a one-off. Deep down, he said, he did not feel like a cheat and remained proud of the work he has done with young cyclists.

'I only ever did it the once. People may find that hard to believe and I have trouble understanding myself why I did it that once,' he said. 'But I won all my races clean outside that 1998 Tour de France. After that race I made a decision not to go there again – ever. I can comfortably sit back and I know that no-one can come along and say I have a positive test anywhere else. In 100 years' time my grandkids' kids won't be hearing any new stories about my racing past. I won Paris-Roubaix and my Olympic gold medal plus all my other Tour de France successes clean. I am happy for all my tests ever taken after 1998 to be re-tested anytime. People say your test came back suspicious – not positive – and why didn't I just tough it out. But once I had opened up to my team manager and told my family there was no going back. I couldn't just try to deny it and then another more in-depth test comes along and I'm made out to be a liar. I told one lie and it's going to haunt me forever. I'm not telling any more.'

Before he went public he had to tell his family, Brian and his mother Faye, his wife Anne-Marie, her parents, his sister Leslie and her husband.

'That was the hardest thing,' he said. 'I just sat them down and let them ask all the questions and I answered them honestly. It's a good thing they were not in Australia – they weren't in the Euro bubble, where I was, and it was less of a drama. But of course they were going to cop it when they got home and I felt really sad about that. They are really great people. All I ever wanted to do was make my parents proud.'

O'Grady said he had not struggled with a guilty conscience 'because I've always thought of myself as one of the good guys. I help the youngsters because that is just my nature. I'm a proud Australian and I believe in the future of Australian cycling.' Knowing that the investigation results were imminent – they were originally going to be released on the day of the Queen stage up Alpe d'Huez but lobbying by riders and others saw that postponed until after the Tour – made the entire three weeks an ordeal.

Even when he and his teammates landed an historic victory in the team time trial in stage four, he couldn't fully enjoy the moment.

Asked what he was thinking on the podium that day, he said: 'I was really worried. I just didn't want to be at the Tour and I knew it was time to retire. I was dreading the Alpe d'Huez stage. I wasn't sure but I knew there was a possibility my name would be there. I really wasn't worrying about myself as much as my friends and family and the team. I felt I had let everyone down.'

Why didn't he just brazen it out?

'Well, once I had opened up to Shayne and then told my family straight after the tour then there was no going back. I actually thought there might be some doubt on my test as I didn't take much EPO and when the Festina saga broke out during that 1998 tour I shit myself and got rid of it. There were people going to jail and it's only a bloody bike race. That was enough to scare me off,' he said.

'Shattered is a good word for how I feel and it only goes part of the way. I feel that I've let a lot of good people down. But deep down I don't feel like a cheat. I made a mistake, yes a big one, but I spent the rest of my career racing hard and tough and true.'

O'Grady said he sourced the EPO and administered it without anyone knowing. His French team GAN was not involved.

He then carried it with him during the Tour but never used it during the race. He said he felt he had no other option and had to use it to survive or be competitive in the race during the sport's dirtiest era.

O'Grady said he destroyed the EPO when the Festina affair, where riders were booted off the Tour after police found a boot full of drugs in a team car, blew up in the first week.

He said he sourced the EPO himself – 'I just had to drive over the border and buy it at any pharmacy' – without his team, GAN or anyone else being involved. It was two weeks before the race and he used only small amounts because he had heard horror stories about side-effects.

O'Grady said part of the reason he went down this avenue was that as a young man far from home, he felt isolated and under pressure in what were very different times. Like all riders, he was under pressure to be competitive.

'After my first Tour (in 1997) when I was dropped after 5km on a mountain day and you're questioning what the hell I am doing in this sport, you're not anywhere near competitive at something you're supposed to be pretty good at.

'It wasn't systematic doping. I wasn't trying to deceive people, I was basically trying to survive in what was a very grey area. We're humans who make mistakes. It was a decision which I made at the time which I thought would basically get me through the Tour. I guess part of me deep down wants to prove that you can do the Tour clean, win Olympic gold medals clean. You can do as much as your natural ability allows you to and I've been riding myself into the ground trying to help young guys, to be the leader, and maybe a small part of that it is to punish myself for my own guilt.'

Despite his guilt, he never intended coming forward.

'Who in their right mind in the environment we've been in the last couple of years would stand up and be crucified?' he said. 'I guess I just wanted this to go away and the only person I've cheated out of all this is myself, my family and friends. I've been the one living with it and trying to smash it out ever since. I want to close this chapter of my life and have a fresh start. I realise there is going to be consequences but I don't want to stand in front of people and lie any more. Deep down, I knew I'd made a mistake and if there is anyone on this planet who has never made a mistake come up and throw the first rock.

'I realise my situation is different to most people but we are human beings. I spent my whole childhood dreaming of racing for Australia and every moral gene in my body was anti-doping and anti-cheating, the whole time I was around the Australian Institute of Sport helped me achieve that. Then all of a sudden I was on my own in Europe getting my arse kicked and knowing it was around you, which opened the option for bad judgement.'

Happily, time does heal most wounds – eventually. When Cycling Australia formed a Hall of Fame in 2015, O'Grady was left out of it even though in normal circumstances he would have been entitled to be one of the first chosen. There have since been three more intakes and he still is excluded. However, he pretty quickly made his peace with the Australian Olympic Committee, and was – with Coates's strong approval – elected president of the South Australian Olympians Club, where he worked hard to help athletes from all sports transition back to everyday life. An offer to help coach the national cycling team was not taken up. 'I hope my experience and knowledge will be of use some day,' he says. It now is. After the 2019 edition of the Tour Down Under, the only World Tour stage race in Australia, the original race director Mike Turter retired and was replaced by – O'Grady. He was officially back on board.

Asked if the affair was still being held against him in any way, he said: 'It's a hard question to answer. I would really hope everyone has moved on. I have never met anybody with anything negative to say to me as yet and I'd hope people have forgiven a mistake I made 20 years ago.'

And yet, the fall-out continues in other ways – and for other people, it seems. That includes me. I have had a long association with the Sport Australia Hall of Fame and in 2019 when that prestigious organisation needed to fill a vacancy on the committee that selects the new inductees and other award winners each year, the Chief Executive Tania Sullivan recommended me because of my deep knowledge of its history, expectations and ethos. The board of directors chose someone else, Sullivan later told me as she departed the job, because they felt I had been too generous in my support of O'Grady the drug cheat. That was disappointing, not because I didn't get a gig I had never aspired to, asked for or even knew was available, but because it demonstrated such a rigid lack of empathy and compassion for a fellow champion.

SURVIVING AND THRIVING ON TOUR 100

Stuart O'Grady wasn't the only one who failed to derive maximum enjoyment from the 2013 Tour de France, the 100th edition of the great race which had begun in 1903 but been suspended for five years while each of the two world wars devastated Europe. His mate John Trevorrow did it hard too. In fact, he was lucky it didn't kill him – and if it had, he probably would have had only himself to blame. But that didn't make another mutual mate Ron Gower and I any less comfortable about heading out for dinner one night soon after the race began in the Mediterranean island of Corsica — Napoleon's birthplace 234 years earlier – not knowing whether we would return to the hotel room the three of us were sharing and find him alive or dead. Just in case it turned out to be the latter, we cracked a couple of bottles of the best local red we could find and toasted him.

Trevorrow, who was in his mid-sixties at the time, might be the most enthusiastic, committed and knowledgeable personality in Australian cycling, then and still. A pretty handy professional rider back in the day, good enough to win multiple national titles and to ride at the 1972 Munich Olympics, the sport has been his life and no part of it has he been more passionate about than the Tour de France, which has rubbed off on many other people, me being one of them, and Melbourne business, sporting and showbiz entrepreneur Gerry Ryan another – the latter with far-reaching results. It led to Ryan forming the GreenEDGE team, Australia's first and only outfit to compete at the top level, the WorldTour.

Trevorrow should never have contemplated making the trip this time because he had recently been diagnosed with cancer of the oesophagus, which is one of the most difficult forms of the deadly disease to combat. He needed major surgery but when the doctors said it would take about three weeks to organise, he decided that was a big enough window for him to fit the Tour in. The doctors did a double take, his wife of many years, Kaye, stamped her foot, something she's had a lot of practice with him over the journey, and Gower and I rolled our eyes before agreeing to help him get through what was obviously going to be a painful and maybe dangerous ordeal. To make it even more daunting, he insisted that he and I press ahead with plans to write a book together about Australia's history across the 110 years that were about to be celebrated, which was going to require a heavy workload for all 21 days of the race and a fair few before and after. Not only that, he was contracted to write a daily column for his home-town *Geelong Advertiser* newspaper.

We weren't off to a good start when my luggage, containing medication that I needed to keep myself alive, never mind my distressed mate, never made it to Corsica and wasn't seen again for a fortnight. (Traveller's tip for slow learners: always pack medication in carry-on.) Luckily we were on good terms with GreenEDGE and its Spanish doctor replaced the pills and potions – and undertook to keep an eye on Trevorrow, known to one and all as 'Iffy,' as in 'if he' gets it right with whatever he's doing all will be good, but 'if he' doesn't then everyone is in trouble, especially him. The doctor's help was greatly appreciated but of limited value when the patient became extremely ill a couple of days into the race and was unable to immediately travel any further, while the teams had sped off several hundred kilometres from where we were on the picturesque island. What to do? The pre-trip advice from Trevorrow's own specialist at home was that his temperature must never be allowed to exceed 39 and if it did, the consequences could be … well, you get the picture. On this night the thermometer in his mouth was showing 38.9. Gower, who is also an old bike racer from way back, and I put him under a cold shower and then back to bed, turned the air conditioning up full blast, darkened the room – and crossed our fingers. Then we went to dinner.

We returned two hours later not knowing what we would find – but, praise the Lord, not only was he still alive, his temperature had dropped by a tenth of a degree. Our expert nursing had worked – just. By the morning, it had dropped marginally further and although he was still a very sick boy he declared himself good to go. Crisis over – well, not quite. Having a drink was not going to be much of an option for the rest of the trip, and nor was his penchant for huge creamy desserts. But he lived to tell the tale, surviving the surgery when he got home, losing about 30kg of weight he definitely didn't need, and of course eventually reigniting his lifelong love affair with good red wine. Like most stories about Iffy, and there are an endless supply of them, he and Gower and I look back and laugh – but seriously, that dinner for two at a table for three was no laughing matter and could have had a very different outcome. Still, at least the vino went down well.

And at least we somehow managed to finish the book, entitled *Green Gold & Bold: Australia at the 100th Tour de France*. It was never a best-seller but that didn't matter because it was a labour of love for both of us, and for that I can thank Iffy, without whom I probably would never have got around to experiencing what is undoubtedly the world's greatest annual sporting event.

He had once spent time riding professionally in Europe himself, contesting one of the three Grand Tours, the Italian Giro, back in the early eighties. He might have done it more than once and might have graduated to the French showpiece if he – yes, 'if he' – hadn't been just as keen on experiencing la dolce vita – the good life – as he was on adding to the impressive racing record he had accumulated in Australia. In 1991, he and another sports journalist mate, Simon Townley, decided to just turn up at the Tour one year, hire a car and sleep where and when they could as they chased the peloton around the country, sampling menus and wine lists as they went. They got by so well, even if it meant sleeping in the car occasionally, that Iffy decided to return seven years later, this time with so many fellow travellers with a love for cycling that two cars were needed. The year or two after, it was three – the party now numbered in the double figures. It had become an earner as well as an annual holiday.

It was made more popular because Iffy realised that back then the media accreditation process wasn't nearly as watertight as it was at other mega-events around the world, such as the Olympics. The Australian media was conspicuous by its almost total absence from Le Tour so he found it easy to pass off multiple 'campers,' as he called his guests, as radio technicians, photographers and official drivers, most of them ostensibly assigned by the paper he did work for himself, the modest provincial daily from Geelong. This proved handy when the authorities eventually began to smell a rat about the numbers collecting the passes because he was able to tell them Geelong was Cadel Evans' home town, which was almost true (Australia's star performer had a house in nearby Barwon Heads beach resort) and that the paper was devoting page after page of news about their local hero every day. That was an exaggeration, of course, but close enough to the truth for him to get away with it. Being accredited meant that the campers could be driven along the actual race route and had access to VIP areas before each day's racing and the media enclosures afterwards, providing opportunities to meet the riders and the entourages of past champions who were always on hand, and to sample the free food and wine that was often provided by stage towns keen to impress the international media.

With the 2003 race – labelled the Centenary edition but in fact the 90th because of the war-related reasons already explained – coming up I decided to join in, having long wondered about the mystique of this colourful carnival that I had been reading about intermittently for years. Despite its obvious importance in the international scheme of things, the Tour had little appeal to the Australian media because, apart from some ground-breaking efforts from Victorian star Phil Anderson in the eighties, there were so few Australian riders that it simply didn't resonate. It was another world, far removed from the diet of cricket, tennis, golf, certain Olympic sports and even soccer that fans were being force-fed. The attitude was summed up a few years later when the editor of the *Herald Sun* in Melbourne told me that he would not pay for me to cover the race 'because no matter what happens in it, I couldn't sell one more paper.' This struck me as a strange stance given that the *Herald*

Sun Tour, sponsored by his paper of course, had been a major cycling event in Victoria since 1952 and until the Tour Down Under emerged as a WorldTour event in Adelaide in 1999, it was the biggest and best bike race in the country – and was still going strong. I reminded him of those words in late 2011 when Evans became the first Australian to win the Tour, one of the nation's greatest-ever sporting feats and huge news in every media outlet, the *Herald Sun* certainly no exception, and again when about 30,000 excited fans packed the city's Federation Square when he made a brief trip home to take a bow, which was more front-page news. The Tour never went uncovered by the *Herald Sun* again.

But back in 2003, the best I could manage was to convince a sports department manager to let me take holidays, pay for the trip myself and claim a modest contributor's fee – beer money, really – for a handful of feature articles in which I would attempt to demystify the event for those readers who could be momentarily distracted from the acres of newsprint being devoted, as always, to the footy season.

Luckily, my timing was good – and it didn't take long to realise that. Normally, the race start – the Grande Departe – is a short time trial, known as a prologue, that takes place somewhere around the country, or maybe another country, with the race ending three weeks later in Paris, with several laps of the Champs Elysees. But because of the historical underpinning of it, the 2003 version began in the charismatic capital, in the shadow of the Eiffel Tower. It was a 6.5km dash against the clock on a treacherous cobbled surface and it was won by one of the seven Australians in the field, Brad McGee, one of the finest all-rounders, track and road, ever to wear the green and gold. That put him in the famous maillot jaune, the leader's yellow jersey, where he stayed for three days. On the third day, McGee's young team-mate in the French team Fdjeux, Victorian Baden Cooke, 22, won stage two, putting himself in the white jersey occupied by the best young rider. And Queenslander Robbie McEwen, also on his way to becoming an all-time great who won 12 stages of both the Tour and the Giro before he was finished, was in the second most important jersey, the green one for the sprint points classification. In other words, three days into the action the Australians –

Le Kangarous – were dominating, and this was without Evans, who had
been prevented from making his debut because of an injured collarbone
suffered in a recent race crash. It had been, as the headline said on my
full-page report in the *Herald Sun*, the 'greatest three days in the history
of Australian cycling.' If the fans Down Under were surprised, Europeans
were astonished. When our car pulled into a roadside bar the next lunchtime for a refreshment, a veteran Swiss journalist who we didn't know
presented us with a bottle of expensive champagne – and we were just
the camp followers, not the riders! The euphoria lasted all the way with
Cook eventually finishing ahead of McEwen in the last stage in Paris
and claiming the green jersey – a significant addition to his palmares, as
cyclists refer to their career records. With Lance Armstrong recording his
fifth successive win, at that stage a stupendous feat with no end in sight,
I had spent my holiday time and money well and the paper had received
extraordinary value for its tiny outlay. Le Tour – and road cycling in
general – had me hooked.

I went back another half a dozen times with Trevorrow as well as
taking in the Giro three times and a tour of Ireland once. They tended to
be eventful forays involving accommodation that could range anywhere
from farmer's barns, rural inns and elegant chateaux, sometimes hours
off the beaten track, with navigation often just hit-or-miss guesswork,
meaning it wasn't uncommon to finally arrive just as the kitchen was
closing – and sometimes the bar, too. But somehow, Iffy would manage
to laugh his way through and we'd all find a way to go to bed fed and
watered and wondering what adventures tomorrow would bring.

Even before he got crook, these could be death-defying – and not just
because of his penchant for driving at only one speed, flat chat. In my
sometimes terrifying experience, all ex-cyclists are like that – because of
their familiarity with negotiating cambers, turns and assorted surfaces
they are good drivers, but not to be recommended to passengers with
faint hearts. And it doesn't matter what's in their way, as I discovered
on one frightening occasion when we – Iffy and I and one other bloke –
pulled in for a pit-stop and were relaxing over a slow glass of something
when we suddenly realised the race was about to go past and we didn't

have time to get back in the car and take off ahead of it, meaning we wouldn't see the finish which our man, our story, McEwen was likely to win. The only option was to get off the race route and take a back road and hope to find our way back in front of the race. This was working out OK except that we kept seeing clumps of burning vegetation on the side of the dirt road. The explanation soon presented itself – a farmer was standing by his stationery motor-cart on which was a huge load of hay, burning fiercely and making the road impassable. We were out of business, obviously. Not to Trevorrow, we weren't. He ordered me to wind up the passenger window and to hold tight – and gunned the car straight through the towering inferno, with the astonished farmer forced to leap for his life. Somehow unscathed, we arrived 10 minutes later at the main road which, of course, was blocked because the peloton was just a minute or two away and there was no way the duty gendarme was letting us through. That is, until he made the rookie error of briefly looking the other way which was all the opportunity Iffy needed to gun the car around the barrier and on towards the finish line, where we arrived just in time to see McEwen win, and to get our interview with him.

Then there was the day the GPS – we had finally graduated to computer navigation after years of time-consuming guesswork – took us down a dirt road in a remote forest which was so narrow that there was no way of turning back. That became awkward when we came to a stream with a rickety little wooden bridge that looked totally incapable of bearing the weight of our fully-loaded SUV – but there was no option but to try, even though it was obvious we would be stranded deep in the woods with no way out if we failed to negotiate not only the inadequate bridge but the many jagged rocks either side of it. Only Iffy would have attempted it, but, guess what, he inched his way across until, bingo, we were back on the road, such as it was – and, although we didn't know it, we were only a click or two from the highway and civilisation. Never in doubt, grinned our pilot, not quite able to disguise the sweaty-palmed relief he was really feeling.

Like everyone else who heard them, Gerry Ryan was mightily amused by these 'Iffy stories,' as they came to be known, and although long drives to barnyard accommodation was never going to be the go for one of Australia's wealthiest businessmen, he did eventually join the party, partly out of curiosity and partly because he was already more than an interested onlooker at bike races. In fact, he had long been deeply and generously involved in a wide range of sports, pouring many millions of dollars into sponsorships. Cycling possibly had a head start with him because he grew up in Bendigo, where it was a thriving sport in the days when he used to sell the evening newspaper, *The Herald*, on street corners to help support his big family. They were far from wealthy. His mother was literally a two-bob (20 cents) punter who lodged a formal objection when the TAB increased the minimum bet to 50 cents and was told that because she was such a good customer she could keep betting at her affordable level. Her ambitious son went on to make an enormous fortune through the establishment of Australia's biggest caravan manufacturing business, Jayco, as well as property development and anything else that caught his entrepreneurial eye, eventually including theatre, wine, hospitality and thoroughbred horse breeding, among many other things. Probably nobody has had such a prominent and generous presence in so many sports, which is why I labelled him 'Australia's most committed sports fan' in a newspaper column. They include racing – he part-owned the Melbourne Cup winner Americain – and three football codes, AFL, rugby league and soccer – as well as international women's basketball and others that have never really been made public.

I have known and dealt with him professionally across most of these sports-related fields, especially the bikes, and also socially through an organisation called the Vingt Cinq Club, which is a collection of mates who have been involved in sport for anything up to half a century, usually at the elite level. Being Melbourne-based, it is footy heavy with champions such as Ron Barassi, Bob Skilton, Allen Aylett, Graham Arthur, Sam Kekovich, John Sharrock, Kevin Sheedy and Murray Weideman among the alumni, together with international cricketers Ian Meckiff, Shaun Graf and Darren Berry, former leviathan racehorse trainer Darren Weir, rugby league Test captain John Ribot, Olympic basketball captain Wayne Carroll and one of Australia's greatest tennis champions, Frank Sedgman.

But plenty of cycling gets talked about over the long lunches, too. That's because Trevorrow is an enthusiastic member, as are Olympic track champion Scott McGrory and track world champion Gordon Johnson, while Alan 'Snowy' Munro – the son of one of first two Australians to ride in the Tour de France and a good performer himself – was a regular until his death a few years ago. And of course, there is Ryan.

His first real involvement in cycling was when a young Kathy Watt approached him for help to train at altitude overseas before contesting the first ever Olympic road race for women in Barcelona in 1992. He gave her $10,000 which she turned into a gold medal on the road and a silver on the track, which Ryan considered to be a pretty handy dividend. He began to help other cyclists, including a young Cadel Evans. He accepted Trevorrow's invitation to join the Tour trips, where he saw the flags of many nations flying on the Champs Elysees but not the Australian one, and wondered why that was and what could be done about it. The first answer, of course, was that cycling teams were extremely expensive to establish and maintain, and a number of consortiums had dipped their toes in the water only to find themselves well out of their depth. One night on tour, I was sitting not far away when I spotted Ryan deep in conversation with a guest of Trevorrow's, one Shayne Bannan who was Cycling Australia's high-performance manager. Not long afterwards Bannan couldn't believe his ears when Ryan rang and asked him to put together a costing for such a team. Before he knew it, the team had been born, Bannan was appointed general manager and his, and Australian cycling's collective dream had come true.

The rest is history – and has continued to be for nearly a decade.

It was an enormous undertaking by Ryan, who does not necessarily get the credit from the broader sporting community that he should for putting Australian sport on the map in a way never before seriously attempted, not that he would be concerned by that. It wasn't just the massive expense – estimated at $15 million a year in the early stages, a large percentage of which came from his own pocket. It was also his willingness to look after the sport as a whole, also forming a highly successful women's team and a development squad for young riders. As well, he was persuaded by the Government's Sports Commission – now Sport Australia – to take on the presidency of Cycling Australia for as long as it took to sort out its chaotic finances. In short, he became Mr Cycling.

The team flew the flag of the Southern Cross proudly, with the original squad of 31 predominantly Australians, 17 of them plus 14 from other countries. The locals included a number of champions who were desperate to be part of something that they had all dreamed of for so long but who had limited futures because their legs were getting tired – Stuart O'Grady was 38, Robbie McEwen 39, Baden Cooke 33, Allan Davis 31 and the journeyman Matt Wilson 34. In keeping with this patriotic philosophy, the early forays into the Tour de France were contested by teams consisting of five Aussies and four others (teams now number eight) but after the first three or four years commercial realities intruded and the balance – both overall and in the Grand Tour teams – tipped the other way, with the Australians in the minority, if only narrowly. Most of the old-timers moved on quickly but some, including McEwen and Wilson, stayed on in non-riding roles. However, the management remained firmly in Australian hands – manager Bannan and sports director, or head coach, Matt White – and the outfit deliberately developed a colourful media presence through the work of a talented young video producer, Dan Jones, who travelled with the team filming everything they did, publicly and behind the scenes and putting it on the internet under the title Backstage Pass. They quickly developed a cult following and, when on the road in France, became a de facto tourist attraction as many hundreds of Australians made the Tour as much a highlight of their European travels as the Eiffel Tower, the Colosseum or the Mona Lisa. The organisers of the great race were delighted with what the entertaining and magnetic Australians brought to the table.

The big question, though, was could they perform? The answer wasn't long coming.

The 2013 Tour was, yes, the 100th for the race itself but for the Australian newcomers it was only their second. At that embryonic stage they had no riders capable of actually winning the Tour – Evans had declined an opportunity to come on board – but they were out to be noticed. They quickly found a bizarre new way to do it. With the peloton just 12km out from completing the 213km first stage from Porto Vecchio to Bastia, the team bus became wedged under the gantry at the finish line. If it hadn't had such potentially disastrous consequences it would have been comical, like something out of a farcical movie. Of course, it wasn't really a laughing matter for anybody intimately involved, with a lot of angry words generated. With very little time to decide what to do when the $500,000 luxury vehicle became stuck, panicked organisers decided to move the finish three kilometres back down the beachfront road, with the riders told to adjust their tactics. But when the Spanish driver Garikoitz Atxk got his bus moving in the nick of time, the original finish was re-instated. Because the driver had been late getting there – if he had been on time he would have been waved through a deviation route – the team was fined 2000 Swiss francs. Watching in bemusement from among the crowd, Ryan declared the money, and the embarrassment, were worth it – the team and its sponsors would be plastered over every front page in Europe. Everybody knew who they were now. 'Money well spent,' he laughed.

There was better, much better, to come. On day three, the team's best rider Simon Gerrans provided it with its first stage win, narrowly prevailing over multiple world champion Peter Sagan of Slovakia on the 145.5km run from Ajaccio to Calvie, and then the next day, back on the French mainland, all nine riders became stage winners when they combined to take out the 25km team time trial into the Riviera resort of Nice by setting the fastest pace for such a race in the tour's history and prevailing by less than a second.

That put Gerrans into the yellow jersey, which he kept for another day before making a gesture in stage six that summed up the mateship and camaraderie within the team. On stage six Gerrans deliberately finished well behind his team-mate Daryl Impey, allowing the popular South African to inherit the yellow jersey and keep it for two days himself. Impey became the first African ever to wear the sacred garment and it made him a hero in his own country as well as giving the sport a huge boost there. 'If you can help someone change their life, why not?' said Gerrans, to applause that echoed right around the cycling world.,

That night in Nice, the consecutive stage wins were celebrated for what they were – not quite the greatest days in Australian cycling history because nothing could beat Evans's historic win, but they did usurp the three days a decade earlier when McGee, McEwen and Cooke put their country on the cycling map so spectacularly.

Ryan declared it a more enjoyable experience than when his horse Americain won the Melbourne Cup just a couple of months before GreenEDGE was born. Why so? 'That was one horse, one jockey, one trainer and a couple of owners, but what you see here is a combination of many people's talent and passion coming through,' he said. Famously Ryan won Australia's biggest race with a horse that was imported from France and trained and ridden by Frenchmen and now here he was assailing France's biggest sporting event with a bunch of Aussies. The connection was taken one enjoyable step further when a copious quantity of France's finest fizz was summoned from behind the bar of the team's hotel, not far from the finish line of the time trial.

Gerrans made an emotional speech about the mateship dynamic within the team, and which he would demonstrate with actions, not words, two days later with the Impey handover. 'It doesn't get better than this because it was a real team effort,' he said. 'Everyone is committed 100 per cent, we work fantastically together, we're a close group of friends – and it shows. The mateship is not something that is put on, that's for sure. You can see the sacrifices we are willing to make for each other. It might look like an individual sport but it's really a team sport and we get a lot of satisfaction from seeing each other do well.'

That said, Gerrans had emerged as the first among equals, head coach Matt White declaring him the most important rider on the team. In fact, with Evans no longer quite the force he was and rising stars such as Richie Porte and Michael Matthews yet to come of age, he was Australia's No 1 rider, not just his team's. Nobody gave Ryan more value for money than Gerrans, who was an inaugural member of the team and stayed until the end of the 2017 season when, by mutual consent and with his legs well on the wane, he spent one final season with Evans's old team, BMC, in order to do what he could to assist Porte achieve his Tour de France dream. Gerrans had been an unlikely star in a sport he took up only after injuring a knee while riding motocross bikes as a teenager, turning to cycling to rehabilitate it with the help of a family friend from a farm down the road, the pioneering road racer Phil Anderson. He finished up with a career that surpassed Anderson's, which in the history of Australian cycling was no small feat. Just as importantly, perhaps, he was a great ambassador for the sport and for his country – modest, courageous, polite and there wouldn't be another sportswriter who would disagree when I say he was a pleasure to deal with.

If the 100th Tour de France had proven nothing else apart from Trevorrow's amazing durability – after recovering from the surgery, he went on to complete 20 successive Tours five years later, which made him eligible for a presentation from the race organisers — it was that Ryan's ambitious venture was going to be a success story. It was here to stay. As far as Ryan was concerned, that was definitely the case because he was deriving immense enjoyment from it — even if it was costing him a lot of money and was changing its name regularly as sponsors came and went.

However, the economic meltdown caused by the coronavirus disaster in 2020 impacted heavily on his business empire, forcing him to close some parts of it and dispense a large number of staff. It would have been no surprise if the team, now operating as Mitchelton-Scott – Mitchelton was his own winery, meaning he was pretty much sponsoring himself – had become an expensive luxury he could no longer justify.

But just before the racing season was due to resume after a long pause because of the pandemic, a solution appeared to have presented himself when Ryan announced that a Spanish philanthropic charity named the Manuela Fundacion would take responsibility for keeping team on the road, wearing its colours. It wasn't made clear how much influence the new player would exert but before anybody could wonder out loud about that, the deal was suddenly off, without any public explanation, less than a week later, with Ryan saying it was back to business as usual with him guaranteeing full funding for another two years.

Needless to say, that was a huge relief to the riders and staff and to the cycling community in general, because if the biggest adventure Australian cycling had ever seen had died on its feet it would have been highly unlikely that any other entrepreneur would have been prepared to make it happen again.

In the end, Ryan's passion for cycling prevailed over all else and it is a debt the sport will never be able to repay.

JOYS OF THE
TOY SHOP

When the celebrated American newspaperman Dave Anderson of the
New York Times won a Pulitzer Prize for commentary many years
ago – an award rarely bestowed on sportswriters – he remarked that
sportswriting was 'part of American culture, just as much as music, art or
anything else.'

It's true of Great Britain too. And it's true where I come from.

In Australia for most of the last two decades, there have been far more
journalists from a multitude of new-age platforms accredited to report on
the Australian Football League, the elite competition of the indigenous
code that is a national obsession in most of the six states and two
mainland territories, than there were in the Parliamentary Press Gallery
or any other area of public interest.

And they weren't even all professional journalists – far from it. 'The
media' became a lucrative after-life for scores if not hundreds of former
players from all mainstream sports. They wrote newspaper columns –
sometimes off their own bats, so to speak, and sometimes with the help
of ghost-writers – and they provided expert commentary on TV, radio
and websites, as well as wheeling out tall tales and true on entertainment
shows where being a good raconteur was just as important as being able
to explain what has just happened out on the field of play.

It became a hard gig to get into because the competition was so fierce.

That went for the pros and the ex-jocks alike.

And what made it even harder was that the most traditional form of
the media, the newspapers, have been fighting a losing battle against
the internet for the past 20 years or so, many of them disappearing or at

least operating with a fraction of the staff numbers that they did in their halcyon days.

The advent of the Coronavirus in 2020 certainly hasn't helped. It accelerated an already depressing trend for outlets to shed good people, sports departments most certainly no exceptions as sport itself, big and small, temporarily disappeared off the map.

I had the immense good fortune to climb aboard while the train was still rattling along, full speed ahead, and rode it through a golden era – from the seventies through to the new millennium, before disembarking in 2016 after more than half a century in the caper. Almost all of that was spent either editing sports sections or travelling around Australia and the world churning out the prose for others to edit – and, hopefully, for hundreds of thousands if not millions of others to read.

I sometimes used to reflect on the 'advice' offered by one of my first bosses when I started this journey on The Standard in Warrnambool where I spent my teenage years. The chief of staff was one Eric Fitzhenry, a weary veteran serving out his final years after an unremarkable career in the big smoke of Melbourne and he was unimpressed that I was one of the town's more enthusiastic young footballers and cricketers and therefore keen to spend as much time as possible writing about those two sports and any others I could learn about, as distinct from sitting in courtrooms, council chambers, police stations or cattle saleyards reporting on the rest of daily life in the bush town. He said he would strongly advise against putting too many of my eggs in that basket because he agreed with a popular theory that if a newspaper could be compared to a department store the sports pages were the toy department and I would never be taken seriously as a journalist if that was the best I had to offer.

The job used to take Fitzhenry about as far as Port Fairy, half an hour down the road, to report on the shire council's deliberations about stray dogs, parking fees, road surfacing and fishing licences.

It took me, eventually, around the world many times, to about 35 countries and every continent, to work on a multitude of Olympic and Commonwealth Games, cricket tours in England, Africa, Asia and the West Indies, the cycling tours of France and Italy, America's Cup yachting, world title fights, world championships in athletics, swimming, cycling and triathlon, major tennis at Wimbledon, golf in Scotland, soccer at Wembley and, of course, a steady stream of all the football codes, horse-racing and still more cricket at home in Melbourne, the self-proclaimed sports capital of the world.

You meet a lot of interesting people doing that – former prime minister Bob Hawke took me and a handful of others to meet Nelson Mandela for a chat about cricket in Johannesburg one day – and you never know quite what the next day, or even the next hour, will bring. As described elsewhere in these pages, I was lucky not to be blown up by terrorist suicide bombers in Sri Lanka one time, which, I must admit, was never a serious threat back in the shire offices in Port Fairy. Even in Melbourne I had to call in the cops one day when I was unwise enough to insult the Italian national soccer team in print, eliciting death threats over the phone which the police took seriously enough to investigate. I've been pepper-gassed during a political protest on the streets of Kuala Lumpur and been threatened with a beating by an off-duty Sydney cop moonlighting as an Australian boxer's bodyguard in Las Vegas, saved only by former world champion Jeff Fenech arriving in the nick of time to talk the thug out of damaging my facial features.

Yes, it's been a roller-coaster ride.

So much has changed – and is still changing.

Methodology, for one.

When I first arrived at the now-defunct Melbourne evening paper *The Herald* in the late sixties you had to master the art of dictating copy off the top of your head on the phone, usually a public call-box – if you could find one unoccupied – requiring a supply of 20 cent coins. In the office, you used typewriters and multi-layered copy paper with carbon paper between the sheets. There were no such things as mobile phones, and so to have any hope of meeting deadlines that came crashing down late morning you would have to ring your contacts at breakfast time, sometimes waking them up and always at risk of them getting their wives to answer the call and tell you they had just left for work – where of course a secretary or colleague would make some other excuse. There were no pocket tape recorders and very few short cuts with research, usually just old clippings – and photographic prints – filed away every day by dedicated library staff.

Looking back, it is difficult to believe how primitive the whole business was – and yet, how well the good operators were able to cope under enormous pressure when a big story was breaking.

The technology revolution arrived in the early eighties and the tiny handful of us assigned to the Los Angeles Olympics in 1984 were the first from our company to use laptops to file copy from a major event. We were issued with little yellow boxes called NECs – the name of the electronics company that manufactured them – which had a tiny screen displaying no more than three lines of rolling type and which had to be connected by an unwieldy coupler to a phone handset until a green light appeared, which meant the copy was being sent. But they were so sensitive that the slightest vibration – such as someone thumping the desk next to you – would cause the light to turn yellow and you would have to repeat the whole procedure again, even if you had been 95 per cent finished before the interruption. It was incredibly frustrating and often more time-consuming that ringing a copytaker would have been.

These days technology advances at breakneck speed but for a long while evolution seemed slow.

On a cricket tour of Pakistan some years later, I spilled lemonade into the keyboard of a more advanced machine with the result that it would produce only unintelligible gibberish. Some unkind colleagues suggested that this was not an uncommon outcome for me except that it usually wasn't lemonade that had anything to do with it. On this occasion, they were overlooking that I was in Pakistan where it is difficult and often impossible to procure any form of stronger drink.

I did find a row of computer shops where one helpful chap said he could not fix my keyboard but he could sell me a full-sized one, meant for an old-fashioned desktop machine, which would operate the laptop. And so it did – sometimes. It did its best work when the sun shone directly into the open-air press box in Peshawar, where I was watching captain

Mark Taylor equal Don Bradman's Australian record Test score of 334, but that was only for a couple of hours each day – and then the laptop and its oversized addition would shut up shop again, forcing me back onto the phone to home base. That, too, was incredibly frustrating but the next match was in Karachi where I was directed to another little workroom up a suburban back alley where a teenage boy and his grandfather told me to come back in a couple of hours and it would be fixed. Amazingly, it was, original keyboard and all, and all for about ten bucks. They also told me the laptop itself had been in poor condition for some time, which had obviously escaped the IT people in Sydney who had issued it to me. That was no great surprise – a lot used to elude them.

So much has changed about sport itself – massively so in most cases.

When I started, the Australian Football League was the Victorian Football League with 11 clubs in Melbourne and one in Geelong playing exclusively on Saturday afternoons with limited TV exposure and not much money involved – in fact most clubs were perpetually broke and relied for their existence on wealthy supporters, if they had any.

Now it is a mega-rich behemoth with 18 clubs – two each in every other state except Tasmania – playing throughout the week with saturation TV coverage financing the ability for the players to be among the best-paid 'workers' in the land, and with even a semi-professional women's competition beginning to thrive. Nothing ever stays the same — the economic impact of the coronavirus has guaranteed that this prosperous state of affairs will take a hit for the foreseeable future.

Back in the day, there was only Test cricket, then the 50-over one-day format arrived – and was energised by TV mogul Kerry Packer's World Series rebel competition, which turned the players into true professionals – and finally the Twenty20 format revolutionised the sport again. Once more, the girls joined in.

Soccer was little more than a niche sport played and followed only by migrant communities with the World Cup, save for one brief foray in the early seventies, just a distant dream.

When I was editing the sports pages of *The Herald* during the eighties we had a designated soccer writer, a Scottish expert who knew his stuff, but because we ran very little copy on the sport he had so little to do that he would spend the bulk of his time editing the racing form-guide, biding his time until he could escape what he unsurprisingly regarded as a cultural purgatory populated by sporting Philistines.

Now the national competition, the A League, is a major presence in every state and it would be a calamity if the Socceroos did not qualify for the World Cup, which they have now done four times in a row. They're still a long way from ever winning it – but the women's team, the Matildas, aren't, especially now that their World Cup will be on home soil in 2023.

Rugby League was practically unheard-of in Melbourne and regarded with something bordering on contempt until a new franchise, the Storm, popped up and immediately started winning premierships much to the shock and horror in the sport's NSW and Queensland heartlands, where they couldn't believe that such a monster could be created let alone take control. The club is now a major presence in the fabric of Melbourne sporting life, not a threat to the AFL in any way but not vulnerable to being put out of business by the obsessively protective AFL either.

During the '70s and '80s Australia's proud presence in the Olympic world – one of only two countries, with Greece, to have been represented at every edition of the modern Games since they were reinvented in 1896 – was as a fringe player, never more so than in Montreal in 1976 when not a single gold medal was won.

Since then the boxing kangaroo has consistently fought well above its weight on and off the field of play, usually finishing in the top 10, sometimes as high as fourth, on the medals table, hosting the Games for the second time in Sydney in 2000 to universal acclaim for the quality of the organisation and presentation, and more recently with its most senior administrator, president John Coates, providing Australia with enormous influence in two stints as senior vice-president of the International Olympic Committee.

It is not hard to remember when that most quintessential of Australian sporting events, the Melbourne Cup – the horse race that famously stops the nation – was purely a local production for not terribly high-class handicappers and of minimal interest to anybody from any further abroad than New Zealand.

Then along came heavyweight Irish trainer Dermot Weld with Vintage Crop in 1993 and the floodgates opened, eventually turning the Cup – and the rest of the Spring Carnival – into a magnet for the biggest and richest racing stables in the world.

If the Australian Open tennis wasn't dead on its feet when it was played at the boutique Kooyong stadium across Christmas and New Year, it was on life support as the bulk of the world's best players ignored it.

Since 1988, the year after Melbourne's Pat Cash won Wimbledon and sparked a surge in interest in tennis, the event has become unrecognisable in its visionary and sophisticated home in the sports precinct close to the city, and is now regarded almost unanimously by the players – and by the huge numbers of visitors it attracts – as the most enjoyable of the four tournaments that make up the Grand Slam.

There was once a car race that used to go by the name of the Australian Grand Prix, but it bore no resemblance to the event that now goes by the same name every March, when it is always the pipe-opener for the Formula One calendar and, like the races and the tennis, contributes enormously to the local economy.

So yes, the sporting world in Australia – and in Melbourne much more than anywhere else – is now from another planet.

So are the people who inhabit it – in the media, at any rate.

Many are on the job 24/7, not merely reporting but pontificating across as many platforms as possible – the papers, TV, radio, websites, podcasts, magazines – and in many cases, across as many sports as they can get to.

Where once they – we – would be pleased to simply have their name printed above a story, now everybody wants to be a personality and naturally the rivalry is fierce and the egos often inflated to unflattering levels, which is less conducive to the social and professional camaraderie that used to exist.

In my view, one of the catalysts for the not altogether subtle change in the relationship dynamics – and this is going back a long way – was Rupert Murdoch's takeover in 1987 of the Melbourne-based *Herald and Weekly Times* group, which put journalists from *The Herald* and

The Sun – later to merge into the *Herald Sun* – into the same bed as their counterparts from his two Sydney dailies, the *Telegraph* and the evening *Mirror*.

It wasn't a comfortable marriage then and never really became one.

It didn't take long for a them-and-us mentality to emerge, with the Sydneysiders regarding themselves as the rightful senior partners.

This manifested itself with unmistakeable clarity at the first major assignment undertaken as a combined operation, the 1988 Olympics in Seoul.

This was overseen by one of Sydney's most senior executives, Brian Hogben, a silver-haired former editor who had commanded a few previous Olympic campaigns and regarded himself as without peer at the caper when, in fact, you only needed to keep your ears open in his pompous presence to realise that he knew very little about the Games history, the various sports or the personalities in the Australian or any other team. And given this was the early days of the technological revolution, he knew very little about that too. He did know how to look after himself alright, turning left at the plane door while we, the troops, settled back in economy and once on the ground in the Korean capital the finest restaurants were rapidly investigated.

There weren't many of us – a couple of individuals were one-out for their own papers but the Group crew included four from Sydney, Ray Kershler, Ian Hanson, Greg Campbell and Mike Hurst – all very good performers, let me stress – and four from HWT, me and Judy Joy Davies from Melbourne, Geoff Kingston from Adelaide and Wayne Smith from Brisbane.

In any Olympics reporting team, especially a small one, there are three main gigs – the swimming, the track and field and roaming colour writing. The Sydney guys were given all three, the rest of us were more or less told to spread out and see what we could come up with – and not, we realised, to get in the road of the others.

It bordered on farcical.

Judy Joy, a lovely and very popular lady who had been an Olympic swimming medallist herself and who had covered the sport with peerless expertise at every Games since her competitive retirement in Helsinki in 1952, was told she would not be assigned to the pool this time, but should go to the modern pentathlon.

The what? Flabbergasted, Judy told Hogben that Australia had only a couple of competitors in that obscure sport and had no chance of winning anything and that it had never been of the slightest interest to Australians.

'Judy,' he said, 'surely you haven't forgotten Bill Roycroft?'

The penny dropped.

He was under the deluded impression that modern pentathlon, which has a horse-riding component, was in fact equestrian, which Roycroft and others had made an Australian specialty, which it still is today.

Judy just looked at me and laughed. I wasn't really laughing back because I had been told to spend the next two days at the rowing. I patiently explained that this would involve only heats and repechages with no medals decided until later and unless some thoroughly unexpected drama burst forth I would be able to contribute nothing more than a few short paragraphs that would duplicate what the agency reporters were doing. In other words, it was a waste of time.

Just do it. So I did. At the end of the second day, I took a call from my own Sports Editor in Melbourne – they were not supposed to do this, all queries and requests to be directed through Hogben – wondering with very good reason when I might be offering something worth publishing under my by-line in my own paper. He sounded as bemused as I was, and possibly just as pissed off.

I was also instructed to not trouble myself by attending the daily, mid-morning Press conferences held by the team boss John Coates because they, too, would be in the hands of one of the Sydney crew.

I rocked up every day anyway and one morning heard Coates announce that a modern pentathlete Alex Watson had failed a drug test and would be sent home. Yes, what irony – the tiny sport had become big news after all, for quite the wrong reason. Coates spoke about 10 minutes before the first edition deadline back in Melbourne which was just enough time for me to grab the nearest phone – no mobiles then – ring the news desk and dictate enough copy off the top of my head for them to replace the front page lead right on the knocker. They rang back an hour later to say they had just got the Sydney version which would have missed the deadline by the best part of half an hour. They told Hogben the same thing – and he didn't say a word to me. Not 'thanks' and not a rebuke for disobeying instructions. Just sullen silence, because 'his' team had been upstaged by the interstate interlopers.

I heard later he had recommended in his debriefing report that I never travel for the company again, although I never found out if that was true. If it was, it wasn't acted on – well, not for another three Olympic cycles.

The ill-will between the two main parts of the Murdoch empire was still evident when the time came to plan and execute the coverage of the 2000 Sydney Olympics, one of the biggest undertakings the company had ever confronted.

A handful of senior Melbourne people, including me, were sent to live in Sydney well in advance of the Games, almost 18 months earlier in my case. I wouldn't say there was overt hostility but there was very little warmth in the welcome. The attitude seemed to be that they knew what they were doing, it was on their turf and they didn't need our help. There was an abundance of good copy available almost every day, even so far out, but I found it difficult to get much of it published in the Telegraph even though it was all emanating from their backyard.

The relationship became strained in various ways.

At one point, the Telegraph, on behalf of the other papers, instituted a weekly Olympics lift out and were so pleased with the first one that it was delivered in advance to the AAP news agency, who then lifted the best news story in it, enabling News's Fairfax rivals to publish it first, which was embarrassing. A Fairfax sports gossip columnist, Geoff McClure, picked up on this and rang me to ask about the circumstances. Why would he ring me, the opposition? Because we were best mates, had worked together for a long time at the HWT and we were best man at each other's wedding. Even so, I told him I couldn't and wouldn't help him because it was obviously a touchy topic and far too close to home. I recommended he talk to one of the lift out's editors, Phil Gardner, who he also knew well and who was also from Melbourne. He did so and ran with the story which did not go down well in the News Olympic bunker and beyond. My relationship with 'Chook' McClure was common knowledge and so I got the blame, and was never able – even years later – to shift it, even though Chook offered on his death bed – almost literally – to make a sworn statement if that would help. By then, it was all a bit pointless.

There was also a brouhaha over accreditations, the much-prized free passes to front-row seats at everything that happens at any Olympics.

Nearly two years out the Carlton & United Brewery offered to sponsor what became known as the Australian Olympic Writers and Photographers Association, which had a number of professional and social objectives. I became the inaugural president and the Sydney Morning Herald's Roy Masters vice-president. CUB threw a lot of money at it mostly in the form of upmarket lunches in Sydney and elsewhere, attended by Coates and other heavyweight Olympic officials, a lot of athletes and coaches and, of course, any journos or snappers who saw themselves as being involved in the Games coverage. They were successful, useful and enjoyable functions but one invitation, issued every time, was always refused. News Ltd's editor in chief John Hartigan never attended, even though his future wife Rebecca Wilson was overseeing the company's Olympic 'war room,' and although he never offered any explanation for his constant disinclination to attend we interpreted it as silent – and mysterious – disapproval.

So it was no great surprise that when Australian Olympic Committee executive Craig McLatchey suggested that the AOWPA, together with the Sydney Ethics Centre, liaise with the International Olympic Committee's media people to allocate the accreditations distribution fairly, Hartigan blew his top.

He wasn't having any of that. News would fight that battle from the top, which they did – and that was fair enough. Accreditation was a crucial element of anyone's and everyone's coverage.

But the issue still had a little sub-plot to play out.

As is always the case, the opening ceremony was declared a ticketed event which meant that an accreditation wasn't enough to get you through the gate, you needed a specific pass as well. These were in high demand so the News heavies were going to be pleased if they could obtain 20 or so and were delighted when 50 turned up. These were given to the writers actually covering the event and to plenty of favoured 'theatre-goers' who were not on duty but just wanted to be there. That meant that quite a few writers who were regulars on the Olympic beat and who had worked tirelessly on the build-up were going to miss out, much to their dismay.

However, I had been around the Olympics for enough years to know that the IOC's old Finnish bloke who was in charge of media passes always kept plenty up his sleeve for just such contingencies, and being an old journo himself he had every sympathy with the AOWPA. So hours before the ceremony he rang me and said to come around to his office with a Fairfax rep where he handed us another 20 or so each, which I was able to distribute to the people who should have got them in the first place. That included a young woman from Adelaide who was desperate to have the full Olympic experience and had worked diligently to earn it. Not long after the Games, she died. Never has a free ticket to anything been put to such good use.

Nonetheless, the appearance of all these extra people in the Press seats did not go unnoticed and was probably another black entry in the book for me.

Given all this uneasiness and the reality that the Group coverage was way overstaffed – some reporters went half-mad trying to find something to write about that wasn't already being covered by someone else – I asked the *Herald Sun*'s editor Peter Blunden if I could work under his direction only (which really meant under my own direction only) with the copy made available to everyone. Knowing I knew my way around the Games better than anyone else on the team, he agreed. Again, it was a move that didn't go down well in Sydney, even though they had people doing the same thing.

When it was all over, Blunden sent me a hero-gram, which said: 'Congratulations and a million thanks for a truly magnificent job covering the games. No journalist in Australia excelled like you did in the *Herald Sun*. Your superb work was there for all to see each day and you can hold up every edition with pride. Your professionalism, brilliant writing, expertise and dedication was instrumental in a coverage we were all delighted with.'

Please excuse the self-indulgence in retrieving that from the archives but I do so only to emphasise the professional quicksand you often have to negotiate when working for the Murdoch operation. In my case, I never worked for them at the Olympics again.

Without any form of explanation, although I have always assumed the McClure incident, of which I was totally innocent, was the main catalyst, I was left out of the large team assigned to Athens four years later. Instead, Coates offered me a semi-executive position in the AOC's media team, flying me there business class just to make the point that he valued my contribution to the movement over, by then, two decades. It was the same in Beijing 2008 and London 2012 – ignored by News, happily engaged by the AOC.

When I protested to Blunden about Athens, he claimed he had simply been out-voted by the editors of the other papers. That's probably true enough but it does sound improbable that the editor-in-chief of the biggest paper in the company could not insist on having his best and most experienced specialist on deck for one of the biggest jobs of the year. He said he could not explain why the situation existed because he didn't know, which, again, sounds odd – surely he was entitled to ask for and get an answer. To add to my bemusement, he also told me he did not like the idea of having one of his best troops helping his main rival, *The Age*, with their coverage, which of course I had to do as part of my brief with the AOC. Later, at Blunden's suggestion – him handballing the issue, I suppose – I wrote to News Ltd's most senior editorial executive Campbell Reid, who had overseen the Olympic coverage in Atlanta in 1996 and had offered high praise for my part in it. I asked him if he could enlighten me on what I had done wrong but all I got back was a highly patronising, slightly absurd note to the effect that other younger people needed to be given opportunities. He did not address the elephant in the room at all, which was just one more frustration. Nobody ever has.

An earlier episode that also strained cross-border relations came early in the 1997 Ashes cricket tour of England, which started with Australian captain Mark Taylor under extreme pressure because of a long run of poor form. On the morning of the last day of the final warm-up match against Derbyshire, I got a call from Sydney to say they had learned Taylor had decided to drop himself from the first Test and I needed to get the story up for their front page immediately. Taylor had already made it clear he had every intention of playing so I, along with the Australian's Malcolm Conn, bailed up coach Geoff Marsh and vice-captain Steve Waugh, both on-tour selectors, who guaranteed us Taylor had said nothing of the sort to them and they would not be party to dumping the Australian captain against his will. I filed this with an assurance that Taylor would play – but was shocked to learn a few hours later that the 'Taylor drops himself' story still appeared on Page One anyway, with my byline attached to someone else's. Naturally, it did not appear in my own paper, the *Herald Sun*.

As it was going to press, Taylor was making a hundred against Derby. That removed all doubt. He saddled up for the Test in Birmingham and made a second innings century there too, his place never in doubt again.

Sydney had nothing to say to me about making me look silly and my own editor, Blunden, rang to tell me he had protested to them on my behalf, and apologised. Neither did Taylor say anything – until about a year later when we were sitting in an airport in Pakistan, discussing an offer from The Telegraph to hold a testimonial dinner for him in honour of the record Test score of 334 not out that he had just compiled in Peshawar. He assured me he knew I wasn't responsible for the misleading front page, that he was used to that sort of thing from his home-town paper, but that he would accept the offer anyway. 'It will put my kids through school,' he said.

All of that said, I am not embedded in the extremely well-populated school of former News people – especially journalists, but also photographers and technology operatives – who have walked away thoroughly unhappy with what they have left behind. In recent years many couldn't wait to get shot of the place, hopefully with a hefty redundancy package in their pocket. The office politics could be savage, and – as I have already indicated – it was often difficult to know where you stood. The last two editors I had hardly spoke to me across the three years or so I worked with each of them.

The saving grace for many, though – including me – was that the work was interesting and enjoyable. By and large, so were the people you do it with – although in newsrooms there is never any shortage of big egos, rampant ambitions and petty feuds. But that's probably the case in most workplaces.

Sports writing used to be heavily populated with colourful characters and still is to a lesser extent.

When I first became Sports Editor of *The Herald* I was 'in charge' – ha! – of three classic examples of the old school, football specialist Alf Brown, racing writer Jack Elliott and golf and tennis guru Don Lawrence, none of whom are still with us.

Brown had the game skun like nobody before him or since. Unusually for this cohort he didn't drink – apparently because he once woke up in a fit of remorse after injuring someone in a pub the night before, and never touched a drop again. Although rarely seen out socially he was on such good terms with every coach in the League, the established ones and the new ones, that they all entrusted him with selection secrets before the teams were published, not just positioning but the reasons why players would be dropped or recalled, which enabled him to produce a full broadsheet page of previews of the main three matches every Friday which were must-reads because they were always spot on with this off-the-record inside information. If a player had, say, squibbed it the previous week, this was the place to find out what the coach thought of him, without being actually quoted. Rookie club officials were often warned by old hands that while they didn't necessarily have to tell Brown the truth, the whole truth and nothing but the truth, they must never tell him a straight-out lie – if they did, there would be hell to pay.

In an era when there were only a handful of full-time footy writers, he stood alone as the doyen – and that respect lives on, with the award for football media identity of the year named after him in perpetuity.

Elliott was an even more formidable presence on the racetrack. Always immaculately attired and with a booming voice, he was one of the first print journalists to gravitate to television. He wielded so much influence from these dual platforms that the leviathan trainer Tommy Smith and the gun jockey Roy Higgins, to name just the two most important examples, allowed him – in fact, encouraged him – to quote them without necessarily going through the formality of ringing them first. 'I knew he wouldn't get me into trouble and even on the rare occasions when he sailed close to the wind there was no point complaining – you'd rather have him on-side than off-side,' Higgins once told me. Smith just understood that any publicity was good publicity and made sure Elliott always had a story about him ready to go.

To say the least, Elliott did not lack a sense of self-importance. He made sure he was the centre of attention, whenever possible, in any gathering, telling tall tales and possibly some true ones about himself and all the famous people he claimed to know, often insisting with a straight face that he was once in a hotel elevator when he was asked, 'excuse me, aren't you Jack Elliott?' – by Frank Sinatra. He did stay in only five-star accommodation, and how! When the editor and the deputy editor arrived at the same hotel in which he was staying in Sydney one time they were invited to his 'room' for a drink, whereupon they discovered that while they were in small, basic dog boxes downstairs their man was living it up in a penthouse suite with a mini-bar well-stocked with fine scotch and champagne. Like Higgins, they knew better than to protest – or, presumably, to ask any questions when the expense sheet eventually lobbed on their desks.

Lawrence mastered the enviable art of turning his hobby – golf – into his meal ticket, although he also had a brief stint in newsroom management. Two of the biggest names in the game, Jack Nicklaus and Greg Norman, were among his fans because he helped both become as famous as they did. It was Lawrence who coined the soubriquet The Golden Bear which Nicklaus was able to parlay into a hugely lucrative marketing tool. Lawrence was on hand when Norman emerged from total obscurity by winning a small tournament in Adelaide and he recognised the personable Queenslander as the possessor of both rare talent and charisma, both unpolished. Norman didn't have much money, just his freshly-pocketed winnings which weren't going to take him far, so Lawrence invited him home as a house guest for the following week's tournament in Melbourne. The Great White Shark – a nickname just as valuable as Nicklaus's, and which Lawrence might have also had some part in coining – never forgot the gesture and did all he could for the rest of his new mate's life to repay the debt. Both superstars contributed live video crosses from America for Lawrence's retirement party.

Sometimes the best sportswriters are not sportswriters at all – except at heart. They are the genius journalists who are at home in any newsworthy environment, brilliant reporters and superb wordsmiths, who are only too happy to take time off from allegedly more weighty matters – war, politics, crime, natural disaster, you name it – to play in 'the toy shop.'

Four of the best I worked with were Les Carlyon, Andrew Rule, Harry Gordon and Bruce Wilson.

Carlyon, who died at 76 in March 2019, was a fine editor and a great writer – a double that is not as common as might be imagined – who wrote two internationally acclaimed books about war and two about his true love, horse racing. He loved the horse sports with a rare passion and wrote about it with a style that reminded me of a quote I once took aboard that asserted there were only three sports that had ever produced genuine literature: cricket, baseball and horse-racing. Regrettably, I have forgotten who said that – but it wasn't Ernest Hemingway. He said: 'There are only three true sports, bullfighting, motor-racing and mountain-climbing – the rest are merely games.' To each his own, I suppose.

Anyway, Carlyon's equine essays – and they weren't about only the horses, but the people too – did qualify as literature and put all other racing writers, and there have been some good ones, in the shade. The great pity was that he stopped producing his newspaper columns, last seen in the Melbourne Age, a decade or so before he died, so that an entire generation of sports fans have grown up without the chance to appreciate his work.

Rule, an all-rounder who specialised in crime reporting, is also a passionate racing man, and in 2019 was judged to be the Australian sportswriter of the year not for his newspaper work – he was hardly ever in the sports pages — but for his book *Winx: The Authorised Biography*, about the Sydney racehorse that became the best galloper in the world and perhaps the best Australia ever saw. The book was a combination of superb writing, in-depth research and a thorough knowledge of the sport/industry, and was dedicated to Carlyon, a career-long mentor.

The award Rule won is named after Gordon, who, like Carlyon, won acclaim as both editor and writer, about both sport and war. They were near contemporaries, Carlyon editing *The Age* and Gordon its rival, *The Sun*, at about the same time and one following the other as editor-in-chief of the *Herald* and *Weekly Times*. Gordon's main contribution to sports writing – other than a passion for the Hawthorn Football Club – was his lifelong immersion in the Olympic movement, eventually becoming the Australian Olympic Committee's official historian. There aren't all that many books about Australia's proud Olympic history and his three are easily the best. Gordon was the first to establish conclusively that Australia is one of only two countries, with Greece, to have attended every modern Games. He was always a great help to me and has continued to be from the grave, the preceding pages of this book bearing frequent testimony to that.

Wilson, one of my best mates, was widely regarded as Australia's best foreign correspondent across lengthy terms in south-east Asia, Washington and London, after making his name on the ground at the Vietnam War. He loved going to war and covered as many international conflicts as he could, but there was nothing he couldn't write about brilliantly. Sport was certainly no exception, especially cricket, rugby and tennis, the latter of which made him a fixture at Wimbledon (and the French Open, if he could) for two decades.

Wislon, as he referred to himself, was one of the great characters of journalism – they are thinner on the ground these days than they once were – and a dedicated disciple of the 'wine, women and song' school.

Married four times, the father of three successful journalists – TV sports presenter and radio host Jim, the late Rebecca, also a sports commentator, and Lizzie, a magazine writer – he was a lover of jazz and fine wine. He possessed the extremely rare – and in his case infinitely valuable – talent for writing even more eloquently after satisfying his prodigious appetite for the grape than he did when cold sober.

I saw that get him into trouble only once.

In 1997, when he was based in England, we covered the aforementioned Ashes cricket tour together, which lasted 116 days of which I was able to take only one off. So the moment it was over, joined by our wives, we repaired to a beach resort in Spain for a spot of R&R. The night we arrived a long, long dinner ended just before a phone call from Sydney ordered him straight back to London because, an hour or so earlier, Princess Diana had been killed.

Wilson immediately scribbled out in longhand his trenchant thoughts about the royal icon, of whom he was no fan, and dictated them for publication. Immediately, a second call arrived, informing him tersely that although the validity of his opinions were not being questioned, it might be much wiser if he waited until her body was at least cold before he expressed them. In the cold light of day, of course, he was in furious, if somewhat abashed agreement.

The misstep didn't last long. He boarded the plane back to London and there, sitting directly across the aisle, was Diana's former lover, the 'cad and bounder' James Hewitt, who agreed to an interview – the first by any member of Diana's entourage, past or current in the immediate aftermath of the tragedy. Wilson was immediately back on the front page – and back in the good books.

A master raconteur and a fierce debater on any and all subjects, it is a great pity that he never wrote a book of his own, especially about his battleground experiences. Sadly, he, too, departed far too young, succumbing rapidly to cancer at 64. With his wife Clare beside him, he was watching a Test cricket match on TV in hospital when a trivia question popped up on the screen regarding a South African batsman. He did not hesitate with the correct answer. 'Peter Kirsten,' he said, looking pleased with himself. They were his last words.

Wislon sometimes said that what he, and we, did was better than real work.

He never got any argument from me on that one.

ACKNOWLEDGEMENTS

To my first family — my parents Bill and Joan and siblings Gail, Jennifer and Colin, all of whom are no longer with me — and my current family — my wife of 45 years Leigh and my son Adam — thank you for the help, support, love and encouragement that has made my journey possible.

I am also grateful to the countless colleagues, many of whom became good friends, who enabled me to navigate half a century in the sometimes uncertain world of newspapers, and to the many sports people — athletes, coaches, administrators and fans — who contributed their time, expertise and experience to make my life easier, and who also became mates in many cases.

In particular, the Australian Olympic Committee, the Melbourne Cricket Club (of which I have been a member for more than 25 years), the Carlton Football Club, Cricket Australia and the Vingt Cinq Club (a Melbourne institution for sports identities who are not as young as they once were) have all played significant roles in keeping me in touch with the wide world of sport.

In putting this book together I have drawn substantially on the work of several fine writers, including Harry Gordon, Les Carlyon, Denis Warner, Hugh Clarke, David Wallechinsky, Roy Tomizawa and Robert Whiting and their insights have been invaluable. I am also indebted to Mark Stiles, the producer of the ABC documentary *Nagasaki Journey*, to Diane Wickson, daughter of my father's co-prisoner and lifelong mate Murray Jobling, and to Andrew Carter, an Australian researcher with a special interest in the Nagasaki POWs and to Maureen Hoyer and my nephew Aaron Savage for their help with my research.

ABOUT THE AUTHOR

Ron Reed is one of Australia's most experienced and acclaimed sports journalists, whose work over more than 50 years has earned numerous awards, including Sport Australia's Lifetime Achievement Award and Australian Sportswriter of the Year. Now a semi-retired freelance writer, he was twice Sports Editor of the Melbourne Herald evening paper, Editor of the old Sporting Globe, and Chief Sportswriter, columnist and feature writer for the Herald Sun, Australia's biggest-selling daily paper. He has covered most of the world's major sports events multiple times, including nine Olympic Games, seven Commonwealth Games, several editions of cycling's Tour de France and Giro d'Italia, numerous cricket tours, major tennis and golf tournaments, world championships in athletics, swimming, road and track cycling, triathlon, hockey and rowing, as well as America's Cup sailing, horse racing and all of the football codes. War Games is his seventh book.